ONE POT OF THE DAY

KATE McMILLAN

PHOTOGRAPHY BY ERIN KUNKEL

weldon**owen**

CONTENTS

A DISH FOR EVERY DAY

From gratins to casseroles, stir-fries to stews, tagines to curries—this collection of scrumptious recipes offers ease, comfort, and flavor for everyday cooking. Whether braised, baked, sautéed, or slow-cooked, you'll find inspiration for combining seasonal ingredients into a delicious one-pot meal.

This colorful, calendar-style cookbook presents 365 main-course dishes that are prepared or served in a pot, baking dish, or on a platter. Emphasizing versatility, this style of cooking allows you to make the most of the seasons, mixing and matching ingredients and techniques throughout the year to create delicious, interesting, and wholesome fare that matches any occasion.

Flexible and adaptable, the one pot approach saves time and makes for smart seasonal cooking. Drawing on fresh offerings as a starting point—asparagus and peas in spring; tomatoes and eggplant in summer; squashes in fall; and sturdy greens and root vegetables in winter—you'll learn how to craft an exceptional dish each day by simply varying the cooking technique and flavor profile. Recipes like paella, Thai red curry with beef, and coq au vin draw on international cuisines and are satisfying enough to make a full meal; other dishes, such as braised salmon with herbs, chicken and basil stir-fry, and pork medallions with roasted nectarines may need only a green salad, a pot of steamed rice, or a loaf of crusty bread to feed and nourish the whole family.

In these pages, you'll find comforting classics like chicken pot pie and meat loaf as well as contemporary fare—cannelloni packed with pumpkin and sage; calamari stuffed with tomatoes, basil, and potatoes; maple-braised pork chops; and baked grits with sausage and kale. There are also numerous meatless offerings, from light and elegant to hearty and filling, that feature easy-to-prepare grains or proteins paired with garden-based ingredients and enticing flavors: vegetarian enchiladas; spinach-feta quiche; baked pasta primavera; gingery tofu stir-fry; and red quinoa sautéed with asparagus and mushrooms.

With this vast collection of recipes as your guide, and gorgeous color photographs to illustrate the way, you're sure to find the perfect one-pot dish to make any day of the year.

Start the year off right with a home full of simmering scents and warming comfort—rich stews and braises showcase aromatic spices and the hearty vegetables of the season. Slow-cooked short ribs nestle atop creamy polenta, cheesy baked pasta is bolstered by winter greens, and seafood is brightened with hints of citrus. From curries and risottos to savory pies and gratins, these dishes soothe all month long.

january

1

BAKED ZITI WITH CAULIFLOWER & GRUYÈRE

serves 4–6

6 Tbsp (3 oz/90 g) unsalted butter

¼ cup (1 oz/30 g) fine dried bread crumbs

3 Tbsp all-purpose flour

3¼ cups (26 fl oz/810 ml) milk, heated

Salt and ground white pepper

6 oz (185 g) Gruyère cheese, shredded

¼ cup (1 oz/30 g) grated Parmesan cheese

1 lb (500 g) ziti

1 large head cauliflower, cut into florets

This recipe is based on one of Britain's favorite comfort foods, "cauliflower cheese." It's a succulent treatment of creamed cauliflower baked until bubbling and golden on the top. It is so delicious that even avowed cauliflower haters are known to love it. Tossing it with pasta tubes makes it a satisfying meal.

In a small frying pan, melt 2 Tbsp of the butter over medium heat. Add the bread crumbs and stir and toss to coat evenly. Set aside.

In a heavy saucepan, melt the remaining 4 Tbsp (2 oz/60 g) butter over low heat. Add the flour and cook, whisking, until a smooth paste forms, about 4 minutes. Slowly whisk in the hot milk and cook, stirring often, until the sauce is smooth and thick enough to coat the back of a spoon, about 15 minutes. Add ½ tsp salt and a few grindings of pepper. Add the Gruyère and stir until melted, about 2 minutes. Stir in the Parmesan, remove from the heat, and cover to keep warm.

Preheat the broiler. Position a rack 8 inches (20 cm) from the heat source.

Bring a large pot of salted water to a rapid boil. Add the pasta and cauliflower and stir well. Cook, stirring occasionally, until the pasta is al dente, according to package directions. Drain the pasta and cauliflower and return to the pot. Add the cheese sauce and toss to coat evenly. Adjust the seasoning with salt and pepper. Transfer to a baking dish. Sprinkle with the buttered bread crumbs. Broil until the surface is bubbling and golden, about 5 minutes, then serve.

2

ITALIAN BRAISED SHORT RIBS

serves 6–8

3 Tbsp all-purpose flour

Salt and freshly ground pepper

5½–6 lb (2.75–3 kg) beef short ribs, English cut

¼ cup (2 fl oz/60 ml) olive oil

2 oz (60 g) pancetta, chopped

2 yellow onions, finely chopped

4 cloves garlic, minced

1 tsp red pepper flakes

2 carrots, finely chopped

2 Tbsp tomato paste

1 Tbsp sugar

1 cup (8 fl oz/250 ml) dry red wine

1 can (14½ oz/455 g) diced tomatoes

1 cup (8 fl oz/250 ml) beef broth

¼ cup (2 fl oz/60 ml) balsamic vinegar

2 bay leaves

2 sprigs each fresh rosemary and thyme

1 Tbsp dried oregano

Meaty short ribs go well with the robust flavors of traditional Italian cooking, and slow cooking coaxes them to fall-off-the-bone tenderness. For an extra flourish, garnish each serving with some of the gremolata traditionally sprinkled over Osso Buco (page 264), and serve atop Creamy Polenta (page 276).

On a plate, stir together the flour, 1 tsp salt, and ½ tsp pepper. Turn the ribs in the seasoned flour, shaking off any excess. In a large, heavy pot, heat the oil over medium-high heat. Working in batches, sear the ribs, turning occasionally, until evenly browned, about 10 minutes. Transfer to a plate.

Add the pancetta to the pot and sauté until mostly crisp, 4–5 minutes. Add the onions and sauté until beginning to soften, about 3 minutes. Stir in the garlic and red pepper flakes and sauté until fragrant, about 30 seconds. Add the carrots, tomato paste, and sugar and cook, stirring often, until well blended, about 1 minute. Add the wine, bring to a boil, and stir to scrape up any browned bits on the pan bottom. Stir in the tomatoes and their juices, broth, and vinegar and bring to a boil.

Preheat the oven to 350°F (180°C). Return the ribs to the pot with the tomato mixture. Add the bay leaves, rosemary and thyme sprigs, and oregano. Cover and cook in the oven until the ribs are very tender, about 2 hours.

Skim as much fat as possible from the cooking liquid and discard the bay leaves. Season with salt and pepper and serve.

3

LEMON-HERB RISOTTO

serves 6

3 cups (24 fl oz/750 ml) chicken or vegetable broth

5 Tbsp (2½ oz/75 g) unsalted butter

3 Tbsp olive oil

3 Tbsp minced shallot

2¼ cups (1 lb/500 g) Arborio or Carnaroli rice

½ cup (4 fl oz/125 ml) fresh lemon juice

¼ cup (⅓ oz/10 g) coarsely grated lemon zest

¾ cup (3 oz/90 g) grated Parmesan cheese, plus shaved cheese for garnish

Salt and freshly ground pepper

¼ cup (⅓ oz/10 g) minced fresh chervil or flat-leaf parsley

A lemony risotto brightens cold winter days. Add the zest at the very end, so its flavor will be fresh; its volatile oils will quickly dissipate if warmed too long. Chicken broth, Parmesan, and creamy grains make this risotto a filling dish on its own, but it is also an excellent side dish for fish.

In a saucepan, combine the broth with 3 cups (24 fl oz/750 ml) water, bring to a gentle simmer over medium heat, and then reduce the heat to low to maintain the simmer.

In a large, heavy saucepan, melt 2 Tbsp of the butter with the oil over medium heat. Add the shallot and sauté until translucent, 2–3 minutes. Add the rice and stir until well coated and translucent, about 3 minutes. Add the simmering broth a ladleful at a time, stirring frequently after each addition. Wait until the broth is almost completely absorbed (but the rice is never dry on top) before adding the next ladleful. Reserve ½ cup (4 fl oz/125 ml) broth.

When the rice is nearly tender to the bite but is still slightly firm in the center and is creamy, after 20–25 minutes, stir the lemon juice into the reserved ½ cup broth. Add the mixture little by little to the rice along with the remaining 3 Tbsp butter, the lemon zest, and the grated Parmesan, stirring constantly. Season with salt and pepper and stir in the chervil. Serve, garnished with shaved Parmesan.

4

FIVE-SPICE CHICKEN SOUP

serves 6

2 lb (1 kg) skinless, boneless chicken thighs

Salt and freshly ground pepper

1 tsp five-spice powder

2 Tbsp peanut oil

1 yellow onion, finely chopped

5½ cups (44 fl oz/1.35 l) chicken broth

Two 1-inch (2.5-cm) pieces peeled fresh ginger

¼ cup (2 fl oz/60 ml) soy sauce

¼ cup (2 fl oz/60 ml) Asian fish sauce

1 Tbsp rice vinegar

4 oz (125 g) rice stick noodles

2 Tbsp chopped fresh basil

2 Tbsp chopped fresh cilantro

1 cup (3 oz/90 g) bean sprouts

½–1 small serrano or jalapeño chile, seeded and thinly sliced

Lime wedges for serving

During the heart of winter, spices are key in creating warming soups and stews. Here, five-spice powder—a mixture of cloves, star anise, fennel, cinnamon, Sichuan peppercorns, and ginger—flavors a Southeast Asian–inspired soup that is topped with crunchy bean sprouts and fresh herbs.

Season the chicken generously on all sides with salt and pepper and the five-spice powder. In a large, heavy frying pan, heat the oil over medium-high heat. Working in batches, add the chicken and sear, turning as needed, until golden brown, about 8 minutes. Drain on paper towels, then transfer to a slow cooker.

Add the onion to the pan and sauté over medium-high heat until golden, 6–7 minutes. Pour in 1 cup (8 fl oz/250 ml) of the broth and stir to scrape up any browned bits on the pan bottom. Transfer the contents of the pan to the slow cooker. Stir in the remaining 4½ cups (36 fl oz/1.1 l) broth, the ginger, soy sauce, fish sauce, and vinegar. Cover and cook on the low setting for 5 hours. The chicken should be very tender.

About 10 minutes before the soup is ready, place the noodles in a bowl with hot water to cover generously and rehydrate. Meanwhile, transfer the chicken to a plate and discard the ginger. Using 2 forks, shred the meat and return it to the soup. Drain the noodles and stir into the soup. Warm through for about 2 minutes on the high setting.

Ladle the soup into bowls. Scatter with the basil, cilantro, bean sprouts, and chile, and serve with the lime wedges.

7

JANUARY

In this classic eastern European comfort food recipe, sweet-and-sour pork stuffing is bundled into winter cabbage leaves, which is then braised until juicy and succulent. The cabbage rolls can be prepared a few hours ahead and reheated.

PORK-STUFFED CABBAGE ROLLS

serves 4

FOR THE CABBAGE ROLLS

1 head green cabbage, about 2 lb (1 kg), bruised outer leaves discarded

1 lb (500 g) lean ground pork

½ cup (2½ oz/75 g) cooked rice

1 egg

3 green onions, white and tender green parts, thinly sliced

¼ tsp freshly grated nutmeg

Salt and freshly ground pepper

4 slices bacon, about 4 oz (125 g) total weight

1 yellow onion, chopped

1 celery rib, chopped

1 carrot, chopped

1 tsp caraway seeds

1 can (28 oz/ 875 g) crushed tomatoes

1 cup (8 fl oz/250 ml) chicken broth

¼ cup (1½ oz/45 g) raisins

1 Tbsp red wine vinegar

To make the cabbage rolls, bring a large, heavy pot of water to a boil. Cut out the core from the cabbage. Lower the cabbage into the boiling water and cook until the leaves soften, about 5 minutes. Set aside to cool slightly.

Gently peel off 12 large outer leaves from the cabbage head. Drain the leaves and let cool. Coarsely chop enough of the remaining cabbage to make ¼ cup (1 oz/30 g).

In a bowl, combine the chopped cabbage, pork, rice, egg, green onions, and nutmeg. Season with ¾ tsp salt and ½ tsp pepper. Using your hands, gently but thoroughly blend the ingredients. Spread the cabbage leaves out on a work surface. Divide the pork filling among the leaves. Fold the core end of each leaf over the filling, then fold in the sides and roll up the leaf.

Preheat the oven to 325°F (165°C). In the pot, cook the bacon over medium heat, turning once, until crisp, about 5 minutes. Set aside to drain on paper towels.

Add the onion, celery, and carrot to the pot and sauté over medium heat until the vegetables are tender, about 5 minutes. Stir in the caraway seeds, tomatoes, broth, raisins, and vinegar. Place the cabbage ⟫

rolls, seam side down, in a single layer in the pot, spooning some of the liquid over the rolls. Cover and bake until the cabbage rolls are tender and the pork filling is cooked through, 1–1½ hours.

Crumble the reserved bacon over the tops of the rolls to garnish, then serve.

8

JANUARY

Potatoes doused in creamy sauce are always comforting, but the addition of firm white fish and sweet, oniony leeks make this a dish fit for company. Toss together a big salad, open a bottle of dry white wine, and dinner is served.

COD, LEEK & POTATO GRATIN

serves 4

Butter for baking dish

1½ lb (750 g) white potatoes, peeled

2 leeks, white and pale green parts, halved

1 lb (500 g) cod or haddock fillets, thickly sliced on the diagonal

Salt and ground white pepper

1 cup (8 fl oz/250 ml) heavy cream

Preheat the oven to 375°F (190°C). Butter a 13-inch (33-cm) oval gratin pan or 4 deep, individual-sized baking dishes. Cut the potatoes crosswise into thin, uniform slices. Cut the leeks crosswise into slices about twice as thick as the potatoes. Season the fish lightly with salt and pepper.

Arrange half of the potato slices in the prepared dish, overlapping them to cover the bottom. Season lightly with salt and pepper. Scatter half of the leeks over the potatoes, then arrange the fish slices over the leeks in a single layer, overlapping the slices as necessary. Top with the remaining leeks, then with the remaining potatoes. Season with salt and pepper. Pour the cream evenly over the layers. Bake for 40 minutes.

Remove from the oven and spoon some of the cooking liquid over the top of the gratin to moisten the potatoes and help them brown. Continue to bake until the top layer of potatoes is tender when pierced with a sharp knife, about 20 minutes. Let stand for 10–15 minutes and serve.

9

SPICY SIMMERED EGGS WITH KALE

serves 4

2 Tbsp unsalted butter

4 green onions, white and light green parts only, chopped

2 cloves garlic, minced

2 bunches kale, tough stems removed, roughly chopped

1 cup chicken or vegetable broth

Salt and freshly ground black pepper

Zest and juice of 1 lemon

4 eggs

Red pepper flakes

This simple, rustic dish is both healthy and hearty. Winter kale is first braised with fragrant garlic, green onions, and lemon juice. Protein-rich eggs are then nestled into the bed of kale, where they gently simmer to perfection. A finishing garnish of chile flakes adds the perfect amount of contrasting heat.

In a large skillet over medium-high heat, melt the butter. Add the green onions and garlic and cook, stirring, until fragrant, about 1 minute. Add half of the kale and sauté, stirring frequently until it begins to wilt, about 2 minutes. Stir in the remaining kale and repeat. Add the chicken broth, ½ tsp salt, and ¼ tsp black pepper. Stir in the lemon zest and juice. Let simmer, stirring occasionally, until the kale softens, about 6 minutes.

Using the back of a spoon, create a pocket for each egg in the kale. Crack one egg into each pocket. Reduce the heat to medium-low, and sprinkle the eggs with salt and black pepper. Cover the pan and let the eggs cook until almost opaque, 4–5 minutes. Turn off the heat and let the eggs rest, covered, until done to taste. Sprinkle with chile flakes and serve.

10

CHICKEN & COCONUT CURRY

serves 6–8

3 Tbsp canola oil

3 lb (1.5 kg) skinless, bone-in chicken thighs

3 cloves garlic, minced

2 shallots, minced

3 Tbsp Madras-style curry powder

1 Tbsp firmly packed dark brown sugar

1 tsp red pepper flakes

Freshly ground pepper

2 lemongrass stalks, center white part only, cut into 1-inch (2.5-cm) pieces

1-inch (2.5-cm) piece peeled fresh ginger, cut into 4 slices

1 cup (8 fl oz/250 ml) chicken broth

1 can (13½ fl oz/420 ml) unsweetened coconut milk

2 Tbsp Asian fish sauce

3 carrots, cut into 1-inch (2.5-cm) chunks

1 sweet potato, about ¾ lb (375 g), peeled and cut into 1-inch (2. 5-cm) chunks

3 Tbsp finely sliced fresh basil

With the infused flavors of ginger, lemongrass, and basil, this classic yellow curry is both fragrant and sweet and will appeal to milder palates. Choose a spicy curry powder if you like more of a kick. Serve over steamed jasmine rice.

In a large, heavy pot, heat the oil over medium-high heat. Working in batches, sear the chicken until nicely browned, about 4 minutes per side. Transfer to a plate.

Add the garlic and shallots to the pot and sauté just until fragrant, about 30 seconds. Add the curry powder, brown sugar, red pepper flakes, 1 tsp pepper, the lemongrass, and the ginger and sauté until the spices are fragrant and well blended with the garlic and shallots, about 30 seconds. Add the broth and stir to scrape up any browned bits on the pot bottom. Stir in the coconut milk and fish sauce and bring to a boil. Add the chicken, carrots, and sweet potato, pushing them into the mixture. Partially cover and cook over low heat until the chicken is opaque throughout and the vegetables are very tender, about 1 hour. Garnish with the basil and serve.

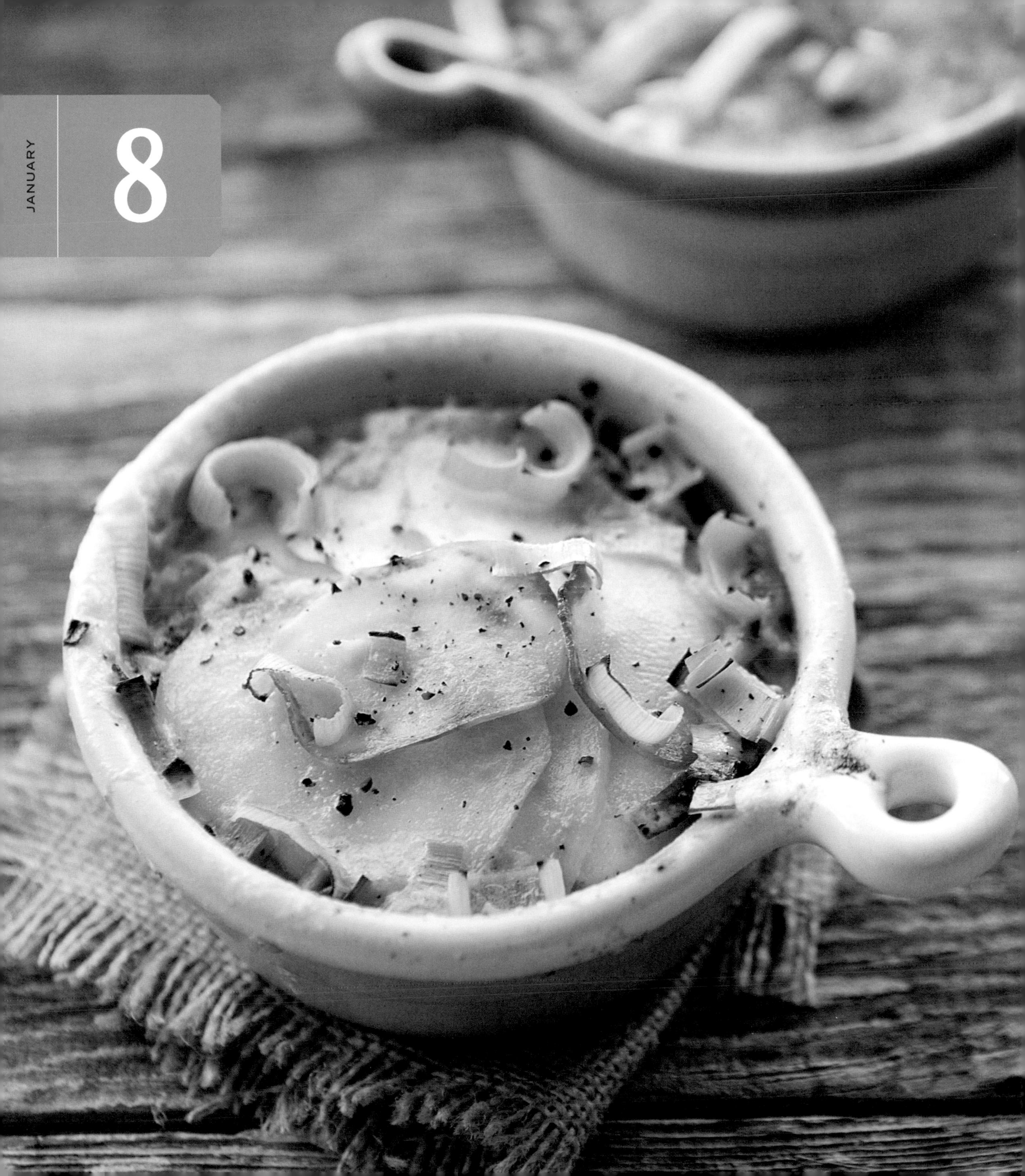

5

LAMB TAGINE WITH DATES & ALMONDS

serves 6–8

3 lb (1.5 kg) boneless lamb from leg or shoulder, cut into 1½-inch (4-cm) chunks

Salt and freshly ground black pepper

3 Tbsp olive oil

2 yellow onions, finely chopped

1 tsp ground cinnamon

1 tsp ground ginger

½ tsp ground cumin

¼ tsp cayenne pepper

¼ tsp saffron threads, crumbled

1½ cups (12 fl oz/375 ml) chicken broth

1 cup (4½ oz/140 g) slivered almonds, toasted

1⅔ cups (10 oz/315 g) pitted dates, halved

2 Tbsp honey

This North African lamb stew combines dried fruits, crunchy nuts, and fragrant hot and sweet spices for a satisfying meal in a pot. Accompany it with a side of instant couscous, which cooks in just minutes.

Put the lamb in a large bowl. Sprinkle with 1 tsp salt and 1 tsp black pepper and toss to coat evenly. In a large, heavy pot, warm the oil over medium-high heat. Working in batches, sear the lamb cubes, turning frequently, until evenly browned on all sides, about 5 minutes. Remove from the pot with a slotted spoon and set aside.

Add the onions to pot and sauté over medium-high heat until just starting to brown, 5–7 minutes. Add the cinnamon, ginger, cumin, cayenne, and saffron and sauté until the spices are fragrant and evenly coat the onions, about 1 minute. Add the broth and stir to scrape up any browned bits on the pot bottom. Bring to a boil.

Return the lamb and any juices to the pot. Cover and cook over very low heat until the lamb is very tender, about 3 hours. Uncover and add the toasted nuts and the dates to the pot. Drizzle with the honey and stir to combine, making sure that the dates are submerged in the cooking liquid. Cover and continue to cook until the dates have softened, about 10 minutes.

Adjust the seasoning with salt and pepper if necessary and serve.

6

CHICKEN & BROCCOLI CASSEROLE

serves 4–6

½ cup (2½ oz/75 g) all-purpose flour

1 Tbsp dried sage

1 tsp sweet paprika

6 skinless, boneless chicken breast halves

3 Tbsp unsalted butter

2 cups (6 oz/180 g) chopped broccoli

6 thin slices lean boiled ham

1 cup (8 fl oz/250 ml) heavy cream

¼ cup (2 fl oz/60 ml) dry sherry

½ cup (2 oz/60 g) grated Parmesan or Romano cheese

Salt and freshly ground pepper

There is sound reason why this retro-fabulous casserole has stuck around. Few kids or adults can resist the charms of tender chicken and crunchy broccoli, especially when topped with a golden, bubbling sauce. Serve it with steamed white rice.

Preheat the oven to 350°F (180°C).

In a sturdy paper bag, mix together the flour, sage, and paprika. Drop the chicken pieces into the bag, one at a time, and shake to coat on all sides. Shake off any excess flour mixture.

In a large frying pan, melt the butter over medium heat. Add the chicken pieces and sauté until golden, 3–4 minutes per side. Transfer to a plate.

Arrange the broccoli in a layer in the bottom of a baking dish. Cover with the chicken and top each piece with a slice of ham.

To make the sauce, pour off the excess oil from the pan and add the cream. Bring to a boil over high heat and stir to scrape up any browned bits on the pan bottom. Add the sherry and boil for 2 minutes. Stir in all but 2 Tbsp of the cheese and season with salt and pepper. Remove from the heat.

Pour the sauce over the ham and chicken. Sprinkle with the remaining 2 Tbsp cheese.

Bake until the chicken is opaque throughout, the broccoli is tender, and the sauce is bubbling, 30–40 minutes. Serve directly from the dish.

11

Slowly cooking duck breasts with sweet and savory spices beautifully complements their rich flavor and texture. The season's crisp bok choy cabbage cooks right alongside in the pot. Serve with steamed jasmine rice.

ALLSPICE DUCK WITH BRAISED BOK CHOY

serves 6–8

3 Tbsp canola oil

Salt and freshly ground pepper

4 lb (2 kg) boneless duck breasts

2 yellow onions, finely chopped

2 cloves garlic, minced

1-inch (2.5-cm) piece peeled fresh ginger, grated

1½ Tbsp ground allspice

1 cinnamon stick

1 star anise, broken into pieces

1½ cups (12 fl oz/375 ml) chicken broth

¼ cup (2 oz/60 g) firmly packed dark brown sugar

¼ cup (2 fl oz/60 ml) soy sauce

3 Tbsp hoisin sauce

6 baby bok choy, each cut lengthwise into quarters

In a large, heavy pot, heat the oil over medium-high heat. In a small bowl, combine 1½ tsp salt and 1 tsp pepper. Rub the mixture all over the duck breasts. Place in the pot, skin side down, and sear, turning once, until well browned, 4–5 minutes per side. Transfer to a plate.

Pour off all but a thin coating of fat from the pot. Add the onions, garlic, ginger, allspice, cinnamon, and star anise and sauté over medium-high heat until the onions begin to soften, about 3 minutes. Add the broth and stir to scrape up any browned bits on the pot bottom. Stir in the sugar, soy sauce, and hoisin sauce and bring to a boil.

Return the duck breasts to the pot. Partially cover and cook over very low heat for 1 hour. Uncover and skim the fat from the surface of the cooking liquid. Arrange the bok choy around the duck breasts, pushing it slightly into the cooking liquid. Partially cover and cook until the duck is very tender and the sauce is thick, about 30 minutes.

Cut the duck breasts on the diagonal into thin slices and arrange on a platter with the bok choy. Spoon the sauce over the top and serve.

12

This dish has a sophisticated flavor and impressive appearance, but the cook's secret is that it really showcases the crab, and requires few other ingredients. Turn this into an elegant multi-course meal by starting with a mixed green salad and finishing with a lemony dessert.

CRAB SOUFFLÉ

serves 4

4 Tbsp (2 oz/60 g) unsalted butter

1 Tbsp grated Parmesan cheese

4 eggs, separated, plus 2 egg whites

2 Tbsp minced shallot

¼ cup (1½ oz/45 g) all-purpose flour

Salt and freshly ground black pepper

⅛ tsp cayenne pepper

1 cup (8 fl oz/250 ml) milk

1 cup (6 oz/185 g) cooked lump crabmeat, picked over for shell fragments, coarsely torn or chopped

Preheat the oven to 375°F (190°C). Use ½ Tbsp of the butter to grease the bottom and sides of a 1-qt (1-l) soufflé dish, then coat with the cheese.

In a bowl, using an electric mixer, beat the 6 egg whites until stiff peaks form, about 4 minutes. In another bowl, using the electric mixer, beat the 4 egg yolks until creamy, about 2 minutes. Set aside.

In a saucepan, melt the remaining 3½ Tbsp butter over medium-high heat. Add the shallot and sauté until translucent, about 1 minute. Remove from the heat and whisk in the flour, 1 tsp salt, ¼ tsp black pepper, and the cayenne. Return to the heat and slowly add the milk, whisking constantly. Cook, stirring often, until a smooth, thick sauce forms, about 5 minutes. Let cool for about 3 minutes.

Whisk the egg yolks into the sauce until well blended. Stir in the crabmeat. Stir 3 Tbsp of the egg whites into the crab mixture to lighten it. Using a rubber spatula, gently fold in the remaining egg whites just until no white streaks remain. Gently spoon the mixture into the prepared dish. Bake until the top has puffed and is golden brown, about 40 minutes. Serve at once.

13

For this rustic pie, a tender beef-and-vegetable stew is topped with creamy mashed potatoes and baked in the oven. Roasted garlic simmers along with the beef, and becomes sweet and mellow in flavor.

BEEF & ROASTED GARLIC PIE

serves 6–8

1 head garlic

4 Tbsp (2 fl oz/60 ml) olive oil

3 Tbsp all-purpose flour

Salt and freshly ground pepper

2½ lb (1.25 kg) lean stewing beef, such as chuck or round, cut into 1½-inch (4-cm) chunks

4 large shallots, finely chopped

½ cup (4 fl oz/125 ml) dry red wine

1 cup (8 fl oz/250 ml) beef broth

3 carrots, chopped

3 celery ribs, chopped

2 bay leaves

1 large strip lemon zest

2 lb (1 kg) Yukon gold potatoes, peeled and cut into 1½-inch (4-cm) chunks

1 cup (8 fl oz/250 ml) heavy cream

2 Tbsp grated Parmesan cheese

2 tsp dry mustard

Preheat the oven to 400°F (200°C). Slice off the top of the garlic head to expose the cloves. Drizzle with 1 Tbsp of the oil. Wrap in foil and bake until the cloves are very soft, about 30 minutes. When cool enough to handle, squeeze the garlic pulp into a bowl.

On a plate, stir together the flour, 1 tsp salt, and 1 tsp pepper. Dredge the beef in the flour, shaking off any excess. In a large, heavy pot, warm the remaining 3 Tbsp oil over medium-high heat. Working in batches, sear the beef, turning as needed, until evenly browned on all sides, 5–7 minutes. Transfer to a plate.

Add the shallots to the pot and sauté until softened, about 1 minute. Add the wine and stir to scrape up any browned bits on the pan bottom. Add the broth and the reserved garlic pulp and bring to a boil, stirring to break up the garlic. Return the beef and any juices to the pot and add the carrots, celery, bay leaves, and lemon zest. Cover and cook at low heat until the beef is very tender, about 2 hours.

About 30 minutes before the beef is done, preheat the oven to 350°F (180°C). Put the potatoes in another pot and cover with salted water. Bring to a boil and cook until ⇢

tender, 15–20 minutes. Drain and return to the pot. Add the cream, Parmesan, and mustard, then mash with a potato masher until smooth. Season with salt and pepper.

When the beef is done, discard the bay leaves and lemon zest. Transfer the beef, vegetables, and sauce to a 9-by-13-inch (23-by-33-cm) baking dish. Using a wooden spoon, press down lightly on the meat chunks to break them up slightly and spread them evenly. Spread the mashed potatoes evenly over the top. Bake until the potatoes are golden brown, about 30 minutes. Serve.

14

Big pasta tubes are a favorite for tossing with other ingredients and baking into one-dish meals. Here, the classic tomato ragu is replaced with strips of Italian ham, sweet peas, and an elegant white sauce.

BAKED PASTA WITH PROSCIUTTO & PEAS

serves 4–6

½ cup (4 oz/125 g) unsalted butter, plus more for greasing

1 lb (500 g) ziti, penne, or other tubular pasta

½ cup (2½ oz/75 g) all-purpose flour

4 cups (32 fl oz/1 l) milk

⅛ tsp grated nutmeg

2 cups (8 oz/250 g) grated Parmesan cheese

1 cup (5 oz/155 g) frozen petite peas

¼ lb (125 g) prosciutto or ham, chopped

½ cup (1 oz/30 g) fresh bread crumbs

Preheat the oven to 425°F (220°C) and butter a 2-qt (2-l) baking dish. Bring a large pot of salted water to a boil. Add the pasta and cook, stirring occasionally, until not quite al dente, about 2 minutes less than the package directions. Drain, rinse with cold water, drain again, and set aside.

In the same pot, melt the ½ cup butter over medium heat. Add the flour and cook, stirring, for 30 seconds. Slowly whisk in the milk, and cook, whisking, until the sauce is thick and creamy, 5–10 minutes. Stir in the nutmeg, cheese, peas, and prosciutto. Add the pasta and toss to combine.

Transfer the pasta and sauce to the prepared dish. Sprinkle with the bread crumbs. Bake until the crumbs are golden and the sauce is bubbling, about 20 minutes. Let cool for about 10 minutes before serving.

15

This classic Mediterranean dish pairs meaty fish with a slightly sweet, vinegary sauce and is served cold or at room temperature. Fragrant with orange zest and garlic, it is finished with a sprinkle of chile flakes, just enough spice to give it a bite.

TUNA IN ESCABECHE

serves 4–6

3 Tbsp olive oil

1½ lb (750 g) albacore or yellowfin tuna fillet, about 1 inch (2.5 cm) thick, cut into 6–8 pieces

1 red bell pepper, seeded and thinly sliced

½ red onion, thinly sliced

1 cup (8 fl oz/250 ml) dry white wine

¾ cup (6 fl oz/180 ml) sherry vinegar

2 cloves garlic, crushed

½ tsp black peppercorns

1 tsp grated orange zest

1 tsp sugar

½ tsp red pepper flakes

Salt

½ cup (2½ oz/75 g) pitted olives

In a large frying pan, warm 2 Tbsp of the oil over medium-high heat. Add the tuna and cook, turning once, until browned on both sides but still translucent in the center, 5–8 minutes. Transfer to a 2-qt (2-l) baking dish.

Add the remaining 1 Tbsp olive oil to the pan. Add the bell pepper and onion and sauté until softened, 3–5 minutes. Add the wine, vinegar, garlic, peppercorns, orange zest, sugar, and red pepper flakes. Season with ¾ tsp salt, pour in ¼ cup (2 fl oz/60 ml) water, and bring to a boil.

Pour the hot liquid and vegetables over the fish and scatter the olives over the top. Let stand until cooled to room temperature. Cover and refrigerate for at least 8 hours or up to 24 hours.

Lift the tuna from the marinade and transfer to a platter. Drain the marinade, reserving the vegetables and olives, and arrange them over the tuna. Let stand for about 15 minutes before serving.

16

If January has you working hard on resolutions and thinking lean, vegetarian curries are your ally. Lentils offer protein and substance, spinach packs iron, and plenty of spice means you won't have to compromise on flavor.

LENTIL, POTATO & SPINACH CURRY

serves 4

1 cup (8 oz/250 g) small green French lentils, picked over and rinsed

1 carrot, cut into 3 pieces

1 celery rib, cut into 3 pieces

1 yellow onion, halved

5 sprigs fresh flat-leaf parsley

2 Tbsp canola oil

2 cloves garlic, minced

1 Tbsp garam masala

2 tsp ground cumin

1 tsp ground coriander

Salt and freshly ground pepper

2 large red-skinned potatoes, cut into 1-inch (2.5-cm) cubes

2 cups (3 oz/90 g) packed baby spinach

Cooked white or brown basmati rice for serving

¼ cup (2 oz/60 g) plain yogurt

In a large, heavy pot, combine the lentils, carrot, celery, half of the onion, and the parsley sprigs. Pour in 4 cups (32 fl oz/1 l) water and bring to a boil over medium-high heat. Reduce the heat to medium-low, cover, and simmer until the lentils are tender, about 35 minutes. Remove and discard the vegetables. Strain the lentils and reserve the cooking liquid in a separate bowl.

In the pot, warm the oil over medium-high heat. Chop the remaining half onion then add and sauté until browned, about 8 minutes. Stir in the garlic, garam masala, cumin, coriander, 1 tsp salt, and ¼ tsp pepper and stir until the spices are toasted and fragrant, about 1 minute.

Add the potatoes, reserved lentils, and 2 cups (16 fl oz/500 ml) of the reserved cooking liquid. If necessary, use water to supplement. Bring to a boil, reduce the heat to medium-low, and simmer, covered, until the potatoes are tender, 15–18 minutes. Stir in the spinach and cook until it wilts, about 2 minutes. Season with salt and pepper. Serve over rice, garnished with the yogurt.

17

Daube is a traditional French stew: rich, hearty, and perfect for the cold-weather months. In this version, white wine, tomatoes, and Dijon mustard are a departure from the red wine-laced original. A little crème fraîche whisked in right at the end adds body and sweetness. Serve over warm buttered noodles, and don't hesitate to braise the beef ahead of time— this dish tastes even better the next day.

BEEF DAUBE
serves 4–6

2 lb (1 kg) stewing beef such as shoulder, chuck, or brisket, cut into 2-inch (5-cm) chunks

Salt and freshly ground pepper

3 Tbsp olive oil

¼ cup (2 fl oz/60 ml) brandy

1 bottle (24 fl oz/750 ml) dry white wine

2 Tbsp Dijon mustard

1 can (14½ oz/400 g) whole peeled tomatoes

3 small yellow onions, thinly sliced

6 cloves garlic, lightly crushed

3 sprigs fresh thyme

3 sprigs fresh tarragon

2 sprigs fresh winter or summer savory or flat-leaf parsley

5 Tbsp (3 oz/80 g) crème fraîche or ¼ cup (2 oz/60 g) sour cream

Season the beef generously with salt and pepper. In a large, heavy pot, warm the oil over medium heat. Working in batches, sear the beef, turning as needed, until evenly browned on all sides, 5–7 minutes. Transfer to a plate.

Preheat the oven to 300°F (150°C). Pour off any excess fat from the pan. Add the brandy and wine to the pot, return to medium heat, and stir to scrape up any browned bits on the pot bottom. Simmer for about 8 minutes. Whisk in the mustard. Add the meat and any juices, tomatoes and their juices, the onions, and garlic. Tie the thyme, tarragon, and savory sprigs tightly together with kitchen string and add to the pot. Cover and cook in the oven until the meat is fork-tender, 2½–3 hours.

Using a slotted spoon, transfer the meat, tomatoes, and onions to a platter. Discard the bundle of herbs. Bring the cooking liquid to a boil and cook until reduced by about one-third, 8–10 minutes. Stir in the crème fraîche until blended. Adjust the seasoning and return the meat and vegetables to the pot to heat through. Serve directly from the pot.

18

Any hard-shell clam variety is good for this creamy soup, such as littleneck, cherrystone, quahog, and so-called chowder clams. To prepare clams for cooking, scrub them well under cold water and discard any that do not close to the touch. Dissolve 2 tsp salt in 4 qt (4 l) cold water, add the clams, and refrigerate for 30 minutes or longer to allow the clams to expel sand and grit. Drain before using.

NEW ENGLAND CLAM CHOWDER
serves 6–8

48 littleneck or cherrystone clams, scrubbed and soaked

4 slices bacon

1 large yellow onion, chopped

2 large russet potatoes, peeled and cut into ½-inch (12-mm) cubes

3 sprigs fresh thyme, or ¼ tsp dried thyme

1½ cups (12 fl oz/375 ml) half-and-half

Salt and freshly ground pepper

Chopped fresh flat-leaf parsley for garnish

In a large pot, combine the clams and 1 cup (8 fl oz/250 ml) water, discarding any clams that do not close to the touch. Cover tightly and bring to a boil. Cook the clams until they open, about 5 minutes. Using tongs, transfer the opened clams to a platter. If some clams fail to open, re-cover the pot, and continue cooking the remaining clams for a few minutes longer. Discard any unopened clams after 10 minutes total cooking time. Reserve the cooking liquid. Let the opened clams stand until cool enough to handle, then remove the meat from the shells and chop coarsely.

Strain the cooking liquid through a fine-mesh sieve into a 1-qt (1-l) glass measuring cup, leaving any grit in the bottom of the pot. Add water as needed to make 4 cups (32 fl oz/1 l) liquid.

Rinse out the pot, add the bacon, and cook over medium heat until crisp and browned, about 6 minutes. Drain on paper towels; leave the bacon fat in the pan. Chop the bacon.

Add the onion to the pot over medium heat and cook, stirring occasionally, until softened, about 3 minutes. Add the potatoes and thyme, stir in the reserved clam liquid, and bring to a boil. Reduce the heat to medium-low, cover, and cook until the potatoes are tender, about 20 minutes. Add the half-and-half and reserved clams and return just to a simmer; do not boil. For a thicker chowder, crush some of the potatoes into the liquid with the back of a large spoon. Season with salt and pepper. Discard the thyme sprigs.

Serve the chowder garnished with the parsley and reserved bacon.

19

These are the classic stuffed shells, filled with fluffy white ricotta cheese and spinach. They are topped with a smooth, flavorful sauce made by slowly simmering tomatoes with just a handful of ingredients. If you're short on time, substitute your favorite bottled marinara sauce.

RICOTTA & SPINACH–STUFFED PASTA SHELLS

serves 4–6

FOR THE SAUCE

1 can (28 oz/875 g) whole peeled tomatoes

1 small carrot, halved

½ small yellow onion, roughly chopped

4 large fresh basil leaves, minced

2 Tbsp olive oil

Salt and freshly ground pepper

FOR THE FILLING

1¼ lb (625 g) spinach, tough stems removed

3½ cups (1¾ lb/875 g) whole-milk ricotta cheese

1 egg, lightly beaten

½ cup (2 oz/60 g) grated Parmesan cheese

⅛ tsp grated nutmeg

½ lb (250 g) large pasta shells

¼ cup (1 oz/30 g) grated Parmesan cheese

To make the sauce, drain the tomatoes, reserving half of their juices. In a saucepan, combine the tomatoes and reserved juices, the carrot, and onion. Bring to a boil over medium-high heat, reduce the heat to medium-low, partially cover, and cook, stirring occasionally, for 45 minutes. Remove from the heat, stir in the basil, and let cool slightly. Pass the mixture through a food mill or a medium-mesh sieve back into the pan. Stir in the oil, season with salt and pepper, and set aside.

Meanwhile, to make the filling, bring a pot of water to a boil and add the spinach and ¼ tsp salt. Cook just until tender, about 2 minutes. Using a slotted spoon, transfer the spinach to a colander to drain. Reserve the cooking water in the pot. Squeeze out excess moisture from the spinach, then finely chop. Add the ricotta to a bowl and stir in the egg until smooth. Add the spinach, the ½ cup Parmesan, the nutmeg, ¼ tsp salt, and a few grindings of pepper and mix well. ⤻

Add water to the reserved spinach water in the pot to total 5 qt (5 l), and bring to a rapid boil. Add 2 Tbsp salt and the pasta shells to the boiling water, stir well, and cook, stirring occasionally, until not quite al dente, about 2 minutes less than the package directions. Drain, rinse with cold water, drain again, and set aside.

Preheat the oven to 375°F (190°C). Smear the bottom of a 9-by-13-inch (23-by-33-cm) baking dish with 2–3 Tbsp of the sauce. Using a teaspoon, stuff the shells with the filling. They should be generously filled but not so stuffed that they are wide open. Place the stuffed shells, side by side and open side up, in the prepared dish. Drizzle with the remaining sauce and sprinkle with the ¼ cup Parmesan. Cover with foil and bake until the sauce is bubbling, about 25 minutes. Let stand for 10 minutes before serving.

20

STIR-FRIED SOBA NOODLES WITH BEEF & CABBAGE

serves 4

The nutty flavor and delicate texture of soba noodles pair particularly well with cabbage. The pure white ribs and bright green curly-edged leaves of napa cabbage make any dish look especially nice.

1 lb (500 g) boneless beef sirloin or tenderloin, partially frozen

¼ cup (2 fl oz/60 ml) toasted sesame oil

¼ cup (2 fl oz/60 ml) soy sauce

¼ cup (2 fl oz/60 ml) plus 1 Tbsp peanut oil

2 Tbsp peeled and grated fresh ginger

2 large cloves garlic, minced

4 green onions, including 3 inches (7.5 cm) of green tops, thinly sliced on the diagonal

1 head napa cabbage, about 2 lb (1 kg), cored and shredded

2 cups (16 fl oz/500 ml) chicken or beef broth

1 Tbsp cornstarch

½ lb (250 g) snow peas, trimmed and halved crosswise

Salt

¾ lb (375 g) dried soba noodles

¼ cup (1 oz/30 g) sesame seeds, lightly toasted

Using a sharp knife, cut the beef across the grain into thin slices, then cut the slices into matchsticks. In a bowl, whisk together the sesame oil, soy sauce, ¼ cup peanut oil, and ginger. Add the beef and stir to coat evenly. Cover and refrigerate, stirring occasionally, for at least 1 hour or up to 3 hours.

Bring a large pot of water to a rapid boil. Add 2 Tbsp salt and the noodles to the boiling water, stir well, and cook, stirring occasionally, until just tender, 5–7 minutes. Drain the noodles.

Meanwhile, in a wok or large frying pan, heat the 1 Tbsp peanut oil over medium-high heat. Add the garlic and green onions and stir-fry until lightly colored, about 1 minute. Raise the heat to high, add the beef and its marinade, and stir-fry until lightly browned, about 8 minutes. Add the cabbage and 1½ cups (12 fl oz/375 ml) of the broth and toss to combine. Cover, reduce the heat to medium-high, and cook until the cabbage wilts, about 4 minutes.

In a small bowl, whisk the cornstarch into the remaining ½ cup (4 fl oz/125 ml) broth. Add the cornstarch mixture to the pan, and stir and toss to incorporate. Add the ⟫→

snow peas, stir and toss to combine, cover, and cook until just tender, about 2 minutes. Take care not to overcook; the snow peas and cabbage should remain crisp.

Add the noodles to the pan and stir and toss until well combined. Garnish with the toasted sesame seeds, and serve.

21

IRISH STEW

serves 6–8

Irish stew is the ideal slow-cooked wintertime meal featuring tender lamb and root vegetables in a meaty broth. Use dark stout for a deeper-flavored sauce, or ale for a lighter touch—and don't hesitate to serve a cold pint of either beer alongside.

2 lb (1 kg) boneless leg of lamb, cut into 1½- to 2-inch (4- to 5-cm) chunks

Salt and freshly ground pepper

2 Tbsp unsalted butter

2 Tbsp canola oil

1 yellow onion, coarsely chopped

3 carrots, cut into large pieces

2 Tbsp all-purpose flour

1½ cups (12 fl oz/375 ml) beef broth

1 cup (8 fl oz/250 ml) stout or ale

3 Yukon gold potatoes, cut into large pieces

2 Tbsp chopped fresh flat-leaf parsley

Preheat the oven to 325°F (165°C).

Season the lamb generously with salt and pepper. In a large, heavy pot, melt the butter with the oil over medium-high heat. Add the lamb and cook, turning often, until browned on all sides, 5–7 minutes. Transfer to a plate.

Pour off all but 1 Tbsp of the fat from the pan. Add the onion and carrots and cook, stirring frequently, until the onion is slightly softened, about 3 minutes. Sprinkle with the flour and cook, stirring, for 1–2 minutes. Pour in the broth and stout and bring to a boil, stirring to scrape up any browned bits on the pot bottom. Return the lamb to the pot, cover, and cook in the oven until the meat is tender, about 1 hour.

Add the potatoes along with 2 cups (16 fl oz/ 500 ml) water to the pot and continue to cook, covered, until the lamb is very tender, about 45 minutes longer. Serve, garnished with the parsley.

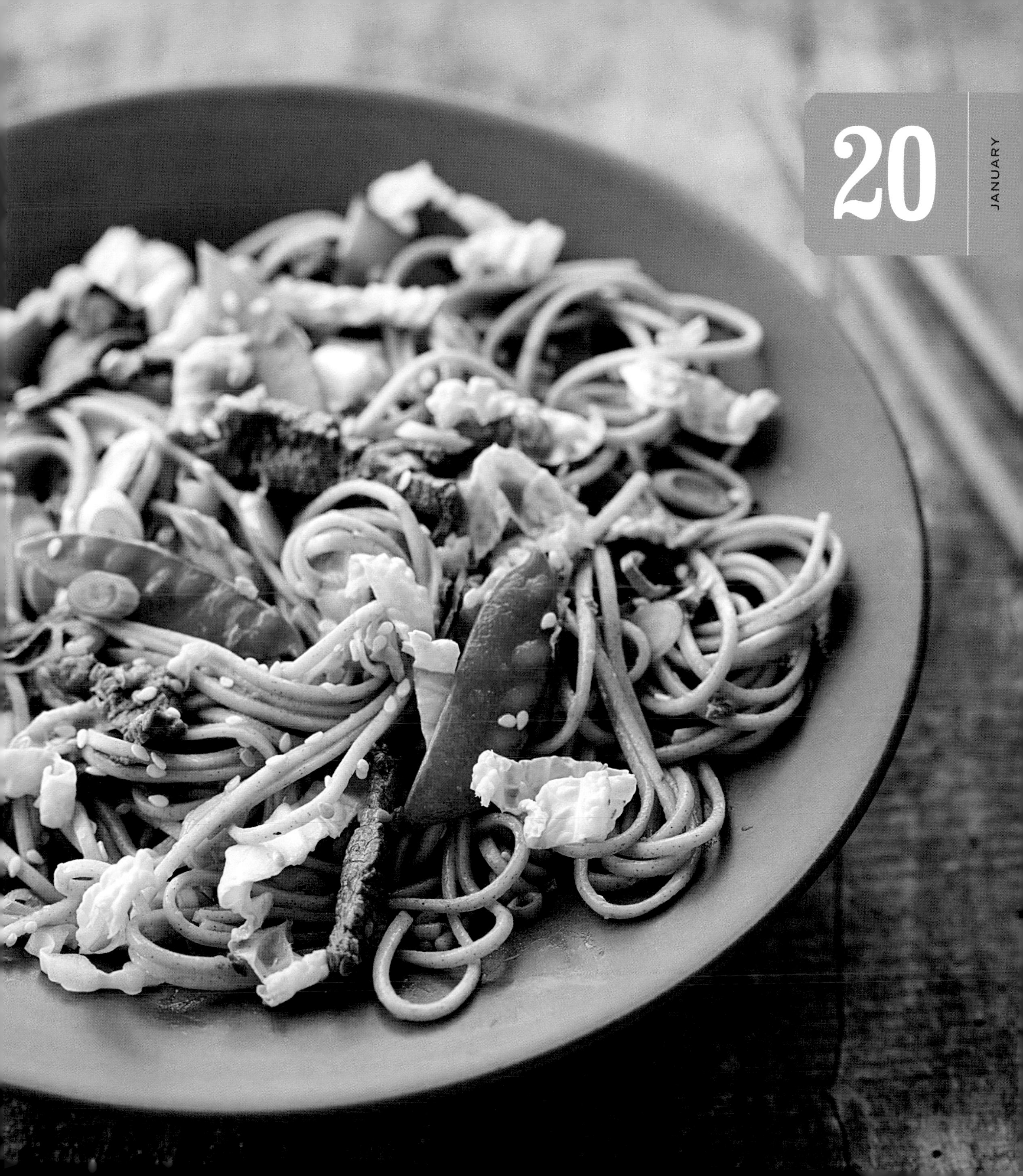

20

JANUARY

22

This is a classic quiche, with a creamy egg custard flavored simply with bacon and Gruyère cheese. It is delicious at any time of day, so try a wedge next to a tangle of salad greens at dinner. You'll want a glass of white wine, preferably one from the Lorraine region, where the dish takes its name.

QUICHE LORRAINE
serves 6

FOR THE TART DOUGH

2 cups (10 oz/315 g) all-purpose flour

Salt and freshly ground pepper

½ cup (4 oz/125 g) cold unsalted butter, cut into ½-inch (12-mm) pieces

6 Tbsp (3 fl oz/80 ml) ice water

3 eggs

1 cup (8 fl oz/250 ml) heavy cream

½ cup (4 fl oz/125 ml) half-and-half

⅛ tsp grated nutmeg

¾ cup (3 oz /90 g) shredded Gruyère cheese

4 thin slices bacon, fried until crisp and cut into ½-inch (12-mm) pieces

Preheat the oven to 375°F (190°C). To make the tart dough, in a bowl, stir together the flour and ½ tsp salt. Scatter the butter over the flour mixture. Using a pastry blender or 2 knives, cut in the butter until pea-sized crumbs form. Add the ice water, 1 Tbsp at a time, while turning the dough lightly with a fork and then with your fingertips; do not overwork the dough or it will become tough. Gather the dough into a ball (it should be a little crumbly), wrap in plastic wrap, and refrigerate for 15 minutes.

On a floured work surface, roll out the dough into a round about 10½ inches (26.5 cm) in diameter and ¼ inch (6 mm) thick. Carefully transfer it to a 9-inch (23-cm) quiche pan or other straight-sided pan with 1-inch (2.5-cm) sides. Press the dough into the bottom and sides of the pan. Pinch the dough around the rim to form a fluted edge. Line the dough with foil and fill with pie weights or dried beans. Bake until the crust is set but not browned, 12–15 minutes. Remove from the oven and lift out the weights and foil. Prick any bubbles with a fork. Bake until the crust is firm and barely colored, about 5 minutes. Transfer to a wire rack. Reduce the oven temperature to 350°F (180°C) and set a rack in the lower third of the oven.

In a bowl, stir together the eggs, cream, half-and-half, ½ tsp salt, ½ tsp pepper, nutmeg, and half of the Gruyère until blended. Scatter the cooked bacon over the pastry crust ≫→

and pour in the egg mixture. Sprinkle the remaining cheese over the top.

Bake on the bottom oven rack until the top is puffed and lightly golden and a knife inserted into the center comes out clean, 25–30 minutes. Transfer to the wire rack and let stand for 15 minutes. Cut into wedges and serve.

23

A sticky-sweet marmalade-based glaze is delicious on roast poultry. Chicken thighs are perfect for roasting, which creates moist and flavorful meat and crispy, savory skin.

ORANGE-GLAZED CHICKEN
serves 4

2 Tbsp olive oil, plus more for greasing

1 tsp ground cumin

Salt and freshly ground pepper

8 skin-on, bone-in chicken thighs, about 3 lb (1.5 kg) total weight

1 Tbsp unsalted butter

1 shallot, minced

1 cup (10 oz/315 g) orange marmalade

¼ cup (2 fl oz/60 ml) cider vinegar

1 Tbsp Dijon mustard

1 tsp cornstarch mixed with 1 Tbsp cold water

Cooked rice for serving

Preheat the oven to 425°F (220°C). Lightly oil a roasting pan large enough to hold the thighs in a single layer.

In a small bowl, stir together the cumin, 1½ tsp salt, and ½ tsp pepper. Brush the chicken thighs on all sides with the 2 Tbsp oil and season with the cumin mixture, pressing it into the skin. Arrange the thighs, skin side up, in the prepared pan. Roast until the skin is lightly golden, about 20 minutes.

Meanwhile, in a saucepan, melt the butter over medium heat. Add the shallot and cook, stirring, until softened, about 2 minutes. Stir in the marmalade, vinegar, mustard, and 1 tsp pepper and stir until the marmalade melts. Stir the cornstarch mixture, add to the pan, and cook, stirring, just until the glaze thickens, about 30 seconds.

Brush the skin side of the chicken thighs generously with the glaze and continue to roast for 5 minutes. Brush again with the glaze and roast until the chicken is opaque throughout, 5–10 minutes. Serve with rice, if desired.

24

BAKED RICE WITH CHICKPEAS & CHORIZO

serves 4–6

Large pinch saffron threads

2 Tbsp olive oil

4 oz (125 g) cured Spanish-style chorizo, cut on the diagonal into rounds ¼ inch (6 mm) thick

1 yellow onion, finely chopped

½ cup (2½ oz/75 g) seeded and chopped red bell pepper

4 cloves garlic, minced

1 cup (7 oz/220 g) Arborio or other medium-grain white rice

1 cup (7 oz/220 g) rinsed and drained canned chickpeas

½ cup (3 oz/90 g) canned crushed tomatoes

2 cups (16 fl oz/500 ml) chicken broth

1½ tsp Spanish smoked paprika

½ tsp ground cumin

Salt

3 Tbsp chopped fresh flat-leaf parsley

Spain boasts many delicious variations on baked rice. This rustic dish from Valenica, called arroz al horno (rice from the oven), is traditionally baked in an earthenware pot. Here, canned chickpeas are used for convenience, but if you simmer your own you can substitute some of their cooking liquid for some of the chicken broth.

In a large, dry frying pan, toast the saffron threads over medium heat, stirring constantly, until fragrant and a shade darker, about 1 minute. Pour into a bowl and crumble with your fingertips.

Preheat the oven to 350°F (180°C).

In the frying pan, warm the oil over medium-high heat. Add the chorizo and onion and sauté until the onion is soft and translucent, 3–5 minutes. Add the bell pepper and garlic and sauté until the bell pepper is softened, about 2 minutes. Add the rice and stir to coat. Transfer the mixture to a 2-qt (2-l) baking dish and stir in the chickpeas and tomatoes.

Combine the broth, paprika, cumin, ½ tsp salt, and the saffron in the frying pan and bring to a boil over high heat. Carefully pour the broth mixture over the rice mixture. Cover with foil and bake until the rice is tender and the liquid is absorbed, 30–40 minutes. Let stand, covered, for 10 minutes.

Fluff the rice with a fork, sprinkle with the parsley, and serve.

25

BEEF WITH ENDIVE & SUN-DRIED TOMATOES

serves 4–6

3 lb (1.5 kg) beef bottom round, cut into large chunks

Salt and freshly ground pepper

5 Tbsp (3 fl oz/80 ml) olive oil

6 cloves garlic, smashed

1⅓ cups (11 fl oz/345 ml) beef broth

¼ cup (2 fl oz/60 ml) dry white wine

3 sprigs fresh thyme

3 bay leaves

2 tsp Dijon mustard

2 Tbsp sherry vinegar

2 Tbsp walnut oil

2 large heads Belgian endive, cored and coarsely chopped

½ cup (2½ oz/75 g) green olives, pitted and chopped

½ cup (4 oz/125 g) oil-packed sun-dried tomatoes, sliced

Grated zest of 1 lemon

2 Tbsp chopped fresh flat-leaf parsley

This dish is perfect for wintertime, when you crave robust flavors but want a relatively light main course—one that will satisfy both salad eaters and meat eaters alike. The mixture of endive, sun-dried tomatoes, and olives imparts a pleasantly sharp note to the slow-braised beef. If you like, accompany with boiled small potatoes tossed with butter and parsley.

Season the beef with salt and pepper. In a large frying pan, heat 2 Tbsp of the olive oil over medium-high heat. Working in batches, sear the beef, turning as needed, until browned on all sides, about 8 minutes. Using a slotted spoon, transfer to a slow cooker.

Pour off most of the fat from the pan and return to medium-high heat. Add the garlic and cook for 1 minute. Pour in the broth and wine and stir to scrape up any browned bits on the pan bottom. Add the thyme and bay leaves and transfer the contents of the pan to the slow cooker. Cover and cook on the low setting for 5–6 hours. The beef should be tender but still moist.

Just before the beef is ready, in a bowl, whisk together the mustard, vinegar, walnut oil, the remaining 3 Tbsp olive oil, ¼ tsp salt, and a few grindings of pepper. Add the endive, olives, sun-dried tomatoes, lemon zest, and parsley and toss.

Using a slotted spoon, transfer the beef to a cutting board and shred with 2 forks. Transfer to a platter. Moisten the beef with some of the braising liquid, mound the endive mixture alongside the beef, and serve.

JANUARY

26

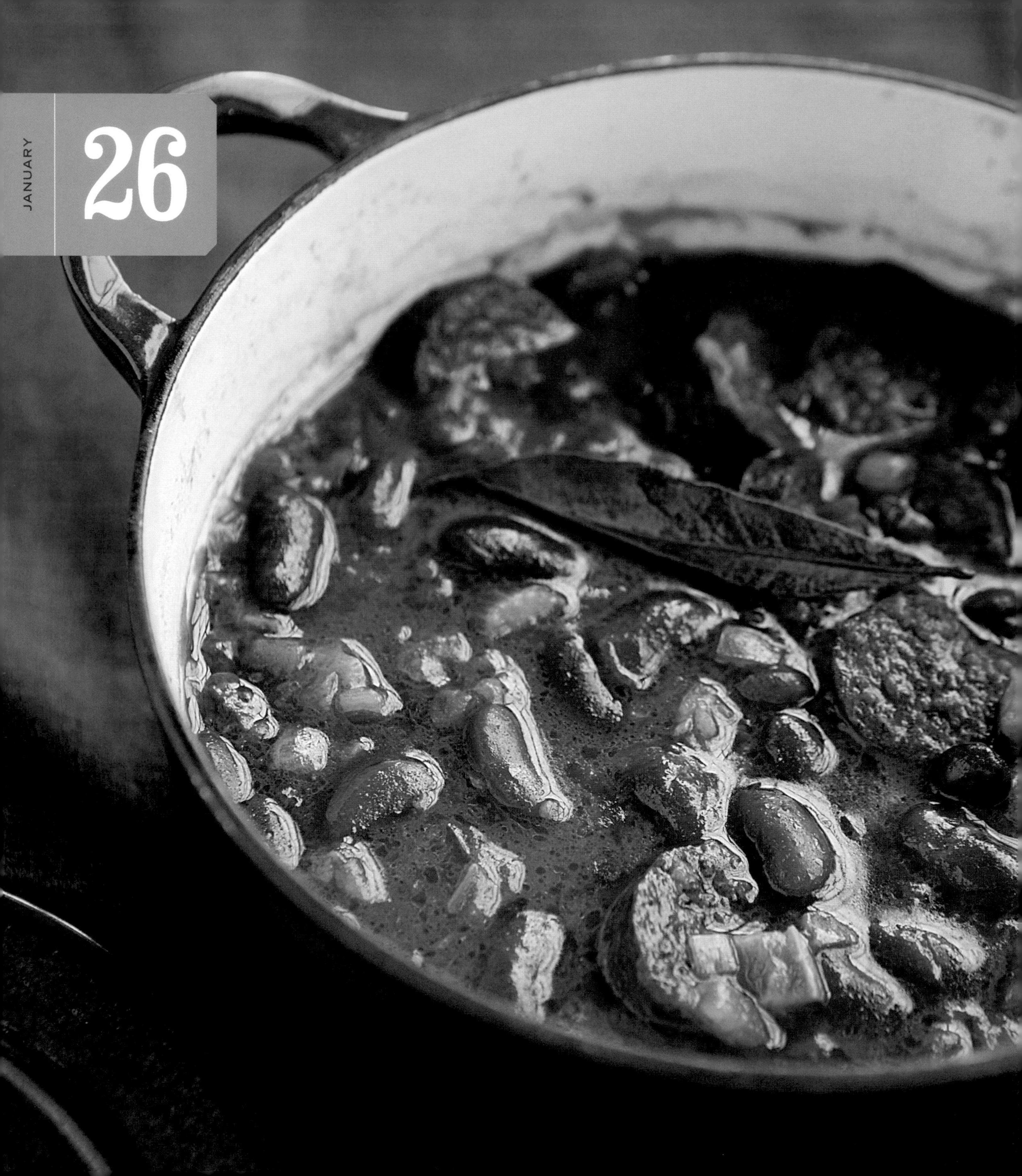

26

SPICY RED BEAN & CHORIZO STEW

serves 6–8

Warm up on cold days with spicy Latin flavors. Chorizo sausage puts a kick into this stew, which is extra satisfying due to the double dose of protein from beans and the meat.

2¼ cups (1 lb/500 g) dried red kidney beans, picked over and rinsed

2 Tbsp canola oil

1 large yellow onion, finely chopped

3 celery ribs, finely chopped

1 green bell pepper, seeded and chopped

6 cloves garlic, minced

Salt and freshly ground pepper

4 cups (32 fl oz/1 l) beef or chicken broth

2 tsp red wine vinegar

½–¾ tsp red pepper flakes

3 bay leaves

1 lb (500 g) cured Spanish-style chorizo, cut into slices ¼ inch (6 mm) thick

Hot-pepper sauce, such as Tabasco

Cooked white rice for serving

Place the beans in a large bowl with cold water to cover and soak for at least 4 hours or up to overnight. (For a quick soak, combine the beans and water to cover in a large pot, bring to a boil, remove from the heat, cover, and soak for 1 hour.) Drain and rinse the beans.

In a large, heavy frying pan, heat the oil over medium-high heat. Add the onion, celery, and bell pepper and sauté until softened and just beginning to brown, about 6 minutes. Add the garlic, season with salt and pepper, and cook for 1 minute. Pour in 1 cup (8 fl oz/250 ml) of the broth and stir to scrape up any browned bits on the pan bottom. Transfer the contents of the pan to a slow cooker and stir in the drained beans, remaining 3 cups (24 fl oz/750 ml) broth, the vinegar, pepper flakes to taste, bay leaves, and chorizo. Cover and cook on the low setting for 6–8 hours, stirring once or twice. The beans should be very tender.

Discard the bay leaves. Season with salt, pepper, and Tabasco. If desired, using the back of a spoon, mash some of the beans against the inside of the cooker to thicken the stew.

Spoon rice into shallow bowls, top with the stew, and serve.

27

FRITTATA WITH GREENS

serves 4

Crinkly leaves of kale and chard reach their sweetest flavor during the winter frosts. Fold your favorite variety into eggs for a quick one-skillet supper, like this Sicilian-inspired version.

About 1 lb (500 g) leafy greens such as kale, chard, broccoli rabe, or spinach, tough stems removed

8 eggs

Salt and freshly ground pepper

¼ cup (2 fl oz/60 ml) olive oil

1 clove garlic, minced

4 oz (125 g) ricotta salata or young pecorino cheese, thinly sliced

In a large pot, combine the greens and 1 cup (8 fl oz/250 ml) water. Cover and cook over medium heat, stirring occasionally, until tender, 3–4 minutes for spinach or up to 10 minutes for the other greens. Drain the greens, let cool, and squeeze to extract the excess liquid. Chop the greens and set aside.

Preheat the broiler.

In a bowl, beat the eggs just until blended. Season with salt and pepper. In a 9-inch (23-cm) ovenproof frying pan, heat the oil over low heat. Add the garlic and sauté until fragrant, about 30 seconds. Add the greens and a pinch of salt, and stir and toss to coat the greens well with the oil. Lightly stir in the eggs and arrange the cheese slices on top. Cook, using a spatula to lift the edges of the egg to allow the uncooked egg to flow underneath, until the edges and bottom are set but the center is still moist, about 5 minutes.

Broil about 4 inches (10 cm) from the heat source until the top is puffed and golden and the cheese is slightly melted, about 1 minute. Slide the frittata onto a plate. Cut into wedges and serve.

28

BARLEY RISOTTO WITH CHICKEN, MUSHROOMS & GREENS

serves 4

6 cups (48 fl oz/1.5 l) chicken broth

1½ Tbsp olive oil

1 yellow onion, chopped

1 clove garlic, minced

2 cups (6 oz/185 g) sliced cremini mushrooms

Salt and freshly ground pepper

½ cup (4 fl oz/125 ml) dry white wine

1 cup (7 oz/220 g) pearl barley

3 cups (4 oz/125 g) bite-sized pieces Swiss chard leaves

2 cups (¾ lb/375 g) shredded cooked chicken

½ cup (2 oz/60 g) grated Parmesan cheese

Barley has a pleasantly chewy texture and a sweet, nutty flavor. When stirred into broth over low heat, it cooks into a creamy risotto-style dish. Meaty mushrooms, shredded chicken, and slightly bitter greens contribute to a balanced one-dish dinner.

In a saucepan, bring the broth to a simmer over medium-high heat. Turn off the heat, cover, and keep warm.

In a large saucepan, heat the oil over medium-high heat. Add the onion and garlic and cook, stirring frequently, until the onion is soft, about 5 minutes. Add the mushrooms, ¼ tsp salt, and a few grindings of pepper. Cook, stirring frequently, until the mushrooms release their liquid and start to brown, 4–5 minutes. Add the wine, bring to a boil, and cook for 1 minute.

Add 5 cups (40 fl oz/1.25 l) of the hot broth and the barley. Cover and simmer over medium-low heat, stirring occasionally and adding more broth ¼ cup (2 fl oz/60 ml) at a time if the barley becomes dry, until the barley is tender, about 45 minutes.

Stir in the Swiss chard and more broth, if necessary. Cook, uncovered, until the greens are wilted, about 2 minutes. Stir in the chicken and cook for 1 minute to heat through. Stir in the Parmesan, season with salt and pepper, and serve.

29

BEEF STEW WITH MUSHROOMS, CARROTS & BACON

serves 6

4 oz (125 g) thick-cut bacon, chopped

3 Tbsp all-purpose flour

Salt and freshly ground pepper

3 lb (1.5 kg) boneless beef chuck, cut into chunks

¾ lb (375 g) cremini mushrooms, halved if large

½ lb (250 g) baby carrots

½ lb (250 g) frozen pearl onions

3 cloves garlic, minced

1 cup (8 fl oz/ 250 ml) dry red wine

1 cup (8 fl oz/ 250 ml) beef broth

2 Tbsp tomato paste

1 Tbsp minced fresh rosemary

This classic beef stew gains a savory edge with the addition of bacon. Bite-sized pearl onions are appealing in stews, and frozen ones offer convenience. If you prefer to use fresh ingredients, substitute 1 yellow onion, chopped.

In a large frying pan, cook the bacon over medium heat, stirring occasionally, until crisp, 5–7 minutes. Drain on paper towels. Pour the drippings into a small heatproof bowl, leaving about 1 Tbsp in the pan. Set the pan, drippings, and bacon aside.

In a resealable plastic bag, combine the flour, 1 tsp salt, and ½ tsp pepper. Add the beef chunks and shake to coat evenly with the flour mixture. Return the frying pan to medium-high heat. Add half of the beef chunks and cook, turning once, until well browned, about 5 minutes on each side. Transfer the beef to a slow cooker. Repeat with the remaining beef chunks, adding the reserved drippings if needed. Scatter the mushrooms, carrots, onions, and garlic over the beef.

Return the pan to medium-high heat and add the wine, broth, and tomato paste. Mix well, bring to a boil, and stir to scrape up any browned bits on the pan bottom. Pour the contents of the pan over the vegetables and beef. Cover and cook on the high setting for 4–5 hours or the low setting for 8–9 hours. The beef should be very tender. Stir in the reserved bacon and the rosemary. Cook, uncovered, on the high setting for 10 minutes to thicken the sauce slightly. Season with salt and pepper and serve in shallow bowls.

30

SPICED CAULIFLOWER & POTATOES

serves 6

1 head cauliflower (1½–2 lb/750 g–1 kg)

2 Tbsp canola oil

1 tsp cumin seeds

3 white potatoes, peeled and cut into 1-inch (2.5-cm) pieces

2–4 Tbsp peeled and grated fresh ginger

4 cloves garlic, minced

¾ tsp ground turmeric

½ tsp cayenne pepper

Salt

¼ cup (⅓ oz/10 g) finely chopped fresh cilantro

½ tsp garam masala

Aloo gobhi is a mild dish, and a favorite of Indian children. Cauliflower and potatoes are cooked in oil laced with cumin and turmeric until smoky and golden yellow. Serve with basmati rice or warmed naan bread, and a dollop of yogurt or fruit chutney.

Separate the cauliflower florets and cut them into 1½-inch (4-cm) pieces. Peel the cauliflower stem and cut crosswise into slices ⅛ inch (3 mm) thick. Chop the leaves, if any, and add to the cauliflower.

In a large saucepan, heat the oil over medium-high heat. Add the cumin seeds and fry until they turn several shades darker, about 30 seconds. Add the potatoes and sauté until lightly crisped, about 5 minutes. Add the ginger, garlic, turmeric, and cayenne and mix well.

Add the cauliflower, 1½ tsp salt, and ¾ cup (6 fl oz/180 ml) water and mix well. Reduce the heat to low, cover, and cook until the cauliflower is very soft, about 7 minutes. Uncover the pan, raise the heat to medium-high, and cook until the excess moisture evaporates, about 5 minutes. Adjust the seasoning. Sprinkle with the cilantro and garam masala and serve.

31

TURKEY & WHITE BEAN CHILI

serves 6

2¼ cups (1 lb/500 g) dried Great Northern or other small white beans, rinsed

1 or 2 serrano chiles or 1 jalapeño chile

3 bay leaves

6 cups (48 fl oz/1.5 l) chicken broth

1 Tbsp canola oil

1 lb (500 g) ground dark-meat turkey

1 large yellow onion, finely chopped

Salt and freshly ground black pepper

5 cloves garlic, minced

2 Tbsp chili powder

1½ Tbsp ground cumin

¼–½ tsp cayenne pepper (optional)

Sour cream for serving

6 green onions, white and tender green parts, finely chopped

⅓ cup (½ oz/15 g) coarsely chopped fresh cilantro

Lean turkey meat and white beans make a light and healthy chili, perfect for recuperating after the holidays. But don't skip on the garnishes—sour cream, green onions, and cilantro—which give this slow-cooked dish a welcome accent. Serve wedges of corn bread alongside.

Put the beans in a large bowl with cold water to cover and soak for at least 4 hours or up to overnight. (For a quick soak, combine the beans and water to cover in a large pot, bring to a boil, remove from the heat, cover, and soak for 1 hour.) Drain and rinse the beans.

Put the beans in a slow cooker. Add the chiles, bay leaves, and broth. The broth should cover the beans by about 1½ inches (4 cm); supplement water if needed. Cover and cook on the low setting for 6 hours. The beans should be tender.

In a large, heavy frying pan, heat the oil over medium heat. Add the turkey and cook, stirring to break up any clumps, until the meat is no longer pink, 8–10 minutes. Add the onion, 1 tsp salt, and several grindings of black pepper and sauté until the onion is soft and lightly golden, about 10 minutes. Add the garlic, chili powder, cumin, and cayenne (if using), and stir for 2–3 minutes to release their aromas. Transfer the contents of the pan to the slow cooker and raise the heat to the high setting. Cover and cook, stirring 2 or 3 times, until slightly thickened, 30–40 minutes. Adjust the seasoning.

Ladle the chili into shallow bowls. Garnish with sour cream, green onions, and cilantro, and serve.

The short days of winter call for hearty and flavorful meals. Whether it's a spicy beef chili or a fragrant chicken tagine spiked with preserved lemons and olives, long-simmered dishes provide nourishment and warmth. Draw on seasonal ingredients such as citrus, broccoli, root vegetables, kale and chard, enlivened with red wine, garlic, and spices to create the stews, braises, gumbos, curries, and chilis popular at this time of year.

1
CHICKEN TAGINE WITH PRESERVED LEMONS & OLIVES
page 34

2
SAUTÉED SHRIMP WITH LEMON & GARLIC
page 34

3
STIR-FRIED TANGERINE BEEF
page 37

8
PORTUGUESE MUSSELS
page 39

9
CHEESE SOUFFLÉ
page 40

10
WINTER VEGETABLE COCONUT CURRY
page 40

15
TEXAS BEEF CHILI
page 45

16
MACARONI WITH FARMSTEAD CHEDDAR & BACON
page 45

17
SLOW-COOKED CUBAN CHICKEN
page 46

22
RED BEAN & VEGETABLE GUMBO
page 49

23
GARLICKY PORK SHOULDER WITH GREENS
page 51

24
PAN-ROASTED CHICKEN WITH FENNEL, LEEKS & CREAM
page 51

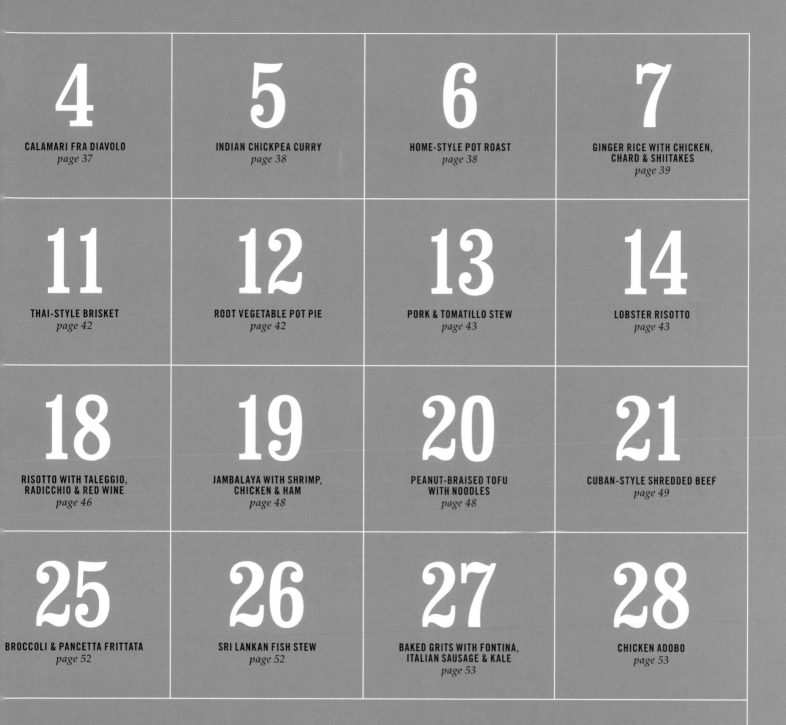

february

1

FEBRUARY

CHICKEN TAGINE WITH PRESERVED LEMONS & OLIVES

serves 4

This colorful Moroccan stew offers deep spices, but stays light and bright with tart citrus, briny green olives, and fresh cilantro. For the most authentic presentation, serve it on a platter or individual plates atop a bed of couscous.

¼ tsp saffron threads

2 large yellow onions, chopped

½ cup (¾ oz/20 g) coarsely chopped fresh cilantro, plus more for garnish

½ cup (¾ oz/20 g) coarsely chopped fresh flat-leaf parsley, plus more for garnish

4 Tbsp (2 fl oz/60 ml) fresh lemon juice

1 tsp ground cumin

½ tsp ground ginger

½ tsp ground turmeric

Salt

2 large cloves garlic, crushed

6 Tbsp olive oil

6 skin-on, bone-in chicken thighs

2 preserved lemons, thinly sliced

½ cup (4 fl oz/125 ml) chicken broth

1½ cups (8 oz/250 g) cracked green olives

In a small bowl, soak the saffron in 2 Tbsp warm water for 10 minutes.

In a food processor, combine the onions, the ½ cup cilantro, ½ cup parsley, and 2 Tbsp of the lemon juice. Add the cumin, ginger, turmeric, and the saffron and its soaking liquid. Season with 1 tsp salt and process to a pulpy purée. Transfer to a large resealable plastic bag. Add the garlic and 3 Tbsp of the oil. Add the chicken pieces, seal the bag, and massage to coat the chicken with the mixture. Refrigerate for at least 8 hours or up to 24 hours.

In a large, heavy pot, warm 1 Tbsp of the oil over medium-high heat. Add the lemon slices and sear until browned, 3–5 minutes. Transfer to a plate. Add the remaining 2 Tbsp oil to the pot. Remove the chicken pieces from the marinade, shaking off the excess and reserving the marinade. Working in batches, sear the chicken pieces, skin side down, until golden brown, 5–6 minutes. Transfer to another plate.

Pour the broth into the pot, stirring to scrape up any browned bits from the pot bottom. Stir in the reserved marinade and add the chicken and any juices. Bring to a boil, ⟫

cover, reduce the heat to medium-low, and simmer until the chicken is opaque throughout, about 40 minutes.

Simmer the olives in a saucepan of boiling water for 5 minutes. Add the olives, the reserved lemon, and the remaining 2 Tbsp lemon juice to the pot. Cover and simmer until the chicken is falling-off-the-bone tender, 10–15 minutes.

Garnish the stew with chopped cilantro and parsley and serve.

2

FEBRUARY

SAUTÉED SHRIMP WITH LEMON & GARLIC

serves 4

Shrimp cook quickly in a hot pan, perfect for weeknight one-pan sautés. Render them irresistible in a hot bath of olive oil and garlic, then spoon this saucy sauté over a bed of steamed rice.

4 Tbsp (2 fl oz/60 ml) olive oil

1¼ lb (625 g) large shrimp, peeled and deveined, tail intact

6 cloves garlic, minced

Salt and freshly ground pepper

2 green onions, white and tender green parts, thinly sliced

2 Tbsp chopped fresh flat-leaf parsley

¼ cup (2 fl oz/60 ml) fresh lemon juice

In a large frying pan, heat 2 Tbsp of the oil over medium-high heat. Add half of the shrimp and cook until pink, about 1 minute. Using tongs, turn the shrimp, add half of the garlic, and cook until the shrimp are pink on the second side, just a few seconds. Season with salt and pepper, toss, and quickly add half of the green onions, parsley, and lemon juice. Toss again and transfer to a platter. Wipe the pan clean and repeat to cook the remaining shrimp and other ingredients, then serve.

3

STIR-FRIED TANGERINE BEEF

serves 4–6

1½ lb (750 g) flank steak

½ tsp sugar

¼ tsp baking soda

Salt

FOR THE SAUCE

1 tsp grated tangerine or orange zest

¼ cup (2 fl oz/60 ml) fresh tangerine or orange juice

1 Tbsp rice wine or dry sherry

1 Tbsp hoisin sauce

2 Tbsp soy sauce

1 tsp chile-bean paste

½ tsp toasted sesame oil

¼ tsp sugar

¼ tsp cornstarch

4 Tbsp (2 fl oz/60 ml) peanut or canola oil

1 small yellow onion, halved and thinly sliced

1 small green bell pepper, seeded and thinly sliced lengthwise

1 red Fresno chile, seeded and thinly sliced lengthwise

2 cloves garlic, minced

2 Tbsp peeled and grated fresh ginger

This stir-fry updates the takeout classic with fresh winter citrus, both the grated zest and the freshly squeezed juice. Baking soda in the marinade helps break down the meat fibers and gives the cooked beef a velvety texture. Spoon the sweet citrusy stir-fry over steamed rice.

Cut the flank steak across the grain into slices ⅛ inch (3 mm) thick. In a large, nonreactive bowl, combine the sugar, baking soda, and 1 tsp salt and stir to mix well. Add the beef slices and stir to coat. Let stand at room temperature for 30 minutes.

To make the sauce, in a small bowl, stir together the tangerine zest and juice, rice wine, hoisin sauce, soy sauce, chile-bean paste, sesame oil, sugar, and cornstarch until the sugar and cornstarch dissolve. Set aside.

Pat the beef slices dry with paper towels. In a large wok or frying pan, warm 2 Tbsp of the oil over high heat. Add half of the beef in a single layer and sear until brown on the first side, about 1 minute. Using tongs, turn and sear until brown on the second side, about 30 seconds. Transfer the meat to a colander to drain. Return the pan to high heat, heat 1 Tbsp of the oil, and repeat to sear the remaining beef. Transfer to the colander to drain. »→

Wipe the pan clean. Reheat the pan over high heat and add the remaining 1 Tbsp oil. When the oil is hot, add the onion and bell pepper and stir-fry until the edges begin to brown, 3–4 minutes. Add the chile, garlic, and ginger and stir-fry for 1 minute. Pour in the sauce and return the beef to the pan. Stir-fry until the beef is heated through and the sauce thickens, about 1 minute. Transfer to a platter and serve.

4

CALAMARI FRA DIAVOLO

serves 4–6

3 Tbsp olive oil

1 yellow onion, chopped

4 cloves garlic, minced

1 can (28 oz/800 g) whole peeled tomatoes

½ cup (4 fl oz/125 ml) fish broth or bottled clam juice

½ cup (4 fl oz/125 ml) full-bodied red wine

3 Tbsp chopped fresh oregano

½ tsp red pepper flakes

2½ lb (1.25 kg) cleaned squid, bodies cut into ½-inch (12-mm) rings and tentacles coarsely chopped

⅓ cup (½ oz/15 g) chopped fresh flat-leaf parsley

Salt and freshly ground pepper

In this classic Italian dish, tender squid rings are smothered with a devilishly spicy tomato sauce. Serve it over a bed of pasta, or pass crusty bread at the table, to help mop up the sauce.

In a small pot, heat the oil over medium heat. Add the onion and sauté until tender and golden, about 5 minutes. Add the garlic and sauté for 30 seconds. Stir in the tomatoes with their juices, breaking them up with the back of a spoon. Add the broth, wine, 2 Tbsp of the oregano, and the red pepper flakes. Reduce the heat to medium-low and cook, uncovered, until the sauce is lightly thickened and the flavors have blended, 15–20 minutes.

Add the squid, cover, reduce the heat to low, and cook until very tender, 25–30 minutes. Stir in the remaining 1 Tbsp oregano and the parsley. Season with salt and pepper and serve.

5

*Known in India
as chana masala,
this classic stew
of chickpeas can
be accompanied by
rice as a vegetarian
main course.
Added at the end of
cooking, a sprinkling
of garam masala
heightens the curry's
flavor and aroma.*

INDIAN CHICKPEA CURRY

serves 6–8

2 Tbsp canola oil

1 yellow onion, finely chopped

2 cloves garlic, minced

1-inch (2.5-cm) piece peeled
fresh ginger, grated

1 cinnamon stick, halved

1 tsp cayenne pepper

1 tsp ground coriander

1 tsp ground cumin

1 tsp brown mustard seeds

1 tsp ground turmeric

1 can (28 oz/875 g) diced tomatoes,
drained

2 tsp sugar

Salt

2 cups (14 oz/440 g) rinsed and drained
canned chickpeas

1 Tbsp garam masala

1 Tbsp fresh lime juice

1 cup (1 oz/30 g) chopped fresh cilantro

In a large, heavy pot, heat the oil over
medium-high heat. Add the onion, garlic,
and ginger and sauté until the mixture
just begins to turn golden, about 5 minutes.
Add the cinnamon, cayenne, coriander,
cumin, mustard seeds, and turmeric. Sauté
until the spices are fragrant and blended with
the onion mixture, about 1 minute. Stir
in the tomatoes, sugar, 2 tsp salt, and 2 cups
(16 fl oz/500 ml) water, stirring to scrape
up any browned bits on the pan bottom.
Bring to a boil. Stir in the chickpeas. Partially
cover and cook over low heat until the
chickpeas are very tender, about 30 minutes.

About 15 minutes before the chickpeas are
done, sprinkle with the garam masala and
lime juice and stir, breaking up some of
the chickpeas with the back of a spoon to
thicken the mixture slightly. Season with
salt. Remove the cinnamon stick and serve,
garnished with the cilantro.

6

*In this recipe,
thickly sliced onions
and paprika boost
the flavor of the
classic one-pot beef
roast. Serve with
roasted or mashed
potatoes to soak up
the ample gravy,
and save leftovers
for sandwiches,
loading crusty
rolls with plenty
of saucy onions.*

HOME-STYLE POT ROAST

serves 4–6

3 yellow onions

1 beef chuck roast, about 2½ lb (1.25 kg)

Salt and freshly ground pepper

¼ cup (1½ oz/45 g) all-purpose flour

3 Tbsp canola oil

4 cloves garlic, minced

1 tsp sweet paprika

1½ cups (12 fl oz/375 ml) beef broth

1½ cups (14½ oz/400 g) canned diced
tomatoes, drained

2 Tbsp chopped fresh flat-leaf parsley,
plus more for garnish

Halve the onions through the stem end, and
cut the halves crosswise into slices about
½-inch (12 mm) thick. Set aside.

Season the roast with ¾ tsp salt and ½ tsp
pepper. Spread the flour on a plate. Coat the
roast with the flour, shaking off the excess.

In a large, heavy pot, heat 2 Tbsp of the oil
over medium-high heat. Add the roast and
cook, turning occasionally, until browned
on all sides, about 8 minutes total. Transfer
the roast to a plate.

Add the remaining 1 Tbsp oil to the pot
and heat over medium-high heat. Add the
onions, cover, and cook, stirring occasionally,
until the onions soften, about 6 minutes. Stir
in the garlic and paprika and sauté until
the garlic is fragrant, 1–2 minutes. Add the
broth, tomatoes, and 2 Tbsp parsley and stir.
Return the beef to the pot, nestling it in the
onions. Bring the liquid to a boil, reduce
the heat to medium-low, cover, and simmer
until the beef is fork-tender, about 2 hours.

Transfer the pot roast to a deep platter. Season
the onion mixture in the pot with salt and
pepper. Skim any fat from the surface. Spoon
the onion mixture around the roast, sprinkle
with parsley, and serve.

GINGER RICE WITH CHICKEN, CHARD & SHIITAKES

serves 4

2 skinless, boneless chicken thighs, cut into bite-sized pieces

1 tsp peeled and grated fresh ginger

1 Tbsp oyster sauce

1 Tbsp soy sauce

1 Tbsp rice wine or dry sherry

1 tsp toasted sesame oil

¼ tsp sugar

Ground white pepper

1½ cups (10½ oz/330 g) jasmine rice

1 bunch Swiss chard, tough stems removed and leaves chopped

6 oz (185 g) shiitake mushrooms, stems discarded and caps thinly sliced

1 green onion, white and tender green part, thinly sliced

In a bowl, combine the chicken, ginger, oyster sauce, soy sauce, rice wine, oil, sugar, and a pinch of pepper, and mix well. Let stand for 10 minutes.

In a heavy saucepan, combine the rice, chard, mushrooms, chicken and its marinade, and 3 cups (24 fl oz/750 ml) water. Bring to a boil over high heat, cover, reduce the heat to low, and cook until the rice has absorbed the water and the chicken is opaque, about 20 minutes. Remove from the heat and let stand, covered, for 10 minutes. Fluff the rice with a fork, transfer to a serving bowl, garnish with the green onion, and serve.

Alternatively, to prepare in an electric rice cooker, combine the rice, chard, mushrooms, chicken and its marinade, and 3 cups (24 fl oz/ 750 ml) boiling water in the cooker, cover, and turn on the cooker. The rice should be ready in about 30 minutes. Let stand undisturbed for 10 minutes before garnishing with green onion and serving.

7

This is a health-savvy rice casserole, featuring jasmine rice, tender chicken, meaty mushrooms, and dark greens. For added flavor, whisk together a quick Asian sauce: In a small bowl, stir together 2 Tbsp oyster sauce, 1 tsp Asian sesame oil, 1 Tbsp rice vinegar, and 1 tsp hot water. Drizzle over the dish before serving.

PORTUGUESE MUSSELS

serves 4–6

¼ cup (2 fl oz/60 ml) olive oil

½ lb (250 g) cured Spanish-style chorizo, linguiça, or other spicy cooked sausage, cut into slices ¼-inch (6 mm) thick

1 yellow onion, chopped

1 green bell pepper, seeded and chopped

4 cloves garlic, minced

2 tsp hot paprika

2 Tbsp chopped fresh marjoram

1 can (28 oz/875 g) whole peeled tomatoes, drained

1 cup (8 fl oz/250 ml) dry white wine

Pinch of red pepper flakes

¼–½ tsp hot-pepper sauce such as Tabasco

Salt and freshly ground pepper

2 lb (1 kg) mussels, scrubbed and debearded

2 Tbsp chopped fresh cilantro

2 Tbsp chopped fresh flat-leaf parsley

In a large, heavy pot, heat the oil over medium-high heat. Add the sausage, onion, and bell pepper, and cook, stirring often, until the vegetables are tender and the sausage is browned, 4–5 minutes. Add the garlic and paprika and cook, stirring, for 30 seconds. Stir in the marjoram, tomatoes, wine, red pepper flakes, and hot-pepper sauce. Bring to a simmer over medium heat, breaking up the tomatoes with the back of a spoon. Season with salt and pepper. Cook, uncovered, until the wine-tomato mixture is reduced by about one-third, 5–6 minutes.

Add the mussels to the pot, discarding any that do not close to the touch. Cover and cook over medium heat until the mussels open, 4–5 minutes. Discard any unopened mussels. Stir in the cilantro and parsley. Transfer to a bowl and serve.

8

Mussels are among the most affordable options at the seafood counter. Tossed into a covered pot, they steam open in just minutes. There are many flavor options, but this hearty version includes spicy chorizo, herbs, and garlic. Accompany with a loaf of crusty bread for mopping up the juices.

9

CHEESE SOUFFLÉ

serves 4

2½ Tbsp unsalted butter,
plus more for greasing

1 cup (4 oz/125 g) shredded Gruyère
or Comté cheese, plus 2 Tbsp

3 Tbsp all-purpose flour

1 cup (8 fl oz/250 ml) milk

4 egg yolks plus 5 egg whites

1 tsp Dijon mustard

Salt and ground white pepper

Pinch of grated nutmeg

Pinch of cream of tartar

1 Tbsp fine fresh or dried bread crumbs

*A classic cheese
soufflé pairs well
with a roast, but
can also serve as
the main event, with
a frisée salad and
a crisp white wine.
The key to success
with a soufflé lies
in beating the egg
whites to their
highest peaks and
folding them in
gently. Start with
a spotless bowl,
add cream of tartar
to help stabilize,
then fold in the fluffy
whites carefully,
using a rubber
spatula and a gentle,
sweeping motion.*

Preheat the oven to 375°F (190°C). Butter
a 6-cup (48–fl oz/1.5-l) soufflé dish and then
coat the bottom and sides evenly with 1 Tbsp
of the cheese.

In a saucepan, melt the 2½ Tbsp butter
over medium heat. Add the flour and cook,
whisking, for 1 minute. Cook until the
mixture is bubbling but still white, about
2 minutes longer. Slowly add the milk,
whisking constantly. Bring to a simmer and
continue to whisk until the sauce is thick
and smooth, about 2 minutes. Let cool for
about 10 minutes.

Add the egg yolks to the cooled milk mixture
and whisk until smooth. Add the mustard,
½ tsp salt, a pinch of pepper, and the nutmeg
and whisk to combine.

In a bowl, using an electric mixer, beat
the egg whites with a pinch of salt and the
cream of tartar until stiff peaks form. Using
a rubber spatula, gently fold half of the egg
whites into the milk mixture to lighten it.
Gently stir in the 1 cup cheese and then fold
in the remaining egg whites just until no
white streaks remain.

Spoon into the prepared dish and sprinkle
with the remaining 1 Tbsp cheese and the
bread crumbs. Bake until the top is puffed
and browned, 30–35 minutes. Serve directly
from the dish.

10

WINTER VEGETABLE
COCONUT CURRY

serves 4

2 tsp canola oil

1 clove garlic, minced

¼-inch (6-mm) slice peeled fresh ginger,
grated

2 tsp Thai red curry paste

1 tsp Asian fish sauce

1 sweet potato, about ½ lb (250 g), peeled
and cut into ½-inch (12-mm) chunks

1 celery root, about ½ lb (250 g), peeled
and cut into ½-inch (12-mm) chunks

3 cups (24 fl oz/750 ml) unsweetened
coconut milk

1 delicata squash, about ½ lb (250 g), peeled
and cut into ½-inch (12-mm) chunks

2 limes

2 Tbsp finely chopped fresh cilantro
for garnish

*Coconut milk lends
richness and exotic
flavor to these
creamy braised
vegetables. It echoes
the sweetness of
both the root
vegetables and
squash, while taming
the spicy red curry
paste, pungent
Asian fish sauce,
and bright lime and
cilantro that season
the broth. Serve over
cooked brown rice.*

In a saucepan, heat the oil over medium heat.
Add the garlic and ginger and sauté until
fragrant but not browned, about 1 minute.
Add the curry paste and cook, stirring, for
1 minute. Add the fish sauce, sweet potato,
and celery root and stir to combine. Reduce
the heat to medium-low, pour in the coconut
milk, and cook, stirring occasionally, for
10 minutes. Add the squash and cook until
the vegetables are just tender but not falling
apart, 12–15 minutes.

Meanwhile, finely grate the zest from the
lime, then cut each lime into wedges. Stir
the lime zest into the vegetables.

Serve, sprinkled with cilantro and topped
with lime wedges.

11

THAI-STYLE BRISKET
serves 6

2 lb (1 kg) beef brisket

Salt and freshly ground pepper

2 Tbsp peanut or canola oil

1 large yellow onion, coarsely chopped

1 carrot, coarsely chopped

5 cloves garlic, smashed

1 stalk lemongrass, center white part only, thinly sliced (optional)

¼ cup (2 fl oz/60 ml) dry white wine

½ cup (4 fl oz/125 ml) chicken or beef broth

¼ cup (2 fl oz/60 ml) soy sauce

Here, beef brisket is recast with Southeast Asian flavors. Make it even more interesting with a pineapple relish: In a bowl, toss together 1 cup (8 oz/250 g) diced pineapple; 2 Tbsp finely diced red bell pepper; 1 Tbsp minced red onion; 1 tsp Thai sweet chile sauce; 1½ tsp Asian fish sauce; 2 tsp soy sauce; 1 tsp minced fresh cilantro; and 6 fresh mint leaves, minced.

Season the brisket generously all over with salt and pepper. In a large frying pan, heat the oil over medium-high heat. Add the brisket and sear, turning as needed, until deep golden brown on all sides, about 10 minutes. Transfer to a plate.

Pour off most of the fat from the pan and return to medium-high heat. Add the onion and carrot and sauté until softened and lightly colored, about 6 minutes. Add the garlic and lemongrass (if using) and cook for 1 minute. Pour in the wine and stir to scrape up any browned bits on the pan bottom. Stir in the broth, soy sauce, and several grindings of pepper. Transfer the contents of the pan to a slow cooker and place the brisket and any juices on top. Cover and cook on the low setting for about 8 hours, turning the brisket halfway through. The meat should be very tender.

Transfer the brisket to a cutting board and let rest for a few minutes. Skim the fat from the surface of the braising liquid, then strain out the vegetables and aromatics. Cut the brisket across the grain into slices. Arrange on a platter, drizzle with some of the braising liquid, and serve.

12

ROOT VEGETABLE POT PIE
serves 4–6

1 sheet frozen puff pastry, thawed

2 carrots, cut into 1-inch (2.5-cm) chunks

1 large yellow onion, chopped

1 sweet potato, peeled and cut into 1-inch (2.5-cm) chunks

2 parsnips, peeled and cut into 1-inch (2.5-cm) chunks

4 sprigs fresh thyme, plus 1 Tbsp leaves

¼ cup (2 fl oz/60 ml) olive oil

Salt and freshly ground pepper

4 Tbsp (2 oz/60 g) unsalted butter

¼ cup (1½ oz/45 g) all-purpose flour

¼ cup (4 fl oz/125 ml) dry white wine

2½ cups (20 fl oz/625 ml) vegetable broth

Pot pies classically feature chicken or turkey, but carrots, parsnips, and sweet potato more than hold their own in this vegetarian version. Choose a good-quality, all-butter puff pastry for the flakiest, most flavorful crust.

Preheat the oven to 400°F (200°C). On a floured work surface, roll the puff pastry to fit a 2-qt (2-l) baking dish. Place the pastry on a sheet of parchment paper and chill in the refrigerator. In the baking dish, toss the carrots, onion, sweet potato, parsnips, and thyme sprigs with the oil. Season with salt and pepper. Spread in an even layer and roast until the vegetables are tender, stirring occasionally about 25 minutes.

Meanwhile, to make the sauce, in a small saucepan, melt the butter over medium-high heat. Add the flour and cook, whisking, for 2 minutes. Add the wine and cook for 1 minute. Stir in the broth and bring to a boil. Stir in the thyme leaves.

Remove the thyme sprigs from the roasted vegetables and discard. Pour the sauce over the vegetables and toss well. Season with salt and pepper. Carefully fit the chilled pastry on top of the vegetables. Bake until the pastry is golden and puffed and the filling is bubbling, 10–12 minutes. Serve directly from the dish.

13

Boneless pork loin becomes meltingly tender through braising, and the sweet, mild meat is the perfect match for the tangy flavor of tomatillos. Serve warm corn tortillas or corn bread alongside big, steaming bowls of this hearty stew.

PORK & TOMATILLO STEW

serves 4

2 Tbsp canola oil

1 boneless pork loin, about 1½ lb (750 g), cut into 2-inch (5-cm) chunks

Salt and freshly ground pepper

1 yellow onion, roughly chopped

1 jalapeño chile, seeded and minced

3 cloves garlic, minced

2 tsp mild chili powder

1 Tbsp ground cumin

Pinch of dried oregano

1 Tbsp all-purpose flour

1¾ cups (14 fl oz/430 ml) chicken broth

1 carrot, cut into ½-inch (12-mm) pieces

¾ lb (375 g) russet potatoes, peeled and cut into 1-inch (2.5-cm) pieces

1 can (28 oz/875 g) diced tomatoes, drained

1 lb (500 g) tomatillos, husked, rinsed, and cut into 1-inch (2.5-cm) pieces

Hot-pepper sauce such as Tabasco

Chopped fresh cilantro for garnish

Blue corn tortilla chips for serving

In a large, heavy pot, heat the oil over high heat. Season the pork generously with salt and pepper. Add to the pot and sear on all sides until browned, about 8 minutes total. Add the onion, reduce the heat to medium, and cook, stirring occasionally, until the onion is softened, about 7 minutes.

Add the jalapeño, garlic, chili powder, cumin, and oregano. Season with ½ tsp salt. Cook, stirring frequently, until the mixture is aromatic, about 3 minutes. Add the flour, stir to make a paste, and cook for 1 minute. Whisk in the broth and bring to a simmer. Add the carrot, potatoes, tomatoes, and tomatillos. Cover partially and simmer over low heat until the pork is very tender, about 45 minutes.

Using a slotted spoon, transfer the pork to a plate. Continue to simmer the stew over medium-high heat until thickened, about 10 minutes. Shred the pork with 2 forks. Return the pork to the pot and season with salt, pepper, and hot-pepper sauce.

Ladle the stew into bowls, garnish with cilantro, and serve with tortilla chips.

14

An indulgent seafood risotto sets the mood for a romantic dinner for two. A splash of wine provides just enough acid to balance the richness of the ingredients, along with some freshness from lemon and tomato.

LOBSTER RISOTTO

serves 4

4 cups (32 fl oz/1 l) chicken broth

3 Tbsp olive oil

½ cup (2½ oz/75 g) finely chopped yellow onion

Pinch of red pepper flakes

1 cup (7 oz/220 g) Arborio or Carnaroli rice

¼ cup (2 fl oz/60 ml) full-bodied white wine, such as Chardonnay

½ tsp grated lemon zest

1 Tbsp fresh lemon juice

Pinch of saffron threads (optional)

Salt

½ lb (250 g) cooked lobster tail meat, coarsely chopped

½ cup (3½ oz/105 g) canned diced tomatoes, drained (optional)

2 Tbsp unsalted butter

In a saucepan, bring the broth to a gentle simmer over medium heat. Reduce the heat to low and maintain the simmer.

In a large, heavy saucepan, heat the oil over medium-low heat. Add the onion and red pepper flakes and sauté until the onion is soft, 7–8 minutes. Add the rice and stir until well coated with oil and translucent, about 2 minutes. Add the wine, lemon zest and juice, and saffron threads, if using, and cook for 2 minutes.

Stir ½ tsp salt into the simmering broth. Add the broth to the rice a ladleful at a time, stirring frequently after each addition. Wait until the broth is almost completely absorbed (but the rice is never dry on top) before adding the next ladleful. After about 20 minutes, when you have added all but ½ cup (4 fl oz/125 ml) of the broth, the rice should be tender to the bite and creamy. If it is still too firm, add the remaining broth and continue cooking.

When the rice is ready, stir in the lobster, distributing it evenly, and then stir in the tomatoes, if using, and the butter. Adjust the seasoning, remove from the heat, and let stand, covered, for 5 minutes before serving.

15

15

TEXAS BEEF CHILI

serves 8

2 tsp cumin seeds, toasted

¼ cup (¾ oz/20 g) pure ancho chile powder

1 Tbsp Spanish smoked paprika

2 tsp dried oregano

4 lb (2 kg) boneless beef chuck roast, cut into ½-inch (12-mm) chunks

Salt and freshly ground pepper

3 Tbsp olive oil

1 large yellow onion, chopped

1 jalapeño chile, seeded and minced

1 large red bell pepper, seeded and chopped

4 cloves garlic, minced

1½ cups (12 fl oz/375 ml) lager beer

1 cup (8 fl oz/250 ml) beef broth

2 Tbsp yellow cornmeal

Shredded Cheddar cheese, chopped red onions, sour cream, and minced jalapeño chiles for serving (optional)

Most Lone Star chili masters eschew beans and tomatoes. To them, chili is all about the meat—beef only— and the seasoning. Purists also claim that toppings turn their bowl of red into a salad bar. But you can opt for anything you like, such as sour cream, shredded cheese, red onions—even a handful of tortilla chips for crunch.

Using a mortar and pestle or a spice grinder, finely grind the cumin seeds. Transfer to a bowl, add the chile powder, paprika, and oregano, and mix well. Set aside.

Season the beef with salt and pepper. In a large, heavy pot, heat 2 Tbsp of the oil over medium-high heat. Working in batches, sear the beef, turning occasionally, until browned, about 5 minutes. Transfer to a plate.

Add the remaining 1 Tbsp oil to the pot. Add the onion, jalapeño, bell pepper, and garlic and reduce the heat to medium. Cover and cook, stirring occasionally, until the onion softens, about 5 minutes. Uncover, add the spice mixture, and stir well for 30 seconds. Stir in the beer and broth. Return the beef to the pot, cover, and reduce the heat to low. Simmer until the beef is fork-tender, 1½–2 hours.

Remove the chili from the heat and let stand for 5 minutes. Skim any fat from the surface. Bring the chili to a simmer over medium heat. Transfer about ½ cup (4 fl oz/125 ml) of the cooking liquid to a small bowl and whisk in the cornmeal. Stir into the chili and cook until lightly thickened, about 1 minute. Season with salt and pepper. Spoon the chili into bowls and serve, garnished with cheese, red onions, sour cream, or jalapeños, if you like.

16

MACARONI WITH FARMSTEAD CHEDDAR & BACON

serves 4–6

4 Tbsp (2 oz/60 g) unsalted butter, plus more for greasing

4 slices baguette or other firm bread, crusts removed and bread torn into bread crumbs

4 slices thick-cut bacon, cut crosswise into ½-inch (12-mm) strips

¼ cup (1½ oz/45 g) all-purpose flour

Salt and freshly ground black pepper

¼ tsp cayenne pepper

3 cups (24 fl oz/750 ml) milk, heated

¾ lb (375 g) Cheddar cheese, preferably farmstead, shredded

½ lb (250 g) elbow macaroni

Aged Cheddar gives this hearty baked pasta a richness that's balanced by the addition of salty, smoky bacon. A layer of toasted coarse bread crumbs provides a crunchy contrast to the creamy casserole.

Butter a shallow 1½-qt (1.5-l) baking dish. In a frying pan, melt 1 Tbsp of the butter over medium-high heat. Add the bread crumbs and fry until golden, about 4 minutes. Transfer to a plate.

In the frying pan, fry the bacon over medium heat until cooked but not crisp, 3–5 minutes. Drain on paper towels. In a saucepan, melt the remaining 3 Tbsp butter over medium-high heat. Add the flour, ½ tsp salt, ¼ tsp black pepper, and the cayenne and whisk until a smooth paste forms. Slowly whisk in the hot milk, reduce the heat to medium, and cook, whisking constantly, until the sauce thickens, about 15 minutes. Add two-thirds of the cheese and stir until melted, about 2 minutes. Remove from the heat.

Preheat the oven to 375°F (190°C). Bring a large pot of salted water to a boil. Add the macaroni, stir well, and cook until al dente, according to package directions. Drain, add to the prepared dish, and toss with the bacon. Pour in the cheese sauce and stir to mix well. Top with the remaining cheese and then the bread crumbs. Bake until the sauce is bubbling and the top is golden, about 30 minutes. Let stand for a few minutes before serving.

17

SLOW-COOKED CUBAN CHICKEN

serves 6

4 lb (2 kg) assorted chicken pieces, skin on and bone in

Salt and freshly ground pepper

3 Tbsp olive oil

8 cloves garlic, coarsely chopped

¾ cup (6 fl oz/180 ml) fresh orange juice

¾ cup (6 fl oz/180 ml) fresh lime juice

1 bay leaf

1 yellow onion, thinly sliced

½ cup (¾ oz/20 g) minced fresh flat-leaf parsley

2 limes, cut into wedges

For this simple yet flavorful recipe, you can substitute 3 lb (1.5 kg) boneless pork shoulder, cut into 2-inch (5-cm) chunks, for the chicken. If using pork, increase the cooking time to 3–4 hours at the high setting or 6–8 hours at the low setting.

Season the chicken pieces with salt and pepper. In a large frying pan, heat the oil over medium-high heat. Working in batches, sear the chicken pieces until golden, turning once, about 8 minutes. Transfer to a slow cooker.

Pour off all but about 1 Tbsp fat from the pan and return it to medium-high heat. Add the garlic and sauté just until fragrant, about 1 minute. Pour in the orange and lime juices. Raise the heat to high, bring to a boil, and stir to scrape up any browned bits on the pan bottom. Pour the contents of the pan over the chicken.

Add the bay leaf, spread the onion on top, and sprinkle with 1 tsp salt. Cover and cook on the high setting for 2½ hours or the low setting for 5 hours. The chicken should be opaque throughout and very tender. Discard the bay leaf. Transfer the chicken to a serving dish. Skim any fat from the cooking juices and season with salt and a generous amount of pepper. Spoon the onion and cooking juices over the chicken, garnish with the parsley, and serve, passing the lime wedges at the table.

18

RISOTTO WITH TALEGGIO, RADICCHIO & RED WINE

serves 6

2 cups (16 fl oz/500 ml) *each* chicken broth and beef broth or 4 cups (32 fl oz/1 l) vegetable broth

1 Tbsp olive oil

2 cups (6 oz/185 g) shredded radicchio (about 1 small head)

2 Tbsp unsalted butter

½ yellow onion, finely chopped

2 cups (14 oz/440 g) Arborio or Carnaroli rice

2 cups (16 fl oz/500 ml) dry red wine

6 oz (185 g) Taleggio cheese, rind removed, cut into small pieces

Salt and freshly ground pepper

⅓ cup (1½ oz/45 g) walnuts, toasted and chopped (optional)

Chopped fresh flat-leaf parsley for garnish (optional)

In this refined and beautifully colored risotto, pleasantly bitter radicchio is balanced by creamy Taleggio cheese, which melts readily, making it a good option to stir into risotto or polenta. Gently swirl in the cheese just before serving.

In a saucepan, bring the chicken and beef broths to a gentle simmer over medium heat. Reduce the heat to low and maintain a simmer.

In a large, heavy saucepan, warm the olive oil over medium-high heat. Add the radicchio and sauté until the edges are golden, about 4 minutes. Drain on paper towels.

In the large saucepan, melt 1 Tbsp of the butter over medium-high heat. Add the onion and sauté until translucent, about 5 minutes. Add the rice and stir until well coated with butter and translucent, about 2 minutes. Add the wine, a little at a time, and cook, stirring constantly, until nearly absorbed, 5–6 minutes.

Reduce the heat to medium and start adding the simmering broth to the rice a ladleful at a time, stirring frequently after each addition. Wait until the broth is almost completely absorbed (but the rice is never dry on top) before adding the next ladleful. After about 20 minutes, the rice will be tender to the bite and creamy.

Stir in the sautéed radicchio, the remaining 1 Tbsp butter, and the cheese. Season with salt and pepper. Spoon into bowls, top with the walnuts and parsley, if using, and serve.

19

The derivation of the word jambalaya is said to come from Spanish, French, and African cultures. All three lay claim to the origins of this quintessential Creole concoction that combines chicken and seafood with rice and assorted seasonings. Use crawfish in place of the shrimp if you can find them. This recipe can easily be doubled to serve a crowd.

JAMBALAYA WITH SHRIMP, CHICKEN & HAM

serves 6

2 Tbsp olive oil, plus more for greasing

3½ lb (1.75 kg) skin-on, bone-in chicken thighs

Salt and freshly ground pepper

3 oz (90 g) cooked ham, diced

1 large yellow onion, chopped

1 green bell pepper, seeded and chopped

3 cloves garlic, minced

1 tsp dried oregano

½ cup (4 fl oz/125 ml) dry white wine

1 can (14½ oz/455 g) diced tomatoes, drained

4 cups (32 fl oz/1 l) chicken broth

2 tsp red wine vinegar

2 cups (14 oz/440 g) long-grain white rice

2 cups (10 oz/315 g) fresh or thawed frozen peas

½ lb (250 g) medium shrimp in the shell

6 green onions, white and tender green parts, thinly sliced

2 Tbsp coarsely chopped fresh flat-leaf parsley

2 lemons, cut into wedges

Oil the insert of a slow cooker. Season the chicken generously all over with salt and pepper. In a large, heavy frying pan, heat the 2 Tbsp oil over medium-high heat. Working in batches, add the chicken and sear, turning as needed, until golden brown, about 8 minutes total. Transfer to a plate.

Pour off most of the fat from the pan and return it to medium-high heat. Add the ham, onion, and bell pepper and sauté until the vegetables start to color, about 7 minutes. Add the garlic and oregano and cook for 1 minute. Add ½ tsp salt, several grindings of pepper, and the wine and stir to scrape up any browned bits on the pan bottom. Transfer the contents of the pan to the slow cooker. Add the tomatoes, broth, and vinegar, then stir in the rice. Nestle the chicken in the rice, cover, and cook on the low setting for 3 hours.

Uncover and check to be sure a little liquid is still visible at the bottom of the cooker. If it appears dry, add 1 Tbsp water. Scatter the peas and shrimp evenly over the top. ⟩⟩

Re-cover and cook until the shrimp are pink, the chicken is opaque throughout, and the rice is tender, 15–20 minutes.

Transfer to a large shallow serving bowl and sprinkle with the green onions and parsley. Squeeze some lemon juice over the top and serve with the remaining lemon wedges.

20

Fresh Chinese noodles and tofu come together quickly on weeknights, and a sauce of coconut milk and creamy peanut butter brings richness and sustenance to a vegetarian meal. Serve with steamed broccoli or bok choy on the side.

PEANUT-BRAISED TOFU WITH NOODLES

serves 4

1 lb (500 g) firm tofu, cut into ¾-inch (2-cm) cubes

1 cup (4 oz/125 g) trimmed and halved snow peas

½ lb (250 g) thin fresh Chinese noodles

½ cup (4 fl oz/125 ml) unsweetened coconut milk

½ cup (5 oz/155 g) creamy peanut butter

1 Tbsp chile paste

1 tsp sugar

¼ cup (2 fl oz/60 ml) vegetable broth

2 Tbsp soy sauce

2 Tbsp fresh lime juice

Line a baking sheet with a double thickness of paper towels. Arrange the tofu in a single layer on the towels. Top with another layer of towels and pat the tofu dry.

Bring a large saucepan of water to a boil. Add the snow peas, cook for 30 seconds, and remove with a slotted spoon and set aside. Add the noodles to the boiling water and cook according to the package directions. Drain the noodles, rinse well with cold water, and drain again.

In the saucepan, stir together the coconut milk and peanut butter until well combined. Stir in the chile paste, sugar, broth, soy sauce, and lime juice. Add the tofu. Cook over medium heat, stirring occasionally, until the sauce is hot and the tofu is heated through, about 2 minutes. Stir in the peas and the noodles and serve.

21

This classic Cuban recipe is slowly simmered until the meat is exceedingly tender. Tossed with a spicy, chile-infused tomato sauce, it's best served over white rice. This is a great make-ahead dish, as the flavors only get better the next day.

CUBAN-STYLE SHREDDED BEEF

serves 6–8

3 lb (1.5 kg) flank steak or lean chuck

Salt

½ white onion, peeled, with root end intact, stuck with 1 whole clove

10 black peppercorns

1 bay leaf

FOR THE TOMATO SAUCE

2 Tbsp canola oil

½ white onion, chopped

1 green bell pepper, seeded and chopped

1 small carrot, chopped

3 cloves garlic, minced

1 Tbsp seeded and minced serrano chile

2 tsp achiote paste or chile paste

1 can (14½ oz/455 g) diced tomatoes, drained or 2 cups (14 oz/440 g) seeded and chopped fresh tomatoes

Pinch of ground cinnamon

Cooked white rice for serving

⅓ cup (2½ oz/75 g) jarred sliced red pimientos, drained

2 Tbsp capers, drained

Place the meat in a large, heavy pot. Add just enough cold water to barely cover the meat. Stir in 2 tsp salt and tuck the onion, peppercorns, and bay leaf around the meat. Bring to a simmer slowly over medium heat. Reduce the heat to low, cover, and cook until the meat is very tender, 2½–3 hours.

Using tongs or 2 forks, transfer the meat to a carving board and let cool. Strain the cooking liquid through a fine-mesh sieve set over a bowl and reserve. Discard the solids.

To make the tomato sauce, in the pot, warm the oil over medium-high heat. Add the onion, bell pepper, carrot, garlic, and chile and cook, stirring frequently, until the vegetables begin to soften, about 2 minutes. Crumble the achiote paste into the pot and cook, stirring, for 2–3 minutes. Add the tomatoes and cinnamon. Cook, stirring frequently, until almost all the liquid has evaporated. Add 1½ cups (12 fl oz/375 ml) of the reserved beef cooking liquid to the sauce and simmer over medium heat for 10 minutes to blend the flavors. ⟩⟩

Shred the meat into bite-size pieces using 2 forks. Add the meat to the simmering sauce and cook until heated through, about 5 minutes.

Serve the stew over the rice, topped with a few pimiento slices and a sprinkling of capers.

22

Protein-rich legumes and cold-weather greens pack lots of nutrients into this nontraditional gumbo, designed to help you recharge in the New Year. Authentic gumbo uses okra as a thickener, but you can substitute 2 Tbsp long-grain rice. Add it to the pot when you cook the vegetables.

RED BEAN & VEGETABLE GUMBO

serves 4

6 cups (¾ lb/375 g) chopped kale leaves

1 green bell pepper, seeded and chopped

1 bunch green onions, white and tender green parts, chopped

1 cup (7 oz/220 g) canned whole peeled tomatoes

4 cups (32 fl oz/1 l) vegetable broth

2 bay leaves

1 tsp dried oregano

1 tsp dried thyme

1 can (15 oz/470 g) red kidney beans, drained and rinsed

8 fresh okra pods, cut into ½-inch (12-mm) pieces, or 1 cup (5 oz/155 g) chopped frozen okra

Salt and freshly ground pepper

Hot-pepper sauce (optional)

Cooked white rice for serving

Combine the kale, bell pepper, green onions, tomatoes and their juices, and broth in a large, heavy pot. Add the bay leaves, oregano, and thyme. Bring to a boil over medium-high heat. Reduce the heat to medium-low, cover, and simmer until the kale is tender, about 30 minutes.

Add the beans and okra to the pot. Re-cover and cook until the okra is just tender, about 15 minutes for fresh, or 5 minutes for frozen. Season with salt and pepper, and with hot-pepper sauce, if using. Discard the bay leaves. Serve the gumbo over the rice.

23

Pork shoulder is a beautifully marbled cut, which emerges fork-tender after long cooking at low temperatures. Rub down the meat with woodsy rosemary and pungent garlic for a boldly flavored, satisfying stew.

GARLICKY PORK SHOULDER WITH GREENS

serves 6

2½ lb (1.25 kg) boneless pork shoulder, cut into 1½-inch (4-cm) chunks

Salt and freshly ground pepper

2 Tbsp olive oil

1 large yellow onion, finely chopped

2 sprigs fresh thyme

15–20 cloves garlic

1 tsp minced fresh rosemary

⅔ cup (5 fl oz/160 ml) dry red wine

1 Tbsp red wine vinegar

⅔ cup (5 fl oz/160 ml) beef or chicken broth

About 1¼ lb (625 g) kale, tough stems removed, leaves cut crosswise into wide strips

Season the pork generously with salt and pepper. In a large frying pan, heat the oil over medium-high heat. Working in batches, add the pork and sear, turning as needed, until well browned on all sides, 6–7 minutes. Using a slotted spoon, transfer to a plate.

Pour off most of the fat from the pan and return to medium-high heat. Add the onion and thyme and sauté until the onion is golden brown, about 5 minutes. Add the garlic and rosemary and cook for 1 minute. Pour in the wine and vinegar and stir to scrape up any browned bits on the pan bottom. Transfer the contents of the pan to a slow cooker. Add the broth and the pork and stir to combine. Cover and cook on the low setting for 5–6 hours, stirring two or three times during the first 2 hours. Stir in the kale, re-cover, and cook for 30–60 minutes. The pork and kale should be very tender.

Using the slotted spoon, transfer the pork and kale to a platter. Skim any fat from the cooking liquid, then drizzle the liquid over the meat and serve.

24

Seared chicken breasts and delicately flavored fennel and leeks cook together in the same pan for an easy but elegant meal. Velvety cream draws together the tastes of the ingredients in an easy pan sauce.

PAN-ROASTED CHICKEN WITH FENNEL, LEEKS & CREAM

serves 4

3–3½ lb (1.5–1.75 kg) assorted chicken pieces, skin on and bone in

Salt and freshly ground pepper

1 Tbsp peanut or grapeseed oil

3 Tbsp unsalted butter

1 large fennel bulb, chopped, any fronds reserved for garnish

3 leeks, white and pale green parts, cut into ½-inch (12-mm) pieces

¼ cup (2 fl oz/60 ml) dry white wine

1 cup (8 fl oz/250 ml) heavy cream

Preheat the oven to 400°F (200°C). Season the chicken with 1½ tsp salt and ½ tsp pepper.

In a large ovenproof frying pan, heat the oil over medium-high heat until very hot but not smoking. Working in batches, sear the chicken, turning once, until golden brown on both sides, about 8 minutes. Transfer to a platter. Pour off the fat from the pan. Return the chicken, skin side up, to the pan, place in the oven, and roast until an instant-read thermometer inserted in the thickest part of a breast away from the bone registers 170°F (77°C), about 30 minutes.

Transfer the chicken pieces to a platter and tent with foil to keep warm. Pour the pan juices into a measuring cup, let stand for 2 minutes, and then skim the fat from the surface. Return the pan to the stove top over medium heat, add 2 Tbsp of the butter, and let it melt. Add the fennel and stir well to coat with the butter. Reduce the heat to medium and sauté until the fennel softens, about 5 minutes. Stir in the leeks and the remaining 1 Tbsp butter and cook, stirring occasionally, until the fennel is tender, about 5 minutes.

Stir in the wine and the cream. Pour the pan juices into the pan. Raise the heat to high and boil until the liquid lightly coats the back of a spoon, about 3 minutes. Adjust the seasoning.

Pour the sauce over the chicken, sprinkle with chopped fennel fronds, if using, and serve.

As spring begins, a wide array of new vegetables becomes available. Sweet peas, asparagus, leeks, dandelion greens, and earthy morels all mingle with the last of the winter greens, bringing life to baked and simmered one-pot dishes. Slow-cooked fish, nutty grains like farro and quinoa, and meltingly tender braised meats are perfect backdrops for this fresh bounty.

march

1

BAKED COD WITH LEEKS, MORELS & BACON

serves 4

Here, elegantly ridged morels partner with smoky bacon and caramelized leeks, for a sophisticated baked fish dish. Just a touch of champagne vinegar adds punch, and a few snips of fresh chives add color.

¾ oz (20 g) dried morel mushrooms

½ cup (4 fl oz/125 ml) boiling water

3 Tbsp unsalted butter

4 slices bacon

2 cups (6 oz/185 g) thinly sliced leeks, white and pale green parts

Salt and freshly ground pepper

1 tsp champagne vinegar

4 cod fillets, about 6 oz (185 g) each

1 Tbsp minced fresh chives

Preheat the oven to 375°F (190°C).

In a small heatproof bowl, soak the mushrooms in the boiling water for 20 minutes. Squeeze dry and roughly chop the larger mushrooms into bite-sized pieces. Set aside.

Melt 2 Tbsp of the butter in a large ovenproof frying pan over medium-high heat. Add the bacon and fry until crispy, about 5 minutes. Drain on paper towels. Pour off all but 3 Tbsp fat from the pan. Add the leeks and ¼ tsp salt, stir until evenly coated with the fat, and cook, stirring often, until tender and beginning to brown, about 10 minutes. Crumble the bacon and add half to the leeks along with the reserved morels and the vinegar. Toss to combine well and spread the leek mixture over the bottom of the pan.

Season the cod fillets with salt and pepper and lay them on top of the leeks. Dot with the remaining 1 Tbsp butter. Bake until the fish flakes with a fork, about 12 minutes. Garnish with the remaining bacon and the chives, and serve.

2

ASIAN BRAISED SHORT RIBS

serves 6–8

Sharp ginger, dark soy, and fragrant lemongrass give these short ribs a fresh Pan-Asian character. The vivid flavors perfectly complement the richness of the meat. Serve with steamed jasmine rice.

3 Tbsp all-purpose flour

Salt and freshly ground pepper

5½–6 lb (2.75–3 kg) beef short ribs, Korean cut

¼ cup (2 fl oz/60 ml) canola oil

4 cloves garlic, minced

4 green onions, white and tender green parts, thinly sliced

2 Tbsp peeled and grated fresh ginger

1 tsp red pepper flakes

1 lemongrass stalk, halved lengthwise, cut into 4 pieces, and crushed

1 cup (8 fl oz/250 ml) beef broth

½ cup (4 fl oz/125 ml) soy sauce

½ cup (4 fl oz/125 ml) hoisin sauce

½ cup (4 fl oz/125 ml) rice vinegar

½ cup (4 oz/125 g) firmly packed dark brown sugar

¼ cup (2 fl oz/60 ml) chile-garlic sauce such as Sriracha

Preheat the oven to 350°F (180°C).

On a plate, stir together the flour, 1 tsp salt, and ½ tsp pepper. Turn the short ribs in the seasoned flour, shaking off any excess. In a large, heavy pot, heat the oil over medium-high heat. Working in batches, cook the ribs, turning occasionally, until evenly browned, 12–15 minutes. Transfer to a plate.

Add the garlic, green onions, ginger, red pepper flakes, and lemongrass to the pot and sauté over medium-high heat until fragrant, about 1 minute. Pour in the broth and stir to scrape up any browned bits on the pot bottom. Stir in the soy sauce, hoisin sauce, vinegar, brown sugar, and chile-garlic sauce. Bring to a boil. Return the ribs to the pot. Cover and cook until the ribs are very tender, about 2 hours. Skim as much fat as possible from the surface of the sauce before serving.

3

FARRO WITH SPRING VEGETABLES

serves 6

3 Tbsp olive oil

½ yellow onion, finely chopped

2 celery ribs, finely chopped

1 oz (30 g) pancetta, finely chopped

1½ cups (10½ oz/330 g) farro, rinsed

½ cup (4 fl oz/125 ml) dry white wine

4 cups (32 fl oz/1 l) chicken or vegetable broth

Salt and freshly ground pepper

1 lb (500 g) asparagus, trimmed and cut into 2-inch (5-cm) pieces

1 Tbsp unsalted butter

2 leeks, white and pale green parts, cut into 2-inch (5-cm) matchsticks

2 cups (10 oz/315 g) fresh or thawed frozen peas

Grated zest and juice of ½ lemon

2 Tbsp chopped fresh flat-leaf parsley

Parmesan cheese for garnish

Farro, an ancient strain of wheat popular in Italian kitchens, holds its shape beautifully as it cooks, making it ideal for salads, side dishes, and soups. Here, it is tossed with peas, leeks, and asparagus in a colorful and healthy meatless dish. It also makes a great side dish for grilled poultry or meat.

In a large, heavy frying pan, warm 2 Tbsp of the oil over medium heat. Add the onion, celery, and pancetta and sauté until the onion is softened and the pancetta is mostly crisp, about 5 minutes. Add the farro and stir to coat with the oil. Cook, stirring, until lightly toasted, 1–2 minutes. Add the wine and stir until it has evaporated, about 5 minutes. Pour in 1 cup (8 fl oz/250 ml) of the broth and stir to scrape up any browned bits on the pan bottom. Transfer the contents of the pan to a slow cooker. Stir in the remaining 3 cups (24 fl oz/750 ml) broth, ¼ tsp salt, and several grindings of pepper. Cover and cook on the low setting until the farro is tender, 2–2½ hours.

Meanwhile, bring a saucepan of salted water to a boil. Add the asparagus and cook until just tender, about 6 minutes. Drain and refresh with cold water, and drain again.

About 5 minutes before the farro is ready, melt the butter with the remaining 1 Tbsp oil in the frying pan over medium heat. Add the leeks and sauté for 1 minute. ⤞

Add the peas and sauté for 1 minute. Add the asparagus and sauté until all the vegetables are just tender and heated through, 1–2 minutes. Stir in the lemon juice.

Stir the vegetables into the farro and transfer to a large shallow serving bowl. Garnish with the lemon zest and parsley. Using a vegetable peeler, shave Parmesan over the top, then serve.

4

BRAISED GARLIC CHICKEN

serves 4–6

3–3½ lb (1.5–1.75 kg) assorted chicken pieces, skin on and bone in

Salt and freshly ground pepper

2 Tbsp canola oil

4 heads garlic, separated into cloves, unpeeled

¼ cup (2 fl oz/60 ml) dry white wine

1 Tbsp chopped fresh thyme

Beautifully magenta-tinged heads of green garlic first appear at the farmers' market in early spring. Simply immature garlic, these bulbs offer a mild and distinctive flavor. Substitute them in equal parts in recipes that call for regular garlic, such as this one, for a distinctive chicken-in-a-pot. This dish is ideal served with tiny boiled red potatoes.

Preheat the oven to 350°F (180°C).

Season the chicken all over with salt and pepper. In a large, heavy pot, heat the oil over medium-high heat. Working in batches, sear the chicken, turning occasionally, until well browned, 7–10 minutes. Transfer to a plate.

Pour off all but 2 Tbsp fat from the pot. Add the garlic and sauté over medium-high heat until lightly browned, about 3 minutes. Pour in the wine and stir to scrape up any browned bits on the pot bottom.

Return the chicken and any juices to the pot. Sprinkle with the thyme, cover, and cook in the oven until the chicken is tender and opaque throughout, about 45 minutes.

Transfer the chicken to a platter and cover loosely with foil. Strain the pan juices back into the pot. Press on the garlic cloves to extract as much liquid and pulp as possible. Bring to a simmer over medium-high heat and season well with salt and pepper. Spoon the sauce over the chicken and serve.

5

Packed with spinach and peppers, this hearty vegetarian lasagna has a twist: a surprise ingredient, tofu, is substituted for part of the cheese, creating a healthy version of a classically high-calorie dish.

SPINACH & ROASTED RED PEPPER LASAGNA

serves 8–10

4 lb (2 kg) fresh spinach or 2 lb (1 kg) frozen chopped spinach

1 lb (500 g) soft tofu

2 cups (1 lb/500 g) part-skim ricotta cheese

2 egg whites

½ cup (2 oz/60 g) Parmesan cheese

1 cup (4 oz/125 g) shredded mozzarella cheese

Salt and freshly ground pepper

8 cups (64 fl oz/2 l) prepared tomato sauce

9 no-boil lasagna noodles

3 large red bell peppers, roasted and seeded

2 large cloves garlic, minced

If using fresh spinach, discard the tough stems and any damaged leaves. Working in batches if necessary, add to a large frying pan, place over medium-high heat, cover, and cook, turning the leaves a couple of times, until wilted but still slightly firm to the bite, 5–6 minutes. Drain well and chop finely. Squeeze the spinach to remove most of the moisture. If using frozen spinach, cook according to the package directions, let cool, and squeeze dry.

Cut the tofu into about 16 pieces. Hold each piece in your hand over the sink or a bowl and gently squeeze to remove some of the water. Crumble the tofu into a large bowl; it should resemble cottage cheese. Add the ricotta and egg whites and stir until well combined. Stir in the Parmesan and half of the mozzarella. Stir in 1 tsp salt and ¼ tsp pepper.

Preheat the oven to 350°F (180°C).

Cover the bottom of a 9-by-13-by-3-inch (23-by-33-by-7.5 cm) baking dish with half of the tomato sauce. Arrange 3 of the noodles on top of the sauce. Cover the noodles with half of the bell peppers, cutting them as needed so they lie flat. There will be spaces. Cover the peppers with half of the spinach, using your fingers to pull apart any clumps. Sprinkle half of the garlic evenly over the spinach. Using a large spoon, dollop half of the cheese mixture on top of the spinach. With the back of the spoon, gently spread the cheese as much as possible without pulling ⟫

up the spinach. There will be some spaces. Top with another layer of 3 noodles, and then the remaining peppers, spinach, garlic, and cheese mixture. Cover with the remaining 3 noodles. Spread the remaining tomato sauce over the top. Cover the baking dish with foil.

Bake until the pasta is almost soft when tested with a knife, about 1¼ hours. Uncover the lasagna. Sprinkle the remaining mozzarella evenly over the top. Replace the foil. Continue to bake until the pasta is soft and the cheese on top is melted, about 15 minutes. Uncover and let the lasagna stand for 20 minutes before cutting into rectangles and serving.

6

Filling white beans and savory ham are a delicious combination. Make it a complete meal with the addition of nutritious leafy greens. Any kind of kale or chard will do, but black kale (also labeled cavolo nero, lacinato, or dinosaur kale) boasts gorgeous color and sweet flavor. It has a devoted following among kale fanatics.

BRAISED KALE WITH HAM & WHITE BEANS

serves 4

2 bunches kale

2 tsp olive oil

2 cloves garlic, thinly sliced

4 oz (125 g) smoked ham such as Black Forest, diced

½ cup (4 fl oz/125 ml) chicken broth

Salt and freshly ground pepper

1 can (15 oz/470 g) cannellini beans, rinsed and drained

½ tsp minced fresh rosemary

Strip the stems and ribs from the kale leaves and discard, then tear the leaves into 2-inch (5-cm) pieces.

In a frying pan, heat the oil over medium-low heat. Add the garlic and sauté until lightly browned, about 1 minute. Add the ham and sauté for 1 minute. Add the kale, cover, and cook, turning occasionally, until the kale leaves just begin to wilt, 2–3 minutes. Add the broth and a pinch each of salt and pepper and cook until the leaves are just tender and the liquid has almost evaporated, 4–5 minutes.

Add the beans and rosemary and raise the heat to medium-high. Cook, tossing gently, until the beans are heated through, about 3 minutes. Adjust the seasoning and serve.

7

In this dish, spring vegetables—leeks, asparagus, and peas—are sautéed in butter and oil just until tender, adding color and garden-fresh flavor to moist, braised salmon. If leeks are unavailable, substitute green onions. If desired, serve with steamed or mashed new potatoes.

SALMON WITH SPRING VEGETABLES

serves 4

1 cup (8 fl oz/250 ml) dry white wine

½ cup (4 fl oz/125 ml) vegetable broth

½ small yellow onion, sliced

3 sprigs fresh tarragon

Salt and freshly ground pepper

4 salmon fillets, about 6 oz (185 g) each

1 lb (500 g) asparagus, trimmed and cut into 2-inch (5-cm) pieces

1 Tbsp unsalted butter

1 Tbsp olive oil

2 leeks, white and pale green parts, cut into 2-inch (5-cm) matchsticks

2 cups (10 oz/315 g) fresh or thawed frozen peas

Grated zest and juice of ½ lemon

Minced fresh chives for garnish

In a slow cooker, combine the wine, broth, onion, and tarragon. Stir in ½ cup (4 fl oz/ 125 ml) water, ½ tsp salt, and several grindings of pepper. Cover and cook on the low setting for 30 minutes. Add the salmon, re-cover, and cook for 1 hour. The fish should be opaque throughout, firm, and very tender.

About 15 minutes before the fish is ready, bring a saucepan of salted water to a boil. Add the asparagus and cook until just tender, about 6 minutes. Drain and refresh with cold water, and drain again.

In a large frying pan, melt the butter with the oil over medium heat. Add the leeks and sauté for 2 minutes. Add the peas and cook for 1 minute, then add the asparagus and sauté until heated through, 1–2 minutes. Stir in the lemon juice and remove from the heat.

Transfer the salmon to a platter. Use the braising liquid to moisten the fish, if desired. Arrange the vegetables around the salmon. Sprinkle with the lemon zest and chives, and serve.

8

Thai green curry paste has a bold, concentrated taste and heat. Tempered by rich, creamy coconut milk, it makes a fragrant simmer sauce for spring chicken, asparagus, and fragrant Thai basil.

THAI GREEN CHICKEN CURRY WITH ASPARAGUS

serves 4–6

Salt

1½ lb (750 g) asparagus, trimmed and cut into 2-inch (5-cm) pieces

4 skinless, boneless chicken breast halves

2 Tbsp peanut or grapeseed oil

1 yellow onion, cut into 8 wedges

1 small red bell pepper, seeded and cut into matchsticks

½-inch (12-mm) piece fresh ginger, peeled and minced

2 cloves garlic, minced

1 can (13 ½ fl oz/420 ml) unsweetened coconut milk (unshaken)

3 Tbsp Thai green curry paste

1 cup (8 fl oz/250 ml) chicken broth

2 Tbsp Asian fish sauce

½ cup (¾ oz/20 g) small Thai basil leaves

1 lime, cut into wedges

Bring a saucepan of salted water to a boil. Add the asparagus and cook just until tender-crisp, about 2 minutes. Drain and refresh with cold water, and drain again. Cut the chicken across the grain on a slight diagonal into slices about ½ inch (12 mm) thick. Season with salt.

In a large frying pan, heat the oil over medium-high heat. Add the onion and bell pepper and sauté until beginning to soften, about 3 minutes. Stir in the ginger and garlic and sauté until fragrant, about 30 seconds. Transfer to a plate.

Open the can of coconut milk (do not shake it) and scoop out 3 Tbsp of the thick cream on the top. Return the pan to medium-high heat. Add the coconut cream and curry paste and stir well. Whisk in the remaining coconut milk, the broth, and the fish sauce. Return the vegetable mixture to the pan, stir in the chicken, and bring to a boil. Reduce the heat to medium-low and simmer, stirring occasionally, until the sauce has reduced slightly and the vegetables are tender-crisp, about 5 minutes. Stir in the asparagus and cook until the chicken is opaque throughout, about 3 minutes. Adjust the seasoning and serve, garnished with the basil and lime wedges.

9

This simple spring vegetable soup can be served either hot or cold. Cold, it is known as vichyssoise, an elegant French soup, which is sometimes topped with a small spoonful of black caviar.

POTATO-LEEK SOUP

serves 6

1 lb (500 g) russet or Yukon gold potatoes

1 lb (500 g) leeks

6 cups (48 fl oz/1.5 l) chicken broth

1 tsp salt

½ cup (4 fl oz/125 ml) heavy cream

3 Tbsp minced fresh chives

Peel the potatoes and then cut into 1-inch (2.5-cm) pieces. Trim the roots from the leeks, then remove the dark green leaves, leaving 2 inches of the pale green parts. Cut each leek in half lengthwise. Rinse the leeks under running cold water, separating the layers to remove any grit. Cut the leeks crosswise into thin slices.

In a large saucepan over medium heat, combine the potatoes, leeks, broth, and salt. Bring to a simmer and cook until the potatoes and leeks are tender when pierced with a fork, about 45 minutes.

Working in batches with a blender or food processor, or using an immersion blender, purée the soup until smooth. Return the soup to the saucepan. Stir in the cream. Taste and adjust the seasoning with salt.

To serve warm, heat the soup gently over medium-low heat until warm. To serve chilled, let the soup cool completely, then cover and refrigerate until cold. Garnish with the chives.

10

If you like, plan ahead and corn your own brisket: In a bowl, combine 8 cups (64 fl oz/2 l) water, 1½ cups (12 oz/ 375 g) kosher salt, ½ cup (4 oz/125 g) sugar, 3 Tbsp pickling spices, and 3 cloves garlic, crushed. Stir until the salt and sugar are dissolved. Submerge one 4 lb (2 kg) brisket in the mixture, cover, and refrigerate for 5–8 days. Remove the brisket, rinse well under cold water, and then proceed with the recipe.

CORNED BEEF & CABBAGE

serves 6–8

3 sprigs fresh thyme

5 sprigs fresh flat-leaf parsley

3½–4 lb (1.75–2 kg) corned beef brisket *(left)*

2 bay leaves

1 tsp peppercorns

12 white boiling onions or 3 small white onions cut into wedges

6 large or 12 small carrots, cut into large chunks or left whole if small

2 lb (1 kg) small red-skinned or mixed-colored new potatoes

1 small head green cabbage, cut into 6–8 wedges

1 cup (8 fl oz/250 ml) heavy cream

3 Tbsp prepared horseradish

Salt

Tie the thyme and parsley sprigs together with kitchen string. Rinse the brisket, put it in a large, heavy pot, and add water to cover by 1 inch (2.5 cm). Bring to a boil over medium-high heat, skimming off any foam from the surface. Add the herb bundle, bay leaves, and peppercorns, reduce the heat to medium-low, cover, and simmer gently until the brisket is almost tender, 2½–3 hours.

Add the onions, carrots, potatoes, and cabbage wedges and return the liquid to a simmer. Cook until the vegetables and brisket are fully tender, about 25 minutes.

Meanwhile, in a bowl, whip the cream until soft peaks form. Fold in the horseradish, then season with salt. Cover and refrigerate the horseradish cream until ready to serve.

Using a slotted spoon, transfer the vegetables to a large platter. Transfer the brisket to a cutting board. Cut the meat across the grain and arrange on the platter with the vegetables. Serve, passing the horseradish cream on the side.

11

Tender chunks of veal star in this light stew fit for the season. The delicate meat is seasoned simply with fresh thyme and bright white wine. Tear open a baguette, and follow the meal with a wedge of Brie or some fresh chevre.

SPRING VEAL STEW

serves 6–8

3 lb (1.5 kg) boneless veal shank or shoulder, cut into 2-inch (5-cm) chunks

Salt and freshly ground pepper

3 Tbsp unsalted butter

3 Tbsp olive oil

2 leeks, white and pale green parts, halved lengthwise and thinly sliced

1 cup (8 fl oz/250 ml) dry white wine

2 sprigs fresh thyme

½ lb (250 g) asparagus, trimmed and coarsely chopped

6 oz (185 g) button or cremini mushrooms, sliced

½ lb (250 g) thawed frozen peas

½ cup (4 oz/125 g) crème fraîche or sour cream

3 Tbsp chopped fresh flat-leaf parsley

Season the veal cubes with salt and pepper. In a large frying pan, melt the butter with the oil over medium-high heat. Working in batches, sear the veal until golden brown on all sides, 7–10 minutes. Add the leeks and sauté until they start to soften, about 3 minutes. Transfer the veal and leeks to a slow cooker.

Return the pan to medium-high heat, add the wine, and stir to scrape up any browned bits on the pan bottom. Bring to a boil and pour the contents of the pan over the veal. Add the thyme sprigs, cover, and cook on the high setting for 3 hours or on the low setting for 6–6½ hours.

Add the asparagus, mushrooms, and peas to the slow cooker and stir to combine. Cover and continue to cook until the vegetables are tender, 20–30 minutes. Discard the thyme sprigs. Stir in the crème fraîche until blended with the cooking juices. Season with salt and pepper. Serve the stew, garnished with the parsley.

12

Jagged dandelion greens can be found at the farmers' market, tucked among the tender leaves of early spring. The pleasantly bitter flavor is an Italian favorite and pairs well with a spicy sausage flecked with fennel in this baked pasta.

BAKED PASTA WITH SAUSAGE & DANDELION GREENS

serves 4

Salt and freshly ground pepper

½ lb (250 g) orecchiette pasta

2 Tbsp olive oil

3 chicken-fennel or other mild sausages

1 bunch dandelion greens, about ¾ lb (375 g), trimmed and coarsely chopped

1 cup (8 oz/250 g) whole-milk ricotta cheese

1 Tbsp unsalted butter

¼ cup (½ oz/15 g) fresh bread crumbs

Bring a large pot of salted water to a boil. Add the orecchiette, reduce the heat to medium, stir once or twice, and cook until al dente, about 15 minutes. Drain and place in a medium baking dish. Drizzle with 1 Tbsp of the olive oil, sprinkle with 1 tsp salt and 1 tsp pepper, and stir to mix well.

Preheat the oven to 350°F (180°C).

In a frying pan, heat the remaining 1 Tbsp oil over medium-high heat. Add the sausages and sauté until browned on all sides, about 10 minutes. Remove from the pan and let cool slightly. Add the dandelion greens to the pan and sauté over medium-high heat until tender but still bright green, about 5 minutes. Remove from the heat.

Cut the sausages into 1-inch (2.5-cm) slices and add to the pasta along with the greens and any pan juices. Toss and stir until the ingredients are evenly distributed. Adjust the seasoning. Spoon the ricotta onto the pasta and spread evenly over the top.

Add the butter to the frying pan, and melt over medium heat. Add the bread crumbs and cook, stirring often, until golden, 3–4 minutes. Sprinkle the toasted crumbs evenly over the ricotta.

Bake until the cheese is lightly browned around the edges, 25–30 minutes. Serve directly from the dish.

13

CHICKEN KORMA

serves 6

¼ cup (2 fl oz/60 ml) canola oil

1 yellow onion, finely chopped

2 cloves garlic, minced

1 Tbsp peeled and grated fresh ginger

1 cinnamon stick

2 bay leaves

1 Tbsp ground coriander

1 tsp ground turmeric

½ tsp *each* cayenne pepper and ground cumin

1½ cups (12 fl oz/375 ml) chicken broth

1 cup (8 fl oz/250 ml) prepared tomato sauce

1 Tbsp sugar

Salt

2 lb (1 kg) skinless, boneless chicken breasts, cut into strips ½ inch (12 mm) wide

½ cup (4 fl oz/125 ml) buttermilk

½ cup (3 oz/90 g) roasted cashew nuts

3 Tbsp chopped fresh cilantro

This dish from northern India is beloved for its creamy sauce, which includes puréed cashew nuts. Other versions may use yogurt or cream to enrich the sauce, but this recipe features buttermilk, a lighter, but no less authentic choice. Serve over steamed basmati rice to soak up the sauce.

In a large, heavy pot over medium-high heat, warm the oil. Add the onion and sauté until it begins to soften, 3 minutes. Add the garlic, ginger, cinnamon, bay leaves, and spices and sauté until the spices are fragrant, about 1 minute. Stir in the broth, tomato sauce, sugar, and 1 tsp salt. Bring to a boil.

Add the chicken, and stir to coat. Reduce the heat to low, cover, and cook until the chicken is tender and the sauce is thickened, about 1 hour.

About 15 minutes before the chicken is done, combine the buttermilk and cashews in a blender or food processor. Blend or process until the nuts are finely puréed and combined with the buttermilk. Add to the chicken and stir to blend into the sauce. Continue cooking until the sauce is completely heated through and thickened, about 5 minutes. Remove and discard the cinnamon stick and bay leaves. Serve, sprinkled with the cilantro.

14

SPICY BRAISED TOFU WITH PORK

serves 4–6

4 Tbsp soy sauce

2 tsp rice wine or dry sherry

2 tsp toasted sesame oil

¼ lb (125 g) ground pork

14 oz (440 g) soft tofu

½ cup (4 fl oz/125 ml) chicken broth

1 Tbsp chile-bean paste

1 tsp sugar

½ tsp cornstarch

Ground white pepper

2 Tbsp canola oil

3 Tbsp minced green onions, white and tender green parts

1 Tbsp peeled and grated fresh ginger

3 cloves garlic, minced

Soft tofu and juicy ground pork make unrivaled partners in this tempting Sichuan preparation, known as ma-po tofu. Traditionally, it's served extra spicy, so add a large pinch of fiery red pepper flakes if you dare.

In a large, nonreactive bowl, stir together 3 Tbsp of the soy sauce, the rice wine, and 1 tsp of the sesame oil. Add the pork and stir to mix well. Set aside.

Bring a small saucepan of salted water to a boil over medium heat. Add the tofu, reduce the heat to low, and simmer gently for 5 minutes to firm up the tofu. Using a slotted spoon, transfer the tofu to a plate. Weight with a second plate to press out the excess water. Set aside for 30 minutes. Just before stir-frying, pour off any water and cut the tofu into ½-inch (12-mm) cubes.

In a small bowl, combine the broth, chile-bean paste, remaining 1 Tbsp soy sauce, the sugar, and cornstarch. Add ⅛ tsp white pepper and the remaining 1 tsp sesame oil and whisk to blend.

In a large work or frying pan, heat the canola oil over medium-high heat. Add the pork and its marinade and stir-fry just until the meat is no longer pink, about 2 minutes. Add 2 Tbsp of the green onions, the ginger, and garlic and stir-fry until fragrant, about 1 minute. Stir in the broth mixture and simmer until the sauce begins to thicken, 2–3 minutes. Add the tofu, reduce the heat to low, and simmer, uncovered, stirring occasionally and gently so the tofu does not fall apart, until most of the sauce is absorbed, about 10 minutes. Serve garnished with the remaining 1 Tbsp green onions.

15

A Chinese wok is best for stir-frying, but a sauté pan or deep frying pan may also be used. Heat the pan before adding the oil, and swirl to coat the sides as well as the bottom. For best results when stir-frying, have ingredients prepped before you begin, and add quick-cooking foods, such as small pieces of meat, fish, or tofu, separately from slower-cooking foods, such as dense vegetables.

STIR-FRIED SHRIMP WITH SUGAR SNAP PEAS & MUSHROOMS

serves 4

2 lb (1 kg) large shrimp, peeled and deveined

1 tsp toasted sesame oil

1 Tbsp tamari or light soy sauce

Salt

2 Tbsp peanut or canola oil

2 cloves garlic, minced

1 Tbsp peeled and grated fresh ginger

½ lb (250 g) mixed fresh mushrooms, such as oyster or cremini

½ lb (250 g) sugar snap peas, halved crosswise

2 green onions, white and tender green parts, cut into 1-inch (2.5-cm) pieces

2 Tbsp rice wine or dry sherry

Fresh cilantro leaves for garnish

Cooked white rice for serving

In a nonreactive bowl, combine the shrimp, sesame oil, tamari, and 1 tsp salt. Toss to coat.

In a wok or large frying pan, heat the peanut oil over medium-high heat. Add the garlic, ginger, and shrimp and stir-fry until the shrimp are evenly pink on both sides, about 1 minute. Using a slotted spoon, transfer the shrimp to a bowl.

Add the mushrooms to the pan and stir-fry over medium-high heat until they soften, about 3 minutes. Add the sugar snap peas and stir-fry until bright green, about 1 minute. Add the green onions and rice wine. Cover and cook until the snap peas are tender-crisp, about 2 minutes. Return the shrimp to the pan and stir-fry just until heated through, about 1 minute. Garnish with cilantro leaves and serve with the rice.

16

In this traditional Italian recipe, the natural sugars of the milk complement the sweetness of the pork, and the liquid cooks down to form a thick sauce that begins to caramelize slightly toward the end of cooking. What results is a tender meat served with a simple, yet very flavorful sauce. Serve over mashed potatoes or an herbed rice pilaf.

ITALIAN BRAISED PORK LOIN

serves 6–8

1 boneless pork loin roast, 2–2½ lb (1–1.25 kg)

Salt and freshly ground pepper

2 Tbsp olive oil

3 slices bacon, about 3 oz (90 g) total, roughly chopped

3–4 cups (24–32 fl oz/750 ml–1 l) milk

2 cloves garlic

Season the pork generously with salt and pepper.

In a large, heavy pot, warm the oil over medium heat. Add the bacon and cook, stirring often, until crisp, 2–3 minutes. Drain on paper towels.

Raise the heat to medium-high. Add the pork to the fat in the pot and cook, turning occasionally, until evenly browned on all sides, about 10 minutes. Transfer the pork to a plate.

Pour off the fat from the pot and return to medium-high heat. Add 3 cups (24 fl oz/ 750 ml) of the milk and stir to scrape up any browned bits on the pan bottom. Bring to a boil.

Add the garlic, reserved bacon, and the pork to the pot. Partially cover and cook over very low heat until the pork is tender and the milk has reduced and thickened, about 2 hours. During the final 30 minutes of cooking, check the milk level and, if necessary, warm some of the remaining milk and add to the pork.

Transfer the pork to a cutting board and cut crosswise into slices about ½ inch (12 mm) thick. Arrange the slices on a platter, top with the sauce, and serve.

21

RED QUINOA WITH ASPARAGUS, PORTOBELLOS & FETA

serves 4

1 cup (5 oz/155 g) red quinoa

2½ cups (20 fl oz/625 ml) chicken or vegetable broth

⅓ cup (1½ oz/45 g) dried currants

¼ cup (2 fl oz/60 ml) olive oil, plus more for drizzling

3 cloves garlic, minced

2 portobello mushrooms, sliced

1 small red onion, halved and sliced

Salt and freshly ground pepper

1 Tbsp balsamic vinegar

1 lb (500 g) asparagus, trimmed and cut into pieces

⅓ cup (½ oz/15 g) chopped fresh flat-leaf parsley

Grated zest of 1 lemon

4 oz (125 g) feta cheese, crumbled

Protein-packed quinoa, tangy feta, hearty portobello mushrooms, and earthy asparagus make this a delicious meatless dinner option. It also works well as a side dish with shredded rotisserie chicken or leftover roasted pork. The dish can be served chilled as part of a spring lunch buffet. Accompany with warm garlic bread and a crisp Sauvignon Blanc.

In a saucepan, bring the quinoa and 2 cups (16 fl oz/250 ml) of the broth to a boil over medium-high heat. Add the currants, reduce the heat to a simmer, cover, and cook until the liquid is absorbed, about 15 minutes. Remove from the heat, but keep covered to stay warm.

In a large frying pan, heat the ¼ cup oil over medium-high heat. Add the garlic, mushrooms, and onion and season with salt and pepper. Sauté until the vegetables soften and begin to brown, 4–6 minutes. Stir in the vinegar and cook until absorbed, about 2 minutes. Add the asparagus and toss to coat with the oil. Add the remaining ½ cup (4 fl oz/125 ml) broth and cook, stirring occasionally, until the asparagus is fork-tender, about 4 minutes. Stir in the quinoa, parsley, lemon zest, and half of the feta. Remove from the heat and season with salt and pepper. Garnish with the remaining feta, drizzle with olive oil, and serve.

22

ITALIAN CHICKEN STEW

serves 6

Large pinch of saffron threads

⅓ cup (3 fl oz/80 ml) plus 3 Tbsp white wine

1 whole chicken, about 3½ lb (1.75 kg), cut into 10 pieces (2 thighs, 2 drumsticks, 2 wings, 4 breast portions)

¾ cup (4 oz/125 g) flour

Salt and freshly ground pepper

2 Tbsp olive oil

1 yellow onion, finely chopped

1 rib celery, finely chopped

10 cloves garlic, smashed

⅓ cup (3 fl oz/80 ml) chicken broth

1 can (28 oz/875 g) diced tomatoes, drained

3 bay leaves

1½ tsp red or white wine vinegar

2 tsp chopped fresh flat-leaf parsley

This chicken stew is elevated by the earthy flavors of saffron and garlic, and brightened with tomatoes and vinegar. If you like, throw in a few quartered red potatoes to simmer with the chicken during the last hour of cooking.

Soak the saffron in the 3 Tbsp white wine for 20 minutes. Pat the chicken pieces dry. In a plastic bag, combine the flour, ¾ tsp salt, and several grinds of pepper. One at a time, add the chicken pieces and toss to coat. Remove from the bag, shaking off any excess flour. In a large frying pan over medium-high heat, warm the oil. When the oil is hot, working in batches, add the chicken and sear, turning, until golden brown, about 8 minutes. Transfer the chicken to a plate.

Pour off most of the fat from the pan and return it to medium heat. Add the onion and celery and sauté until softened and golden, about 5 minutes. Add the garlic and cook for 1 minute. Pour in the remaining ⅓ cup wine and the broth and stir to dislodge any browned bits on the pan bottom. Bring to a rapid simmer and cook to reduce slightly and to concentrate the flavor, 10 minutes. Transfer the contents of the pan to a slow cooker and stir in the tomatoes, the saffron mixture, and the bay leaves. Stack the chicken on top. Cover and cook on the low setting for 5–6 hours. The chicken should be very tender.

Using a slotted spoon, transfer the chicken to a plate. Stir the vinegar into the braising liquid, then skim away the fat from the surface with a large spoon. Serve the stew, garnished with the parsley.

23

BEER-BRAISED PORK ROAST

serves 4–6

1 pork butt roast, about 4 lb (2 kg), trimmed

Salt and freshly ground pepper

2 Tbsp canola oil

2 yellow onions, thinly sliced

1 carrot, chopped

2 cloves garlic, minced

1 Tbsp tomato paste

3 Tbsp all-purpose flour

1 bottle (12 fl oz/375 ml) dark beer or ale

½ cup (4 fl oz/125 ml) apple cider

1 cup (8 fl oz/250 ml) chicken broth

1 Tbsp apple cider vinegar

5–6 sprigs fresh thyme

In this recipe the pleasant flavor of beer permeates the pork during slow cooking. The butt, used here, is the top end of a whole leg of the pig. The shoulder, although a little fattier and with more connective tissue, makes a good alternative for beer-braising. Serve with buttered egg noodles or polenta.

Season the pork generously with salt and pepper. In a large, heavy pot, heat the oil over medium-high heat. Add the pork and cook, turning occasionally, until browned on all sides, about 10 minutes total. Transfer to a plate.

Preheat the oven to 300°F (150°C). Pour off all but 1 Tbsp fat from the pot. Add the onions, carrot, and garlic and sauté over medium-high heat until softened, about 5 minutes. Stir in the tomato paste and cook, stirring frequently, until the mixture starts to become dry, about 2 minutes. Add the flour and cook, stirring constantly, for 2 minutes. Pour in the beer and stir to scrape up any browned bits on the pot bottom. Cook until the liquid starts to thicken, about 10 minutes. Stir in the cider, broth, vinegar, and thyme. Season with salt and pepper and bring to a boil.

Return the pork to the pot, cover, and cook in the oven for about 3 hours. Uncover and continue to cook, basting frequently with the braising liquid, until the pork is tender, about 1 hour longer.

Transfer the pork to a cutting board and cover loosely with foil. Skim the excess fat from the surface of the cooking liquid. Cut the pork across the grain into thin slices. Arrange the slices on a platter, spoon the cooking juices over the top and serve.

24

SUGAR SNAP PEA RISOTTO

serves 4

5 cups (40 fl oz/1.25 l) chicken or vegetable broth

3 Tbsp unsalted butter

1 small yellow onion, finely chopped

Salt

1½ cups (10½ oz/330 g) Arborio or Carnaroli rice

1 tsp finely grated lemon zest

½ cup (4 fl oz/125 ml) dry white wine

10 oz (330 g) sugar snap peas, trimmed and halved crosswise

⅓ cup (1 oz/30 g) grated Parmesan cheese, plus more for garnish

Brisk sunny days welcome the first fresh green peas to market. If you can resist snacking on crisp sugar snaps on their own, try them in this quintessential springtime risotto. The creamy texture of the rice is a welcome foil against the signature bite of the sweet pods.

In a saucepan, bring the broth to a gentle simmer over medium heat. Reduce the heat to low and maintain a simmer.

In a large, heavy saucepan, melt 2 Tbsp of the butter over medium heat. Add the onion and a pinch of salt and sauté until the onion is soft, about 8 minutes. Add the rice and stir until well coated with butter and translucent, about 3 minutes. Add the lemon zest and wine and cook, stirring, until the wine is absorbed. Add the simmering broth to the rice a ladleful at a time, stirring frequently after each addition. Wait until the broth is almost completely absorbed (but the rice is never dry on top) before adding the next ladleful.

After about 15 minutes, add the snap peas and continue to cook, adding ladlefuls of the remaining broth, until the rice is tender to the bite and creamy, about 10 minutes. Turn off the heat, stir in the remaining 1 Tbsp butter and the ⅓ cup Parmesan, and let stand for 2 minutes. Season with salt. Sprinkle with Parmesan and serve.

29

BELGIAN BEEF STEW

serves 6–8

4 Tbsp (2 oz/60 g) unsalted butter

4 slices bacon, about 4 oz (125 g), roughly chopped

4 yellow onions, thinly sliced

2 tsp firmly packed dark brown sugar

2 cloves garlic, minced

3 Tbsp all-purpose flour

Salt and freshly ground pepper

3 lb (1.5 kg) chuck steak or round steak, cut into chunks about 3 inches (7.5 cm) wide

2 Tbsp olive oil

2 cups (16 fl oz/500 ml) dark beer

Carbonnade, the name of this traditional Belgian dish, comes from the Latin root for "carbon." The word reflects that the stew was originally cooked very slowly in a cast-iron pot over the coals in an open hearth. It undoubtedly also refers to the caramelized onions and dark beer that give the finished dish a burnished color and rich, deep flavor. Serve it with boiled or mashed potatoes and ice-cold beer.

In a large, heavy pot, melt 2 Tbsp of the butter over medium-high heat. Add the bacon and cook, turning, until crisp, about 3 minutes. Transfer the bacon to a paper towel to drain.

Add the onions to the pot, sprinkle in the sugar, and sauté until the onions turn a deep caramel brown, about 35 minutes. Stir in the garlic. Transfer the onion mixture to a plate.

On another plate, stir together the flour, 1 tsp salt, and 1 tsp pepper. Turn the steak pieces in the seasoned flour, shaking off any excess.

Melt the remaining 2 Tbsp butter with the olive oil in the pot over medium heat. Working in batches, sear the steak, turning occasionally, until browned on all sides, about 10 minutes. Transfer to a plate. Pour in the beer and stir to scrape up any browned bits on the pot bottom. Bring to a boil.

Return the onion mixture and the steak to the pot. Cover and cook over low heat until the meat is very tender, about 2 hours. Divide the stew among shallow bowls and serve.

30

SMOKED SALMON FRITTATA WITH GOAT CHEESE & CHIVES

serves 8–10

½ lb (250 g) hot-smoked salmon

10 eggs

¼ cup (2 fl oz/60 ml) milk

Salt and freshly ground pepper

4 oz (125 g) fresh goat cheese, crumbled

1 bunch chives, chopped

1 Tbsp olive oil

Fold your favorite seasonal ingredients into fluffy eggs for a meal in a skillet. Delicate smoked fish, tangy goat cheese, and fresh, oniony chives evoke spring. Serve with a big bowl of baby greens and a crisp white wine.

Preheat the oven to 350°F (180°C). Skin the salmon and break the flesh into bite-sized pieces. In a large bowl, whisk together the eggs, milk, ¼ tsp salt, and ¼ tsp pepper. Gently stir in the salmon, cheese, and chives.

Heat the oil in a 12-inch (30-cm) ovenproof frying pan over medium-high heat. Pour the egg mixture into the pan and reduce the heat to medium. Cook for 1 minute, then transfer to the oven and bake until the frittata is set in the center and slightly puffed up, 25–30 minutes. Let cool in the pan for 5 minutes before serving.

31

WILD RICE & MUSHROOM PILAF

serves 6

1 Tbsp unsalted butter

1 small leek or 4 ramps, white part only, chopped

1 lb (500 g) mixed fresh mushrooms, sliced

1 cup (6 oz/185 g) wild rice, rinsed and drained

¼ cup (⅓ oz/10 g) finely chopped fresh flat-leaf parsley

Salt and freshly ground pepper

Seek out ramps at the farmers' market. A type of wild onion harvested in early spring, they have a distinctive onion-garlic flavor, and are an interesting substitute for leeks. With its nutty grains and tender mushrooms, this pilaf would also be excellent alongside broiled salmon.

In a saucepan, melt the butter over medium heat. Add the leek and mushrooms and sauté until the leek is translucent and the mushrooms begin to brown, about 8 minutes.

Add the wild rice and parsley, season with salt and pepper, and add water to cover by 1 inch (2.5 cm). Bring to a boil, reduce the heat to low, cover, and cook until tender, about 45 minutes. Drain off any excess water. The cooking time will vary with different batches of rice. The rice is ready when the grains puff up, and the inner, lighter part is visible. Transfer to a dish and serve.

The abundance of tantalizing produce adds vigor to one-pot favorites. Tender baby artichokes, peas, fingerling potatoes, or sautéed leeks are perfect for tucking into fluffy frittatas or simmering in ragouts; sugar snap peas, lemon zest, and mint enliven stir-fries and braises; and risottos are a natural canvas for sweet peas and asparagus spears. From bourbon-glazed ham and mustard-crusted salmon to lamb chops braised with Moroccan spices, springtime calls for food that's fresh, flavorful, and easy.

april

1

MUSTARD-CRUSTED SALMON WITH RED POTATOES

serves 4

1 lb (500 g) red-skinned potatoes, quartered

2 Tbsp olive oil

Salt and freshly ground pepper

¼ cup (2 oz/60 g) Dijon mustard

2 Tbsp dry mustard

4 salmon fillets, about 6 oz (185 g) each, skin removed

4 Tbsp (1 oz/15 g) panko or fresh bread crumbs

¼ cup (½ oz/15 g) chopped fresh flat-leaf parsley

Spicy mustard rubbed onto fish imparts a quick infusion of flavor. The whole meal goes into the oven at the same time, as waxy new potatoes roast alongside the salmon. Add a salad of peppery arugula or fresh petite peas, and whisk a dollop of mustard into the vinaigrette to bring it all together.

Preheat the oven to 375°F (190°C). In a large roasting pan, toss the potatoes with the olive oil and season with salt and pepper. Spread the potatoes evenly in the pan. Roast until the potatoes are golden, about 10 minutes.

Meanwhile, in a small bowl, stir together the Dijon and dry mustards. Coat one side of the salmon fillets with the mustard mixture, then sprinkle evenly with the panko, gently pressing to adhere.

Arrange the fillets in the pan, breaded side up, next to the potatoes. Bake until the fillets are barely opaque, the topping is golden brown, and the potatoes are tender, 15–18 minutes. Arrange the salmon fillets alongside the potatoes on a platter or individual plates, sprinkle with the parsley, and serve.

2

ARTICHOKE & LEEK FRITTATA

serves 4

Juice of 1 lemon

8 baby artichokes, about 1 lb (450 g) total

Salt and freshly ground pepper

2 Tbsp unsalted butter

2 or 3 leeks, white and pale green parts, halved lengthwise and thinly sliced

6 eggs

¼ cup (1 oz/30 g) grated Parmesan cheese

2 Tbsp minced fresh flat-leaf parsley

Nutty artichokes and oniony leeks join forces in this springtime frittata, which is just as good at room temperature as it is straight from the oven. Leftover frittata, sliced and layered in a baguette with a little mayonnaise, makes a wonderful sandwich the next day.

Fill a bowl with water and stir in the lemon juice. Snap the outer leaves off each artichoke until you reach the tender, pale green inner leaves. Cut about ½ inch (4 cm) from the top of the leaves and trim away the stem. Add the trimmed artichokes to the lemon water.

Bring a pot of salted water to a boil. Drain the artichokes, add to the boiling water, and cook until tender, 5–7 minutes. Drain and transfer to a bowl of ice water. Drain again. Cut the artichokes in half lengthwise, then cut lengthwise into slices ¼ inch (6 mm) thick.

In a 10-inch (25-cm) ovenproof frying pan, melt the butter over medium-low heat. Add the leeks and cook, stirring occasionally, until soft, 10–12 minutes. Stir in the artichokes, season with salt and pepper, and cook for about 2 minutes.

In a bowl, whisk together the eggs, cheese, and parsley just until blended. Add the egg mixture to the pan and stir to distribute the vegetables evenly. Reduce the heat to low and cook until the eggs are almost completely set but still a little moist in the center, 15–20 minutes.

Preheat the broiler and position a rack about 8 inches (20 cm) from the heat source. Broil the frittata until the top is lightly colored and the center is firm to the touch. Cut into wedges and serve.

3

Mint leaves add a fresh, bracing quality to an easy chicken stir-fry of pure, simple flavors. Sugar snap peas provide their natural sweetness and irresistible crunch, while fragrant lemon zest and juice add a welcome brightness.

STIR-FRIED CHICKEN WITH SUGAR SNAP PEAS & LEMON

serves 4–6

2 skinless, boneless chicken breast halves, about 6 oz (185 g) each

Salt and freshly ground pepper

1 lemon

1 cup (8 fl oz/250 ml) chicken broth

2 Tbsp Asian fish sauce

1 tsp sugar

1 tsp cornstarch

4 Tbsp (2 fl oz/60 ml) peanut or grapeseed oil

2 green onions, white and tender green parts chopped, green tops thinly sliced

½-inch (12-mm) piece peeled fresh ginger, grated

2 cloves garlic, minced

½ lb (250 g) sugar snap peas, trimmed

3 Tbsp coarsely chopped fresh mint

Cut the chicken across the grain on a slight diagonal into slices about ½ inch (12 mm) thick. Season with 1 tsp salt and ¼ tsp pepper.

Grate the zest from the lemon, and then squeeze 2 Tbsp juice. In a small nonreactive bowl, stir together the broth, fish sauce, sugar, and lemon zest and juice. In another small bowl, mix the cornstarch with 1 Tbsp cold water.

In a wok or very large frying pan, heat 2 Tbsp of the oil over medium-high heat until hot. Add the chicken and stir-fry until opaque throughout, about 3 minutes. Transfer to a plate. Return the pan to medium-high heat, add the remaining 2 Tbsp oil, and heat until very hot but not smoking. Add the chopped green onions, ginger, and garlic and stir-fry until fragrant, about 15 seconds. Add the sugar snap peas and ¼ cup (2 oz/60 ml) water, cover, and cook, stirring occasionally, until the peas turn bright green, about 1 minute.

Return the chicken to the pan and add the sliced green onions and the mint. Stir the broth mixture, add to the pan, and bring to a boil, stirring constantly. Stir the cornstarch mixture, stir into the pan, and cook until the sauce is slightly thickened, about 15 seconds. Adjust the seasoning and serve.

4

Succulent, fork-shredded pork is baked into a richly spiced casserole with a thick and creamy polenta crust—perfect for a Sunday meal with the family. If you like, increase the amount of pork you are braising and save the leftovers to tuck into tortillas with cheese and salsa.

MEXICAN PORK & POLENTA PIE

serves 6

2½ lb (1.25 kg) boneless pork shoulder, cut into 1-inch (2.5-cm) chunks

Salt

2 Tbsp olive oil

4 cloves garlic, minced

3 Tbsp chili powder

4½ cups (36 fl oz/1.1 l) chicken broth

1 can (14½ oz/455 g) crushed tomatoes

1 tsp crumbled dried oregano

1 cup (7 oz/220 g) quick-cooking polenta

Generously season the pork with salt. Add the oil to a large ovenproof frying pan and warm over high heat. Add the pork and cook, stirring frequently, until browned, about 5 minutes. Add the garlic and 6 cups (48 fl oz/1.5 l) water. Bring to a boil, reduce the heat to low, and simmer, uncovered, until most of the water has evaporated, 1½–2 hours.

Preheat the oven to 350°F (180°C). Raise the heat to medium-high, sprinkle the pork with the chili powder, and cook, stirring, for about 1 minute. Add 2 cups (16 fl oz/500 ml) of the broth, the tomatoes, and the oregano and simmer until the flavors are blended, 2–3 minutes.

In a saucepan over high heat, bring the remaining 2½ cups (20 fl oz/625 ml) broth to a boil. Whisk in the polenta and 1 tsp salt. Reduce the heat to low and cook, stirring frequently, until the polenta is thick and creamy, about 5 minutes. Spoon over the top of the pork.

Bake in the oven until the polenta is browned, about 15 minutes. Serve.

9

PARMESAN-CRUSTED MEAT LOAF

serves 6–8

Meat loaf is one of those dishes that tastes far better than it sounds, especially with the addition of herbs, a bright citrus accent, and elegant, flavorful ingredients like pancetta and Parmesan cheese. The panko topping provides a pleasingly crunchy texture.

Olive oil for greasing

4 slices country-style bread, each about ⅓ inch (9 mm) thick, crusts removed and torn into small pieces

1 cup (8 fl oz/250 ml) milk

1 lb (500 g) ground beef chuck (20 percent fat)

1 lb (500 g) ground veal

2 eggs, lightly beaten

4 oz (125 g) pancetta, finely chopped

¾ cup (3 oz/90 g) plus 2 Tbsp grated Parmesan cheese

⅓ cup (½ oz/15 g) minced fresh flat-leaf parsley

⅓ cup (½ oz/15 g) minced fresh dill

Grated zest of 1 lemon

Salt and freshly ground pepper

3 Tbsp panko or plain dried bread crumbs

Oil a rimmed baking sheet. In a bowl, soak the bread in the milk for 10 minutes. In a large bowl, combine the ground beef and veal, eggs, pancetta, the ¾ cup Parmesan, parsley, dill, and lemon zest. Season with ¾ tsp salt and plenty of pepper. Squeeze the bread to remove the excess milk, then coarsely chop. Add to the meat. Using a fork, mix gently until the ingredients are evenly distributed; do not overmix. Transfer to the prepared baking sheet and shape into a cylindrical loaf just under 12 inches (30 cm) long and 4 inches (10 cm) wide. Refrigerate for 15 minutes.

Preheat the oven to 500°F (260°C).

Place the baking sheet in the oven and cook the meat loaf for 15 minutes. Remove from the oven and scatter the panko and remaining 2 Tbsp Parmesan in a line down the center of the loaf. Reduce the oven temperature to 325°F (165°C). Continue to cook until the crust is golden brown and an instant-read thermometer inserted in the center of the loaf registers 150°F (65°C), 15–20 minutes. Transfer the loaf to a platter, tent loosely with foil, and let stand for about 10 minutes. Cut into thick slices and serve.

10

ARROZ CON POLLO

serves 6

This classic Latin dish, which means "rice with chicken" is like a simplified version of paella. Saffron-infused rice is simmered with onion, peppers, and tomatoes and topped with pan-seared chicken for a simple and comforting one-pan meal.

4 large cloves garlic, minced

2 tsp red pepper flakes

1 Tbsp white vinegar

Salt and freshly ground pepper

3 lb (1.5 kg) chicken pieces, skin on and bone in

3 Tbsp olive oil

4 cups (32 fl oz/1 l) chicken broth

½ tsp saffron threads

1 red onion, chopped

2 bell peppers, seeded and chopped

1 large jalapeño chile, seeded and minced

4 plum tomatoes, chopped

1 tsp ground cumin

2 bay leaves

2 cups (14 oz/440 g) long-grain white rice

In a large bowl, stir together the garlic, red pepper flakes, vinegar, 1 tsp salt, and ½ tsp pepper. Add the chicken pieces, toss to coat, and refrigerate for at least 1 hour or up to overnight.

In a large frying pan with a lid, heat the oil over medium heat. Remove the chicken and brush off the marinade, reserving it in the bowl. Arrange the chicken in the pan, skin side down, and cook without turning, until golden brown, 10–15 minutes. Turn the chicken, cover the pan, and cook until golden on the second side, about 10 minutes. Meanwhile, in a saucepan, warm the broth over medium-high heat. Remove from the heat, crumble in the saffron, and let steep.

Transfer the chicken to a plate and pour off all but 2 Tbsp fat from the pan. Add the onion, bell peppers, and jalapeño and sauté until softened, about 3 minutes. Add the tomatoes and cook, stirring, for 1 minute. Add the cumin, bay leaves, and rice and cook, stirring constantly, until the rice has absorbed the pan juices, 3–5 minutes. Pour the reserved marinade and saffron broth into the pan and stir briefly. Place the chicken on top. Raise the heat to medium-high and bring to a boil. Reduce the heat to low, cover, and simmer until the chicken is opaque throughout, the rice is tender, and the liquid has been absorbed, about 25 minutes. Let stand for 5–10 minutes before serving.

15

BRAISED MOROCCAN LAMB CHOPS

serves 6–8

¼ cup (1½ oz/45 g) all-purpose flour

Salt and freshly ground pepper

4 lb (2 kg) lamb shoulder chops, each about 1 inch (2.5 cm) thick

3 Tbsp olive oil

1 yellow onion, finely chopped

1 tsp ground cumin

1 tsp paprika

2 cups (16 fl oz/500 ml) beef broth

Juice of 1 lemon

1½ cups (7½ oz/235 g) green olives, pitted if desired

½ cup (¾ oz/20 g) minced fresh mint

Tender lamb chops are a springtime treat and pair naturally with the spices common to Moroccan cuisine. Simmer them just until tender in this fragrant braise, then serve them over a bed of fluffy couscous, to soak up all the juices.

On a large plate, stir together the flour and 1 tsp salt. Coat the lamb chops evenly with the flour mixture, shaking off the excess; reserve the remaining flour mixture. In a large frying pan, heat the oil over medium-high heat. Working in batches, sear the lamb chops, turning once, until browned, about 3 minutes. Transfer to a slow cooker.

Pour off all but about 1 Tbsp fat from the frying pan and return the pan to medium-high heat. Add the onion and sauté until translucent, 2–3 minutes. Sprinkle with the cumin, paprika, and reserved flour mixture and sauté briefly, just until fragrant. Pour in the broth and lemon juice. Raise the heat to high, bring to a boil, and stir to scrape up any browned bits on the pan bottom. Pour the contents of the pan over the lamb.

Cover and cook on the high setting for 3–4 hours or the low setting for 6–8 hours. The lamb should be very tender. About 1 hour before the lamb is done, add the olives. When the lamb is ready, transfer it to a platter and cover with foil to keep warm. Skim any fat from the surface of the braising liquid. Season with salt and pepper and stir in the mint. Spoon the sauce over the lamb and serve.

16

SPRING VEGETABLE RAGOUT

serves 4–6

6 oz (185 g) new potatoes or small red potatoes, cut into 1-inch (2.5-cm) pieces

3 leeks, white and pale green parts, cut into slices about ¼ inch (6 mm) thick

1 lb (500 g) baby artichokes, trimmed and halved lengthwise, or 1 package (14 oz/440 g) frozen artichoke hearts, thawed and halved lengthwise

1 cup (6 oz/185 g) cherry or grape tomatoes, halved

10 cloves garlic, smashed

½ yellow onion, finely chopped

¼ cup (2 fl oz/60 ml) dry white wine

¼ cup (2 fl oz/60 ml) vegetable or chicken broth

2 Tbsp olive oil

4 tsp white wine vinegar

2 sprigs fresh thyme

Salt and freshly ground pepper

4 thin slices pancetta (optional)

1½ cups (7½ oz/235 g) fresh or thawed frozen peas

1 Tbsp chopped fresh mint

1 Tbsp chopped fresh basil

This bright green, seasonal vegetarian dish is the perfect way to use spring's bounty of vegetables. Instead of the oven-baked pancetta, you can use crisp crumbled bacon. If you have very tiny potatoes or tomatoes, you can leave them whole. You can also serve this as a side dish alongside roast chicken or baked ham.

In a slow cooker, combine the potatoes, leeks, fresh artichoke hearts (if using), tomatoes, garlic, onion, wine, broth, oil, vinegar, and thyme sprigs. Season with ½ tsp salt, and several grindings of pepper and stir to mix well. Cover and cook on the low setting for 3 hours. If using frozen artichoke hearts, add them to the slow cooker after 2 hours of cooking, and stir well.

Meanwhile, if using the pancetta, preheat the oven to 300°F (150°C). Line a rimmed baking sheet with parchment paper. Place the pancetta slices in a single layer on the prepared pan and cover with a second sheet of parchment. Top with a second baking sheet of the same size. Bake until the pancetta is golden and crisp, 45–50 minutes. Drain on paper towels.

About 5 minutes before the ragout is ready, add the peas to the slow cooker, re-cover, and cook until heated through. When the ragout is ready, remove and discard the thyme sprigs. Stir in the mint and basil. Crumble the pancetta into large pieces, scatter over the top, and serve.

17

INDIAN FISH CURRY

serves 6–8

⅓ cup (3 fl oz/80 ml) canola oil

1 yellow onion, finely chopped

2 cloves garlic, minced

2 small hot green chiles,
seeded and minced

1-inch (2.5-cm) piece peeled fresh
ginger, grated

1 Tbsp ground cumin

2 tsp ground coriander

2 tsp brown mustard seeds

2 tsp ground turmeric

2 tomatoes, chopped

1 Tbsp sugar

Salt

2 lb (1 kg) tilapia, cod, halibut, or other firm,
white fish fillets cut into 1-inch (2.5-cm)
chunks

3 Tbsp chopped fresh cilantro

Vivid yellow from turmeric and brightly seasoned from a medley of spices, this fish curry is typical of those found in the eastern Indian province of Bengal. The fish itself needs very little time to cook, but slow simmering of the sauce in advance helps develop the complex bouquet that flavors the mild seafood.

In a large, heavy pot, heat the oil over medium-high heat. Add the onion and sauté until it starts to turn golden, 5–7 minutes. Stir in the garlic, chiles, ginger, cumin, coriander, mustard seeds, and turmeric, and sauté until the spices are fragrant and evenly coat the onion, about 1 minute. Add the tomatoes, sugar, and 1 tsp salt and sauté until the tomatoes begin to release their juices. Pour in 1½ cups (12 fl oz/375 ml) water and stir to scrape up any browned bits on the pot bottom.

Partially cover and cook over low heat for about 15 minutes. Uncover and add the fish, stirring gently to coat with the sauce. Partially cover and cook until the fish is opaque throughout and the sauce is thick, about 30 minutes. Check the sauce halfway through the cooking time; if it seems to be getting too thick, stir in more water, about ½ cup (4 fl oz/125 ml) at a time. Season with salt. Serve the curry, garnished with the cilantro.

18

BAKED RIGATONI WITH FENNEL, SAUSAGE & PEPERONATA

serves 6

2 Tbsp extra virgin olive oil, plus more
for greasing

1 lb (500 g) rigatoni

1 fennel bulb

¾ lb (350 g) sweet Italian sausage, casings
removed, crumbled

1 *each* red, yellow, and orange bell pepper,
seeded and cut into matchsticks

Salt and freshly ground black pepper

1 tsp sugar

1 Tbsp red wine vinegar

1 cup (8 fl oz/250 ml) prepared tomato sauce

1½ cups (12 fl oz/375 ml) heavy cream

2 cups (8 oz/250 g) shredded fontina cheese

¼ cup (1 oz/30 g) grated Parmesan

Golden brown and bubbling, this perennial dish is welcome at the table any time of year. Sweet Italian sausage, colorful peppers, and fragrant fennel add heft to this one-pan baked pasta. A touch of cream finishes the dish and rounds out the tangy tomato sauce.

Preheat the oven to 425°F (220°C). Lightly oil a 9-by-13-inch (24-by-33-cm) baking dish.

Bring a pot of salted water to a boil. Add the pasta and cook until al dente, 7–8 minutes, or according to the package directions. Drain and place in a large bowl.

Remove and discard the stalks and core from the fennel bulb and dice the bulb. In a frying pan, heat 1 Tbsp of the oil over medium heat. Add the crumbled sausage and cook, stirring occasionally, until lightly browned, 3–4 minutes. Add the fennel and cook, stirring, until tender, 4–5 minutes. Add to the bowl with the pasta.

Add the remaining 1 Tbsp oil to the pan, along with the bell peppers and a pinch each of salt and black pepper. Cook, stirring occasionally, until the bell peppers are tender with a bit of a bite, 3–4 minutes. Add the sugar and vinegar and continue cooking until the vinegar has reduced to a syrup, 1–2 minutes. Add the tomato sauce and cream and cook, stirring, until lightly thickened, 4–5 minutes. Transfer to the bowl with the pasta, add the fontina, and stir well.

Pour the pasta mixture into the prepared dish and top with the Parmesan. Bake until the top is golden brown and the sauce is bubbling around the sides, 10–15 minutes. Serve directly from the dish.

23

BOURBON-GLAZED HAM

serves 12–14, with leftovers

20 lb (10 kg) fully cooked, bone-in ham

2½ cups (17½ oz/545 g) firmly packed dark brown sugar

⅓ cup (3 fl oz/80 ml) bourbon

15–20 whole cloves

A glistening whole ham forms a striking centerpiece for an Easter dinner or brunch. Take inspiration from the American South, and slip some bourbon into the glaze, for a hint of sweet and spice. This would be delicious served with a basket of fluffy biscuits and a green salad.

Preheat the oven to 325°F (165°C). Line a roasting pan with foil and set a roasting rack in the pan. Cut away and discard any skin from the ham and trim the fat to ½ inch (12 mm) thick. Place the ham, fat side up, on the rack in the pan. Roast until the ham is fully warmed through and an instant-read thermometer inserted into the thickest part of the ham (but not touching the bone) registers 140°F (60°C), 3–3½ hours.

Remove the ham from the oven. Raise the oven temperature to 425°F (220°C). In a bowl, combine the sugar and bourbon and mix to form a paste. Score the fat on the upper half of the ham in a diamond pattern, cutting about ¼ inch (6 mm) deep. Rub the paste over the surface of the fat, then insert the cloves at random intersections of the diamonds. Return the ham to the oven and bake, basting several times with the pan juices, until the surface is shiny and beginning to brown, 15–20 minutes.

Transfer the ham to a cutting board and tent loosely with foil. Let stand for 20–30 minutes. Remove the cloves. Carve half of the ham, arrange on a platter, and serve. Carve the remaining ham as needed.

24

CHICKEN WITH BEANS, BACON & CHEDDAR

serves 4

1 Tbsp olive oil

4 skin-on whole chicken legs

Salt and freshly ground pepper

4 slices thick-cut bacon

1 small yellow onion, chopped

3 cloves garlic, minced

2 cans (15 oz/470 g each) pinto beans, rinsed and drained

2 plum tomatoes, chopped

2 Tbsp chopped fresh flat-leaf parsley

½ cup (2 oz/60 g) grated white Cheddar cheese

Whole, bone-in chicken legs stay tender and juicy during cooking. Fast enough to be a weeknight meal, this warm and hearty dish pleases everyone.

Preheat the oven to 400°F (200°C).

In a large, ovenproof frying pan, heat the oil over medium-high heat. Season the chicken legs with salt and pepper. Add to the pan, skin side down, and cook until browned, about 5 minutes. Turn and cook until almost cooked through, about 5 minutes more. Transfer to a plate.

Return the pan to medium-high heat, arrange the bacon slices in a single layer, and fry until crispy, about 7 minutes, turning once. Drain on paper towels, then break into big pieces.

Add the onion and garlic to the pan and sauté over medium-high heat until soft, 5 minutes. Add the beans and tomatoes and cook until the tomatoes begin to release their juices, about 3 minutes. Stir in the parsley and bacon and season with salt and pepper.

Return the chicken to the pan, nestling the pieces in the bean mixture. Sprinkle with the Cheddar. Cook in the oven until the cheese browns and the chicken is opaque throughout, about 10 minutes. Spoon onto plates or serve directly from the pan.

29

BEEF WITH MUSHROOMS & BARLEY

serves 4–6

1 oz (30 g) dried mushrooms, such as porcini

2 cups (16 fl oz/500 ml) boiling water

2 Tbsp unsalted butter

2 lb (1 kg) beef chuck, cut into 2-inch (5-cm) pieces

2 yellow onions, finely chopped

2 cloves garlic, minced

1 lb (500 g) small cremini or other fresh mushrooms, trimmed

2 cups (16 fl oz/500 ml) beef broth

½ cup (4 oz/125 g) pearl barley

3 carrots, finely chopped

2 parsnips, peeled and finely chopped

Salt and freshly ground pepper

2 Tbsp chopped fresh dill

Tender chunks of stewed beef, meaty mushrooms, and pleasantly chewy grains create a bowl brimming with texture and flavor. Look to any varieties of wild mushrooms that are still in season, before they vanish with the spring showers.

Put the dried mushrooms in a bowl, add the boiling water, and soak for 20 minutes. Line a fine-mesh sieve with a double layer of cheesecloth, place over a bowl, and drain the mushrooms, reserving the soaking liquid. Rinse the mushrooms with cold water and chop finely.

Preheat the oven to 300°F (150°C). In a large, heavy pot, melt the butter over medium-high heat. Working in batches, sear the beef in the butter, turning frequently, until browned on all sides, about 10 minutes. Transfer to a plate.

Add the onions and garlic and sauté until softened, 5–7 minutes. Stir in the rehydrated mushrooms. Add the fresh mushrooms, reduce the heat to medium, and sauté until they start to brown and release their liquid, about 5 minutes. Stir in the mushroom soaking liquid and the broth. Return the beef to the pot and stir to combine. Cover and cook in the oven until the beef is tender, about 2 hours.

Stir in the barley and 1 cup (8 fl oz/250 ml) water and cook, covered, for 1 hour. Stir in the carrots and parsnips and cook, covered, until the barley and vegetables are tender, about 30 minutes. Season with salt and pepper. Garnish with the dill and serve.

30

POTATO & CAULIFLOWER GRATIN

serves 4–6

Butter for greasing

2 cups (16 fl oz/500 ml) heavy cream

3 cloves garlic, crushed

2 sprigs fresh thyme

Salt and freshly ground pepper

1 small head cauliflower, cut into florets

2 lb (1 kg) Yukon gold potatoes, peeled and thinly sliced

2 cups (8 oz/250 g) shredded Gruyère cheese

1 cup (4 oz/125 g) grated Parmesan cheese

¼ cup (½ oz/15 g) fresh bread crumbs

Both potatoes and cauliflower shine in a good cheese sauce. Throw the two together, and it only improves on a good thing. Serve this hearty vegetarian dish with a lightly dressed butter lettuce salad.

Preheat the oven to 400°F (200°C). Butter a 2-qt (2-l) baking dish.

In a saucepan, combine the cream, garlic, and thyme. Season with 1 tsp salt and ¼ tsp pepper. Bring to a boil over high heat, add the cauliflower, reduce the heat to low, and simmer until the cauliflower is just tender and the sauce has thickened, 8–10 minutes. Discard the garlic and thyme.

Layer the potatoes in the prepared dish and sprinkle evenly with ½ cup (2 oz/60 g) each of the Gruyère and Parmesan. Using a slotted spoon, remove the cauliflower from the sauce and arrange in the dish. Top with the remaining cheeses. Pour the sauce evenly over all and sprinkle with the bread crumbs. Bake until the potatoes are just tender and the top is golden brown, about 30 minutes. Let cool for about 5 minutes before serving.

As the weather warms, heartier one-pot meals make way for lighter fare. Pair favorite proteins with the plethora of spring greens—fava beans, asparagus, pea shoots, and spinach—in simple braises, curries and quiches, quick sautés, and fragrant tagines. Try artichokes stuffed with bread crumbs and cheese or tender calamari packed with herbs and tomatoes. Add slow-braised carnitas to tacos and burritos for a real crowd-pleaser.

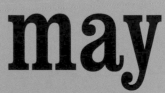

may

1

Colorful zucchini, yellow squash, and cherry tomatoes nestle in this creamy pasta. Lemon zest brightens the dish, and fresh bread crumbs on top add a delightful crunch. Cut all the vegetables to about the same size to ensure that they cook evenly. Substitute other seasonal vegetables to make this recipe year-round.

BAKED PASTA PRIMAVERA

serves 6

2 Tbsp olive oil, plus more for greasing

½ yellow onion, chopped

3 cloves garlic, minced

2 small yellow summer squash, cut into ¾-inch (2-cm) pieces

2 small zucchini, cut into ¾-inch (2-cm) pieces

1 large carrot, cut into ¾-inch (2-cm) matchsticks

Salt and freshly ground pepper

1 cup (6 oz/185 g) small cherry tomatoes

¾ lb (375 g) gemelli pasta, cooked according to the package directions

1 Tbsp unsalted butter

1 tsp grated lemon zest

1 Tbsp all-purpose flour

1 cup (8 fl oz/250 ml) milk

1 cup (4 oz/125 g) grated Parmesan cheese

2 Tbsp cream cheese

1 cup (4 oz/125 g) shredded mozzarella cheese

1 cup (2 oz/60 g) fresh bread crumbs

Preheat the oven to 400°F (200°C). Oil a 9-by-13-inch (23-by-33-cm) baking dish.

In a large frying pan, heat the 2 Tbsp oil over medium-high heat. Add the onion and two-thirds of the garlic and sauté until translucent, about 4 minutes. Add the squash, zucchini, and carrot, and season with salt and pepper. Sauté until the vegetables are very soft and just beginning to brown, about 5 minutes. Add the tomatoes and cook just until they start to soften but still hold their shape, about 3 minutes. Transfer to a bowl and add the cooked pasta.

In a small saucepan, melt the butter over medium heat. Add the remaining garlic and the lemon zest and sauté just until the garlic softens, about 2 minutes, being careful not to burn the garlic. Add the flour and cook, stirring constantly, for 1 minute. Slowly add the milk and bring to a simmer. Reduce the heat to low and cook, stirring frequently, until thickened, 4–5 minutes. Add ¾ cup (3 oz/90 g) of the Parmesan and the cream cheese and whisk until the cheeses melt. Season with salt and pepper. »→

Pour the cream sauce into the bowl with the pasta and the vegetables and toss to combine. Transfer to the prepared dish. Sprinkle with the mozzarella, the remaining Parmesan, and the bread crumbs.

Bake until the pasta is warmed through and the bread crumbs are golden brown, about 15 minutes. Spoon onto plates and serve.

2

This Italian-American classic takes a healthful turn with the addition of leafy green kale and pan-seared— not fried—chicken breasts. But while it cuts out the calories, it doesn't cut out the comforting flavor.

CHICKEN PARMESAN WITH GREENS

serves 4

4 skinless, boneless chicken breast halves, about 1½ lb (750 g) total weight

Salt and freshly ground pepper

2 Tbsp olive oil

1 bunch kale, tough stems removed and leaves torn into large pieces

2 cups (16 fl oz/500 ml) marinara sauce, warmed

8 thick slices fresh mozzarella cheese

½ cup (2 oz/60 g) grated Parmesan cheese

Preheat the oven to 400°F (200°C). Season the chicken generously with salt and pepper. In a large ovenproof frying pan over medium-high heat, warm the oil. Add the chicken and cook, turning once, until golden brown, about 7 minutes total. Transfer to a plate and set aside.

Add the kale to the frying pan and sauté over medium-high heat until wilted, about 1 minute. Add the chicken back to the frying pan with the kale and pour the marinara sauce over the chicken. Place 2 mozzarella slices on each chicken breast. Sprinkle evenly with the Parmesan. Bake until the cheese is golden and the chicken is opaque throughout, about 20 minutes, then serve.

3

PORK SMOTHERED IN LEEKS

serves 4

9 leeks, white parts only,
halved lengthwise

1¾ lb (875 g) boneless pork shoulder,
cut into 1-inch (2.5-cm) chunks

Salt and freshly ground pepper

1 Tbsp olive oil

1 yellow onion, chopped

1 cup (6 oz/185 g) canned diced tomatoes

1 small celery rib, chopped

Leeks are often relegated to the supporting cast, as the starting point for soups and stocks. Here, they star in a simmering sauce for tender pork shoulder and make the dish sing out with fresh spring flavor.

Put the leeks in a deep sauté pan with a lid with 1½ cups (12 fl oz/375 ml) water and bring to a boil over medium-high heat. Reduce the heat to medium-low and simmer for 10 minutes. Drain, then rinse with cold water, and drain again. Set aside.

Sprinkle the pork pieces lightly with salt and pepper. Add the oil to the sauté pan and warm over medium-high heat. Working in batches, sear the meat, turning as needed, until browned on all sides, about 8 minutes. Transfer to a plate.

Pour off all but 1 Tbsp fat from the pan. Add the onion and sauté until lightly browned, about 5 minutes. Return the meat and any juices to the pan. Add the tomatoes, celery, and about 2 cups (16 fl oz/500 ml) water; the meat should be almost covered by liquid. Bring to a simmer and stir to scrape up any browned bits from the pan bottom. Reduce the heat to medium-low, cover, and simmer gently until the meat is almost tender, about 45 minutes.

Spread the leeks over the pork, cover, and simmer until the meat and leeks are very tender and have absorbed most of the liquid, about 30 minutes. Adjust the seasoning and serve.

4

STIR-FRIED CALAMARI & PEA SHOOTS

serves 4

4 Tbsp (2 fl oz/60 ml) peanut or canola oil

2 Tbsp minced garlic

1 Tbsp peeled and grated fresh ginger

1 lb (500 g) green pea shoots,
tough parts removed

½ cup (1½ oz/45 g) chopped green onions

¼ cup (2 fl oz/60 ml) chicken broth

Salt and freshly ground pepper

1 Tbsp soy sauce

1 tsp chile paste

1 tsp sugar

1 tsp toasted sesame oil

¾ lb (375 g) cleaned squid,
cut into bite-size pieces

Cooked rice for serving (optional)

Pea shoots are the delicate leaves and tendrils that grow from the vines of the pea plant. Tender and sweet, they are delicious when eaten raw or sautéed. Look for them at the farmers' market in the spring and early summer. Here they are flash-cooked in a hot pan with tender squid rings and tentacles and lots of lemon.

In a wok or large frying pan, heat 2 Tbsp of the peanut oil over medium-high heat. Add the garlic and ginger and stir-fry until fragrant, about 30 seconds. Add the pea shoots and green onions and stir-fry for 3 minutes. Add the broth, ½ tsp salt, and ⅛ tsp pepper and cook until the shoots are tender-crisp, about 2 minutes. Using a slotted spoon, transfer to a plate. Wipe out the pan.

In a small bowl, mix together the soy sauce, chile paste, sugar, and sesame oil.

Warm the remaining 2 Tbsp peanut oil in the pan over medium-high heat. Add the squid and stir-fry until opaque, about 2 minutes. Return the pea shoots to the pan, add the soy sauce mixture, and stir-fry, tossing to combine and heat through, about 1 minute. Using the slotted spoon, transfer the greens and squid to a platter. Serve over rice, if desired.

9

SAVORY BREAD PUDDING WITH ASPARAGUS & FONTINA

serves 6–8

8–12 thick slices stale bread, halved

2½ cups (20 fl oz/625 ml) milk, plus more if needed

1½ tsp unsalted butter, cut into small pieces, plus more for greasing

5 eggs

Salt and freshly ground pepper

1 lb (500 g) asparagus, trimmed and cut into 2-inch (5-cm) pieces

½ cup (¾ oz/20 g) mixed chopped fresh herbs, such as chives, flat-leaf parsley, tarragon, thyme, and marjoram

¼ cup (1 oz/30 g) grated *pecorino romano* cheese

½ lb (250 g) shredded fontina cheese

Slivers of fontina cheese are dotted throughout this savory pudding and offer bursts of nutty flavor; the pecorino brings a hint of saltiness. Heavy breads make a dense pudding, lighter ones yield a softer texture. Save up your leftover bread for a week, including baguette heels.

Place the bread in a shallow baking dish and pour the 2½ cups milk over the slices. Let soak until the bread has absorbed the milk and softened. Depending on the hardness of the bread, this will take 5–30 minutes. Squeeze the bread to extract the milk. Measure the extracted milk; you should have ½ cup (4 fl oz/125 ml). Add more milk if necessary. Set the bread and milk aside.

Preheat the oven to 350°F (180°C). Butter a large 12-inch (30-cm) shallow baking dish or two 8-inch (20-cm) baking dishes or ramekins.

In a bowl, beat together the eggs, 1 tsp salt, 1 tsp pepper, and the reserved milk. Arrange the bread in the prepared baking dish. Set 6–8 asparagus tips aside and top the bread with the remaining asparagus pieces and the herbs. Sprinkle the cheeses over the asparagus. Pour the egg mixture over the top, and dot with the 1½ tsp butter.

Bake until the top is crusty brown and a knife inserted into the middle of the pudding comes out clean, about 45 minutes. During the last 5 minutes of cooking, top with the reserved asparagus tips. Let the pudding stand for 15 minutes before serving.

10

BRAISED CHICKEN & ARTICHOKES

serves 4–6

1 lemon, halved

1 lb (500 g) baby artichokes

3 Tbsp all-purpose flour

Salt and freshly ground pepper

2 *each* skinless, bone-in chicken breast halves, thighs, and drumsticks

2 Tbsp olive oil

4 cloves garlic, slivered

1 shallot, slivered

1 Tbsp *each* minced fresh basil, tarragon, and flat-leaf parsley

1 Tbsp Dijon mustard

1 cup (8 fl oz/250 ml) dry white wine

½ cup (4 fl oz/125 ml) chicken broth

3 plum tomatoes, seeded and chopped

Baby artichokes require some trimming, but you won't need to wrestle with removing the choke, which is negligible in the small vegetables. The rewards will be well worth your efforts. Out of season, you can use 1½ cups (12 oz/ 375 g) thawed, frozen hearts or drained marinated hearts, and add them with the tomatoes.

Fill a large bowl with water and add the juice of ½ lemon. Trim the stem of each artichoke. Snap off the outer leaves until you reach the tender inner leaves. Cut off the top one-third of the artichoke. Halve each artichoke lengthwise, and if they seem large, cut each half in half. Add the artichokes to the lemon water.

Spread the flour on a plate, season well with salt and pepper, then lightly toss the chicken in the seasoned flour, shaking off the excess. In a large frying pan, heat the oil over medium-high heat. Add the chicken and cook, turning once, until lightly browned, 4–6 minutes. Transfer to a platter, and season with salt and pepper.

Pour off all but 2 Tbsp fat from the pan. Add the garlic and shallot and sauté until softened, 1–2 minutes. Stir in the herbs and mustard. Add the wine and broth, bring to a boil, and stir to scrape up any browned bits on the pan bottom. Add the tomatoes.

Return the thighs and drumsticks to the pan, reduce the heat to medium, and simmer for 10 minutes. Add the breasts and cook for another 10 minutes. Drain the artichokes, add to the pan, and cook until the chicken is opaque throughout and the artichokes are tender, about 10 minutes. Transfer to a deep platter and serve.

15

American cooks use the term scampi to describe sautéed jumbo shrimp in a buttery, white wine sauce. Scallops are good with this sauce, too. Small bay scallops will cook in about the same amount of time as the shrimp. If you like, serve the saucy scampi over fresh pasta.

GARLICKY SHRIMP SCAMPI

serves 4

½ cup (2½ oz/75 g) all-purpose flour

Salt and freshly ground pepper

2 Tbsp olive oil, plus more as needed

1½ lb (750 g) jumbo or extra-large shrimp, peeled and deveined, tails intact

12 Tbsp (6 oz/185 g) unsalted butter

3 cloves garlic, minced

¼ cup (2 fl oz/60 ml) dry white wine

Grated zest of 1 lemon

2 Tbsp fresh lemon juice

2 Tbsp finely chopped fresh flat-leaf parsley

Lemon wedges

In a shallow bowl, stir together the flour, ½ tsp salt, and ¼ tsp pepper. In a large frying pan, heat the 2 Tbsp oil over medium-high heat. Toss half of the shrimp in the flour mixture to coat evenly, shaking off the excess. Add to the pan and cook, turning occasionally, until opaque throughout, about 3 minutes. Transfer to a plate and tent with foil. Repeat with the remaining shrimp, adding more oil as needed.

Reduce the heat to medium-low, add 2 Tbsp of the butter and the garlic, and cook, stirring frequently, until the garlic softens and is fragrant but not browned, about 2 minutes. Add the wine and the lemon zest and juice and bring to a boil over high heat. Cook until reduced by half, about 1 minute. Reduce the heat to very low. Whisk in the remaining 10 Tbsp butter, 1 Tbsp at a time, letting each addition soften into a creamy emulsion before adding more.

Return the shrimp to the sauce and mix gently to coat well. Remove from the heat and season with salt and pepper. Transfer to a serving dish and sprinkle with the parsley. Serve, passing the lemon wedges at the table.

16

This dish is a brilliant use for leftovers. Stale chips, leftover rotisserie chicken, and any melting cheese can all be put to good use. If you like your Mexican food spicy, add a punch by using serrano peppers instead of jalapeños. Keep in mind that the tortilla chips add some salt to begin with, so taste as you go and take care not to overseason.

MEXICAN NACHO CASSEROLE

serves 4–6

2 lb (1 kg) plum tomatoes, halved lengthwise

2 jalapeño chiles

6 cloves garlic, unpeeled

1 Tbsp plus 2 tsp olive oil, plus more for greasing

Salt and freshly ground pepper

¼ cup (½ oz/15 g) fresh cilantro leaves

1 white onion, ½ chopped and ½ thinly sliced

6 oz (185 g) corn tortilla chips

1½ cups (9 oz/280 g) shredded cooked chicken

1 can (15 oz/470 g) pinto beans, rinsed and drained

¾ cup (3 oz/90 g) shredded Cheddar cheese

¾ cup (3 oz/90 g) shredded Monterey jack cheese

Sour cream, prepared fresh salsa, and avocado slices

Preheat the broiler.

Combine the tomatoes, chiles, and garlic on a rimmed baking sheet. Drizzle with 2 tsp oil, season with salt and pepper, and toss to coat. Arrange in a single layer, placing the tomatoes cut side down. Broil until the vegetables are lightly charred, about 12 minutes. Let cool, then pull the stems from the chiles and peel the garlic. Put the vegetables and cilantro in a blender and purée.

Preheat the oven to 350°F (180°C). Oil an 8-by-10-inch (20-by-25-cm) baking dish.

In a large frying pan, heat the remaining 1 Tbsp oil over medium-high heat. Add the chopped onion and sauté until translucent, about 5 minutes. Add the puréed vegetables and cook, stirring, for 5 minutes. Season with salt and pepper. Pour half of the purée into the prepared dish. Top with the tortilla chips, laying them flat on each other, breaking them if necessary.

Top the chips evenly with the chicken, then with the beans, the remaining purée, the cheeses, and finally with the sliced onion. Bake until warmed all the way through and the cheese is melted and slightly browned, about 25 minutes. Serve with sour cream, salsa, and avocado.

21

Tender chicken, verdant English peas, and gooey cheese define this sweet and simple risotto. It's charming enough for adult dinner guests, but won't fail to satisfy younger appetites. If you have them on hand, sprinkle a few pea shoots on top for a pretty garnish.

RISOTTO WITH CHICKEN, PEAS & PARMESAN

serves 4

5 cups (40 fl oz/1.25 l) chicken broth

2 Tbsp unsalted butter

1 small yellow onion, finely chopped

1½ cups (10½ oz/330 g) Arborio or Carnaroli rice

¾ cup (6 fl oz/180 ml) dry white wine

2 cups (about 10½ oz/330 g) bite-sized pieces roasted chicken

1 cup (5 oz/155 g) fresh or thawed frozen peas

⅔ cup (2½ oz/75 g) grated Parmesan cheese, plus more for sprinkling

Salt and freshly ground pepper

Chopped fresh flat-leaf parsley for garnish

In a saucepan, bring the broth to a gentle simmer over medium heat. Reduce the heat to low and maintain a simmer.

In a large, heavy saucepan, melt the butter over medium heat. Add the onion and sauté until softened, about 3 minutes. Add the rice and cook, stirring often, until opaque, about 3 minutes. Add the wine and cook, stirring constantly, until almost completely absorbed.

Stir in a ladleful of the simmering broth and cook, stirring frequently, until nearly all the liquid is absorbed. Continue adding the broth, a ladleful at a time, and stirring until almost absorbed (but the rice is never dry on top) until the rice is tender but still slightly firm at the center, 20–25 minutes. (If all of the broth is used before the rice is tender, add hot water.) During the last 3 minutes, stir in the chicken and peas. When the rice is just cooked, add about ⅔ cup (5 fl oz/160 ml) broth or hot water to give the risotto a creamy consistency.

Remove from the heat and stir in the ⅔ cup cheese. Season with salt and pepper. Spoon into shallow bowls, sprinkle with cheese and parsley, and serve.

22

Although tri-tip is often grilled, its leanness makes it a better candidate for stir-frying. When stir-fried, the meat can absorb the flavors of the other ingredients, rather than drying out from the heat of the grill. Pleasantly bitter radicchio crisps in the same pan, and peppery watercress provides a refreshing accent.

STIR-FRIED TRI-TIP WITH RADICCHIO

serves 4

1 tri-tip roast or top sirloin steak, about 1 lb (500 g)

1 large head radicchio, 8–9 oz (250–280 g)

Salt and freshly ground pepper

2 Tbsp olive oil

2 Tbsp unsalted butter

1 large shallot, minced

1 small bunch watercress, tough stems removed

1 tsp white or red wine vinegar

Put the beef in the freezer for 20 minutes to firm it up for slicing thin. Meanwhile, core the radicchio and cut lengthwise into quarters. Cut each quarter crosswise into thin slivers.

Cut the partially frozen beef in half lengthwise, then cut each half across the grain into slices about ¼ inch (6 mm) thick. Season the slices generously with salt and pepper.

In a large wok or frying pan, heat 1 Tbsp of the oil over medium-high heat. Add half of the beef, distributing it evenly, and cook without moving it for about 20 seconds. Continue to cook the beef, tossing and stirring it every 15–20 seconds, until browned but still slightly pink inside, 2–3 minutes. Transfer to a platter. Repeat to cook the remaining beef in the remaining 1 Tbsp oil, and transfer to the platter with the first batch.

Pour off most of the oil from the pan. Reduce the heat to medium and add the butter. Add the radicchio and shallot, and stir-fry until the radicchio is wilted and tender, 3–4 minutes. Season with salt and pepper. Return the beef and any juices to the pan. Add the watercress and vinegar. Stir-fry for about 1 minute to warm the beef and wilt the watercress, then serve.

23

Quiche was traditionally offered as a first course, but now it is more commonly served as a main course at brunch or lunchtime. Take it into dinner with early summer greens and tangy goat cheese. Spinach particularly complements the rich egg custard and flaky pastry crust.

SPINACH-FETA QUICHE

serves 8

FOR THE TART DOUGH

1⅓ cups (7 oz/220 g) all-purpose flour

1 Tbsp sugar

Salt

½ cup (4 oz/125 g) cold unsalted butter, cut into small pieces

4 Tbsp (2 fl oz/60 ml) ice water, or more as needed

1 cup (1 oz/30g) steamed fresh spinach or thawed frozen spinach, drained and squeezed completely dry

3 eggs

Salt and freshly ground pepper

Pinch of grated nutmeg

¾ cup (6 fl oz/180 ml) heavy cream

¾ cup (6 fl oz/180 ml) milk

1 cup (5 oz/155 g) crumbled feta cheese

1 Tbsp unsalted butter, cut into ¼-inch (6-mm) pieces

To make the tart dough, in a food processor, combine the flour, sugar, and ¼ tsp salt. Pulse to mix. Add the butter and pulse 8 times. Add the 4 Tbsp ice water and pulse about 10 times. If the dough crumbles, add more ice water, a Tbsp at a time, and pulse just until the dough holds together. Transfer the dough to a floured work surface, shape into a 6-inch (15-cm) disk, wrap in plastic wrap, and refrigerate for at least 1 hour or up to overnight.

Preheat the oven to 400°F (200°C). On a floured work surface, roll out the dough into a round about 10½ inches (26.5 cm) in diameter and ¼ inch (6 mm) thick. Carefully transfer it to a 9-inch (23-cm) quiche pan or other straight-sided pan with 1-inch (2.5-cm) sides. Press the dough into the bottom and sides of the pan. Pinch the dough around the rim to form a fluted edge.

Line the dough with foil and fill with pie weights or dried beans. Bake until the crust is dry, about 15 minutes. Remove from the oven and lift out the weights and foil. Transfer to a wire rack. Reduce the oven temperature to 350°F (180°C) and set a rack in the bottom third of the oven. ↦

Arrange the spinach evenly in the prebaked crust. In a large bowl, whisk together the eggs, ½ tsp salt, ⅛ tsp pepper, and the nutmeg. Add the cream and milk and whisk until well blended. Slowly pour the egg mixture over the spinach in the crust. Dot the top with the cheese and the butter.

Bake on the bottom oven rack until the top is lightly browned and the filling is just barely set, 40–45 minutes. Transfer to the wire rack and let stand for 5 minutes. Cut into wedges and serve.

24

Lentils cook gently in the slow cooker, with garlic and a smoky ham hock. To add a cucumber-mint salad: In a bowl, whisk together 1½ Tbsp sherry vinegar, ¼ cup (2 fl oz/60 ml) olive oil, ¼ tsp salt, and several grinds of pepper. Add ½ English cucumber, peeled and cut into matchsticks; 4 green onions, including the light green tops, finely chopped; and 2 Tbsp finely chopped fresh mint. Mix together.

GARLICKY LENTILS WITH HAM

serves 4–6

1 smoked ham hock, about 1½ lb (750 g)

2½ cups (20 fl oz/625 ml) chicken broth

½ cup (4 fl oz/125 ml) dry red wine

½ yellow onion, halved through the stem end

1 carrot, finely chopped

1 celery rib, cut into 2-inch (5-cm) lengths

20 cloves garlic

3 bay leaves

2 sprigs fresh thyme

1 tsp ground cumin

1½ cups (10½ oz/330 g) small green French lentils, picked over and rinsed

Salt and freshly ground pepper

Combine the ham hock, broth, wine, onion, carrot, celery, garlic, bay leaves, thyme, and cumin in a slow cooker, and stir to mix well. Cover and cook on the low setting for 3 hours. Stir in the lentils, re-cover, and cook for about 1½ hours. The lentils should be tender but not mushy.

Remove the ham hock, bay leaves, onion and celery pieces, and thyme sprigs. Pull the meat off the ham hock and discard the bone, cartilage, skin, and fat. Shred the meat. Stir the shredded meat back into the lentils. Season with salt and pepper.

Using a slotted spoon, transfer the lentils to a shallow serving bowl, and serve.

29

Cherries have a short season, heralding the start of summer. They pair well with duck or pork in savory dishes, bringing out the natural sweetness of the meat. A cherry pitter will make short work of the stones. When fresh cherries aren't in season, use dried cherries.

BRAISED PORK CHOPS WITH CHERRIES
serves 4

4 bone-in, center-cut pork loin chops, each 1 inch (2.5 cm) thick

Salt and freshly ground pepper

1 Tbsp minced fresh rosemary

3 Tbsp unsalted butter

2 leeks, white and pale green parts, halved lengthwise and thinly sliced

1 cup (8 fl oz/250 ml) chicken broth

¼ cup (2 fl oz/60 ml) Port wine

2 Tbsp balsamic vinegar

½ cup (2 oz/60 g) dried cherries or 1 cup (4 oz/120 g) fresh pitted cherries, halved

Season the pork chops with salt and pepper and sprinkle with the rosemary, patting the seasonings firmly to adhere to the meat. In a sauté pan with a lid, melt 2 Tbsp of the butter over medium-high heat. Add the pork chops and cook, turning once, until golden on both sides, about 6 minutes. Transfer to a plate.

In the same pan, melt the remaining 1 Tbsp butter over medium heat. Add the leeks and sauté until softened and beginning to brown, 3–4 minutes. Stir in the broth, stir to scrape up any browned bits on the pan bottom, and cook for 1 minute. Stir in the wine, vinegar, and cherries.

Return the pork chops and any juices to the pan and spoon the liquid over them. Cover, reduce the heat to medium-low, and simmer until the pork is tender and barely pink in the center, about 15 minutes. Divide the chops among plates, spoon the cherry mixture over the top, and serve.

30

Here, sweet, anise-like tarragon adds color and garden-fresh flavor to moist, braised salmon. For a perfect side dish, while the fish braises, sauté some fresh green vegetables—asparagus, peas, and leeks—in butter and oil just until tender.

WHITE WINE–BRAISED SALMON WITH TARRAGON
serves 6

½ cup (4 fl oz/125 ml) vegetable broth

1 cup (8 fl oz/250 ml) dry white wine

½ small yellow onion, sliced

3 sprigs fresh tarragon, plus 1 tsp minced

Salt and freshly ground pepper

6 salmon fillets, about 5 oz (155 g) each

In a slow cooker, stir together the broth, wine, onion, and tarragon sprigs. Season with ½ tsp salt and several grindings of pepper. Pour in ½ cup (4 fl oz/125 ml) water and stir to combine. Cover and cook on the low setting for 30 minutes. Add the salmon fillets (they can overlap), cover, and cook for 1 hour. The fish should be opaque throughout, firm, and very tender.

Transfer the salmon fillets to plates and moisten with the braising liquid, if desired. Garnish with the minced tarragon and serve.

31

A fluffy frittata, which begins on the stove and finishes in the oven, makes a savory meal at any time of day. Choose from summer's bounty and try sweet basil and tender zucchini, which will add speckles of green. Serve with crusty French bread.

ZUCCHINI-BASIL FRITTATA
serves 2

5 eggs

Salt and pepper

1 Tbsp olive oil

2 zucchini, cut into matchsticks

⅓ cup (2½ oz/75 g) ricotta cheese

Leaves from 2 sprigs fresh basil, torn into small pieces

Preheat the oven to 350°F (180°C).

Beat the eggs in a bowl until blended and season lightly with salt. In an 8-inch (20-cm) ovenproof frying pan, heat the oil over medium heat. Add the zucchini and sauté for 1–2 minutes. Season lightly with salt and pepper. Stir in the ricotta and basil, mixing well, and then pour in the eggs. Reduce the heat to low and stir for 1 minute.

Place the pan in the oven and bake until the frittata has gently risen and is set, 8–12 minutes.

Using a spatula, transfer the frittata to a large plate. Cut into wedges and serve.

Early summer heralds the start of the garden's bounty—and a desire for dishes that showcase ingredients like sweet peppers, tangy tomatillos, and peppery arugula, along with summer's first corn and basil. One-pot recipes like baked pasta with eggplant, summer squash, and tomatoes; steak piperade; or roasted halibut with tomatillo salsa reflect the offerings. For easy weeknight suppers, serve a Mexican-style casserole with corn and green chiles, chicken breasts with balsamic-spiked cherry tomatoes, or a simple yet elegant shellfish stew.

june

1

RISOTTO RUSTICA WITH PROSCIUTTO & ARUGULA

serves 6

Mild and sweet, thinly sliced prosciutto provides a savory contrast to peppery arugula and creamy risotto. Serve it with country-style bread and a rustic red wine.

7–8 cups (56–64 fl oz/1.75–2 l) chicken broth

¼ cup (2 fl oz/60 ml) olive oil

½ cup (2½ oz/75 g) finely chopped yellow onion

3 cups (21 oz/655 g) Arborio or Carnaroli rice

1 cup (8 fl oz/250 ml) dry white wine

2 Tbsp unsalted butter

Salt and freshly ground pepper

6 large, thin slices prosciutto

1 bunch arugula, tough stems removed

Parmesan cheese for serving

In a saucepan, bring the broth to a gentle simmer over medium heat. Reduce the heat to low and maintain a simmer.

In a large, heavy saucepan, heat the oil over medium heat. Add the onion and sauté until softened, about 4 minutes. Add the rice and stir until well coated with oil and translucent, about 3 minutes. Add the wine and stir until completely absorbed.

Add the simmering broth a ladleful at a time, stirring frequently after each addition. Wait until the broth is almost completely absorbed (but the rice is never dry on top) before adding the next ladleful. Reserve ¼ cup (2 fl oz/60 ml) broth to add at the end.

When the rice is tender to the bite but slightly firm in the center and looks creamy, after about 20 minutes, remove from the heat and stir in the butter and reserved ¼ cup broth. Season with salt and pepper.

Line a shallow serving bowl with the prosciutto slices. Top with the risotto. Make a well in the risotto and fill with the arugula, tearing large leaves into bite-sized pieces. Using a vegetable peeler, shave Parmesan cheese over the top, then serve.

2

VEGETABLE ENCHILADAS

serves 4–6

Tender zucchini and kernels of fresh sweet corn star in this Tex-Mex classic. Wrapped up in tortillas and smothered in a tangy green sauce and gooey, melted cheese, this is a light but comforting vegetarian meal.

12 corn tortillas, each 8 inches (20 cm) in diameter

2 Tbsp canola oil

Salt

1 cup (4 oz/125 g) shredded Monterey jack cheese

1 cup (4 oz/125 g) shredded white Cheddar cheese

2 cups (12 oz/375 g) fresh or thawed frozen corn kernels

2 zucchini, halved lengthwise and thinly sliced

1 large yellow onion, halved and thinly sliced

2 jars (12½ oz/390 g each) tomatillo salsa

¼ cup (2 oz/60 g) Mexican crema or sour cream

Preheat the oven to 300°F (150°C). Brush the tortillas with the oil, sprinkle with salt, and arrange on a baking sheet. Bake until warm and softened, about 1 minute. Remove from the oven and increase the oven temperature to 375°F (190°C).

In a small bowl, stir together half of the Monterey jack cheese, half of the Cheddar cheese, the corn, zucchini, and onion. Cover the bottom of a 9-by-13-inch (23-by-33-cm) baking dish with 1 jar of the salsa.

To assemble the enchiladas, place a tortilla on a work surface, add a few tablespoons of the vegetable filling down the center, and roll up the tortilla. Place it, seam side down, in the baking dish. Repeat with the remaining tortillas and filling. Spread the remaining jar of salsa over the top and sprinkle with the remaining cheese.

Cover the dish with foil and bake until the vegetables are tender and the cheese has melted, about 20 minutes. Uncover and continue to bake until the cheese is golden, 10–15 minutes. Let stand briefly before serving. Pass the crema at the table.

7

Throw together something fresh for dinner with this easy vegetable stir-fry. For a heartier dish, add ½ lb (250 g) pork loin or skinless, boneless chicken, cut into thin strips. Add to the pan after stir-frying the ginger and garlic and cook just until cooked through, 3–4 minutes, then proceed as directed.

VEGETABLE CHOW MEIN

serves 4

½ lb (250 g) fresh Chinese noodles

5 Tbsp (3 fl oz/80 ml) corn or peanut oil

2 Tbsp oyster sauce

2 Tbsp soy sauce

2 Tbsp rice vinegar

1 Tbsp toasted sesame oil

1 tsp sugar (optional)

½ yellow onion, thinly sliced

1 red bell pepper, seeded and thinly sliced lengthwise

4 oz (125 g) shiitake mushrooms, stemmed and thinly sliced

1 zucchini, cut into matchsticks

1 Tbsp peeled and grated fresh ginger

2 cloves garlic, minced

Bring a large pot of water to a boil. Add the noodles, boil for 2 minutes, drain, and rinse well with cold water. Place in a bowl, add 1 Tbsp of the corn oil, and toss to coat evenly.

In a small bowl, stir together the oyster sauce, soy sauce, vinegar, sesame oil, and sugar (if using). Add 3 Tbsp water and stir to dissolve the sugar.

In a wok or large frying pan, heat 2 Tbsp of the corn oil over high heat. Add the onion and bell pepper and stir-fry just until tender, about 2 minutes. Add the mushrooms and zucchini and stir-fry until golden brown, about 2 minutes. Using a slotted spoon, transfer the vegetables to a bowl.

Return the pan to high heat and heat the remaining 2 Tbsp corn oil. Add the ginger and garlic and stir-fry until fragrant, about 5 seconds. Add the noodles and cook until heated through, about 5 minutes. Return the vegetables to the pan, add the oyster sauce mixture, and continue to stir and toss until all the ingredients are well combined and heated through, about 1 minute. Transfer to a platter and serve.

8

Piperade, a basque-style mixture of sweet peppers and onions, is an excellent topping for quick-cooking steaks. Searing the steaks in a pan leaves some meaty flavor for the peppers, but you could also fire up the grill.

STEAK PIPERADE

serves 4

1½ lb (750 g) skirt or flank steak

Salt and freshly ground pepper

2 Tbsp unsalted butter

2 Tbsp olive oil

1 red onion, chopped

3 red or yellow bell peppers, seeded and thinly sliced crosswise

3 cloves garlic, minced

1 Tbsp chopped fresh thyme

½ cup (4 fl oz/125 ml) dry white wine

1 can (14½ oz/455 g) diced tomatoes

Season the steak generously with salt and pepper. In a large frying pan, melt 1 Tbsp of the butter with 1 Tbsp of the oil over high heat. Add the steak and cook, turning once, for 4–6 minutes for medium-rare, or until done to your liking. Transfer the meat to a carving board and tent with foil.

Melt the remaining 1 Tbsp butter with the remaining 1 Tbsp oil in the same pan over medium heat. Add the onion, bell peppers, garlic, and thyme and sauté until the onion is barely softened, 3–4 minutes. Add the wine, bring to a boil, stir to scrape up any browned bits on the pan bottom, and cook for about 30 seconds. Stir in the tomatoes and their juice and simmer until the liquid is slightly reduced, about 5 minutes. Season with salt and pepper.

Cut the meat thinly across the grain on the diagonal. Arrange the slices on a warm platter, spoon the pepper sauce over the slices, and serve.

9

SPANISH PAELLA

serves 4–6

2 Tbsp olive oil

1 lb (500 g) cured Spanish-style chorizo or other spicy smoked sausage, cut into slices ½ inch (12 mm) thick

1 yellow onion, chopped

1 red bell pepper, seeded and chopped

3 cloves garlic, minced

Salt and freshly ground pepper

2 cups (14 oz/440 g) long-grain white rice, such as basmati

½ tsp saffron threads (optional)

4 cups (32 fl oz/1 l) chicken broth

1–2 lb (500 g–1 kg) small clams, such as littleneck or Manila, scrubbed

1 lb (500 g) large shrimp, peeled and deveined

1 cup (5 oz/155 g) thawed frozen baby peas

Paella is the national dish of Spain, where there are many different variations on the theme. Here, the flavorful rice dish includes clams and shrimp, but you can add or substitute mussels, if you like. The mussels should be scrubbed and debearded before cooking. Make sure to purchase dried Spanish-style chorizo, rather than the fresh Mexican-style sausage.

In a large frying pan or paella pan, heat the oil over medium-high heat. Add the sausage slices and cook, turning occasionally, until browned on both sides, about 3 minutes. Add the onion, bell pepper, and garlic and sauté until softened, 3–4 minutes. Season with salt and pepper. Add the rice, crumble in the saffron (if using), and cook, stirring, until the grains are well coated, about 2 minutes. Pour the broth into the pan and stir in 1½ tsp salt. Bring to a boil, reduce the heat to low, cover, and cook until the rice has absorbed nearly all of the liquid, about 20 minutes.

Press the clams, hinge side down, into the rice, discarding any that do not close to the touch. Spread the shrimp over the rice and top with the peas. Cover and cook until the shrimp are opaque and the clams have opened, about 5 minutes longer. Discard any unopened clams, and serve.

10

BRAISED CHICKEN WITH TOMATILLOS & CILANTRO

serves 6

2 Tbsp canola oil

3½ lb (1.75 kg) assorted chicken pieces, skin on and bone in

1 large yellow onion, finely chopped

2 cups (16 fl oz/500 ml) chicken broth

3 Anaheim or poblano chiles, roasted and peeled (page 131), and finely chopped

6 cloves garlic, minced

1½ lb (750 g) tomatillos, husked and cut into quarters *(left)*

3 Tbsp finely chopped fresh cilantro, plus whole leaves for garnish

½ tsp ground cumin

1 Tbsp fresh lime juice

Salt and freshly ground pepper

Warm tortillas for serving

Small, round, and green, tomatillos look like unripe tomatoes—they're even known as tomates verdes in Mexico. (Both tomatoes and tomatillos are members of the nightshade family.) Tomatillos have a tart herbal taste and can be used in salsa verde, soups, and stews. To remove the husks, hold the fruit under warm running water, strip off the husks, and rinse off the sticky residue coating the skins.

In a large sauté pan with a lid, heat the oil over medium-high heat. Working in batches, sear the chicken, turning once, until browned, 7–8 minutes. Transfer to a plate.

Reduce the heat to medium and add the onion and sauté until softened, 3–5 minutes. Add the broth, stirring to scrape up any browned bits on the pan bottom. Add the roasted chiles, garlic, tomatillos, chopped cilantro, and cumin. Bring to a boil, then reduce the heat to low. Return the chicken and any juices to the pan, cover, and simmer, turning once, until the chicken is opaque throughout, about 20 minutes. The white meat and smaller pieces will be done first. Transfer the chicken to a platter and tent with foil to keep warm.

Add the lime juice to the pan and cook the sauce over high heat until slightly reduced and thickened. Season with salt and pepper. Pour the sauce over the chicken and garnish with the cilantro leaves. Serve with the tortillas alongside.

15

RISOTTO WITH FRESH CORN & BASIL OIL

serves 4

¼ cup (⅓ oz/10 g) fresh basil, chopped

¼ cup (2 fl oz/60 ml) extra-virgin olive oil

5 cups (40 fl oz/1.25 l) chicken broth

2 Tbsp unsalted butter

1 cup (3 oz/90 g) thinly sliced leeks, white and pale green parts

1½ cups (10 oz/315 g) Arborio or Carnaroli rice

Kernels from 2 or 3 ears of corn

Salt and freshly ground pepper

2 Tbsp minced fresh chives

Corn lovers eagerly anticipate its arrival at markets during the summer. Purists insist on cooking corn on the cob only until warmed through, either boiled or steamed, to preserve its sweetness and crunch. Cut from the cob, the fresh kernels are added raw to this creamy risotto, and cook in the gentle heat. A drizzle of basil oil provides a distinctive finish.

In a blender, combine the basil and olive oil and process until combined. Set aside.

In a saucepan, bring the broth to a gentle simmer over medium heat. Reduce the heat to low and maintain a simmer.

In a large, heavy saucepan, melt the butter over medium heat. Add the leeks, stir to coat, cover, reduce the heat to medium-low, and cook until translucent, about 5 minutes. Raise the heat to medium, add the rice, and stir until translucent, about 3 minutes. Add the simmering broth a ladleful at a time, stirring frequently after each addition. Wait until the broth is almost completely absorbed (but the rice is never dry on top) before adding the next ladleful. After 10 minutes, stir in the corn. After about 20 minutes, the rice should be tender to the bite and creamy. If you need more liquid, use heated water. Season with salt and pepper.

Remove from the heat and stir in the chives and 2 Tbsp of the basil oil. Divide among bowls, drizzle with more basil oil, and serve.

16

CHICKEN, CORN & GREEN CHILE CASSEROLE

serves 4–6

2 Tbsp unsalted butter, plus more for dish

1 yellow onion, chopped

2 cloves garlic, minced

1 Tbsp plus 1 tsp ground cumin

Salt and freshly ground pepper

1 Tbsp all-purpose flour

1½ cups (12 fl oz/375 ml) milk

3 cups (18 oz/560 g) shredded cooked chicken

3 cups (18 oz/560 g) fresh corn kernels (from about 6 ears) or thawed frozen corn kernels

1 can (4 oz/125 g) diced fire-roasted green chiles

FOR THE CORNMEAL TOPPING

1 cup (5 oz/155 g) all-purpose flour

½ cup (2½ oz/75 g) yellow cornmeal

2 tsp baking powder

3 green onions, white and tender green parts, chopped

1 cup (8 fl oz/250 ml) milk

3 Tbsp unsalted butter, melted

Latin spices inspire a modern take on chicken and dumplings, with fresh corn, roasted chiles, and a crunchy cornmeal topping. This is an excellent way to use leftover rotisserie or grilled chicken. When entertaining, bake and serve in individual ramekins, alongside a butter lettuce salad with avocado, citrus sections, and a zesty vinaigrette.

Preheat the oven to 375°F (180°C). Butter an 8-by-10-inch (20-by-25-cm) baking dish.

In a large frying pan, melt the 2 Tbsp butter over medium-high heat. Add the onion and garlic and sauté until translucent, 5 minutes. Add the cumin and 2 tsp salt and cook, stirring, for 2 minutes. Add the flour and cook, stirring constantly, for 1 minute. Stir in the milk and bring to a boil. Reduce the heat to medium-low and simmer, stirring occasionally, until the sauce thickens, 4–5 minutes. Add the chicken, corn, and chiles and stir to combine. Season with salt and pepper. Transfer to the prepared dish.

To make the topping, in a bowl, stir together the flour, cornmeal, baking powder, ½ tsp salt, and the green onions. Add the milk and melted butter and stir to combine. Using a large spoon, drop the cornmeal mixture in large mounds on top of the chicken mixture.

Bake until the topping is lightly browned and the chicken mixture is bubbly, about 20 minutes. Spoon onto plates and serve.

17

ROASTED HALIBUT FILLETS WITH TOMATILLO SALSA

serves 4

¾ lb (375 g) tomatillos, husked and rinsed

2 serrano chiles

½ cup (¾ oz/20 g) chopped cilantro, plus more for garnish

½ cup (2 oz/60 g) chopped yellow onion

4 cloves garlic

2 Tbsp lime juice

2 Tbsp cider vinegar

1 tsp sugar

Salt and freshly ground pepper

3 Tbsp olive oil

4 halibut fillets, each about 6 oz (185 g)

Plump, meaty halibut fillets are ideal for this brightly flavored tomatillo salsa. Delicious on its own as a one-pot meal, you could also tuck the saucy fish into corn tortillas for a new spin on fish tacos.

Preheat the broiler. Spread the tomatillos and chiles on a baking sheet and broil until browned and blackened in spots, about 15 minutes. Let cool, then transfer to a blender along with the ½ cup cilantro, onion, garlic, lime juice, vinegar, and sugar. Season with ¼ tsp salt, pour in ¼ cup (2 fl oz/60 ml) water, and purée.

Preheat the oven to 425°F (220°C).

In a large, overproof frying pan, warm 2 Tbsp of the oil over medium heat. Add the tomatillo purée and cook until it thickens slightly, about 5 minutes. Remove from the heat and season with salt and pepper. Spoon about one-third of the salsa into a bowl and set aside.

Nestle the fillets in the frying pan. Season with salt and pepper. Spoon some of the salsa over the top of each fillet. Bake until the fish is opaque throughout, 10–12 minutes.

Garnish with cilantro and serve with the remaining salsa.

18

STEAMED TOFU WITH GREENS & PEANUT SAUCE

serves 4

½ cup (5 oz/155 g) creamy peanut butter

½ cup (4 fl oz/125 ml) light coconut milk

3 Tbsp lime juice

2 Tbsp firmly packed golden brown sugar

1½ Tbsp soy sauce

1½–2 tsp Asian red chile paste

¾ lb (375 g) chopped green or savoy cabbage

6 oz (185 g) baby spinach

1 lb (500 g) firm tofu, cut into slices ½ inch (12 mm) thick

This is a virtuous vegetarian supper, with nutrients from the cabbage and spinach, and protein from the tofu. The steaming technique is quick and lean, limiting the fat content to the healthy fats from coconut milk and peanut butter in the rich sauce.

In a blender, combine the peanut butter, coconut milk, lime juice, brown sugar, soy sauce, and chile paste and process until smooth. Transfer the peanut sauce to a bowl.

Set a steamer rack inside a large pot filled with about 2 inches (5 cm) of water. Arrange the cabbage on the steamer and bring the water to a boil. Cover the pot and steam until the cabbage is wilted, about 7 minutes. Place the spinach leaves and tofu on top of the cabbage. Cover and steam until the spinach is wilted and the tofu is heated through, about 5 minutes longer.

Mound the cabbage, spinach, and tofu on a platter, drizzle with the peanut sauce, and serve.

23

BRAISED CHICKEN WITH SHALLOTS & MUSHROOMS

serves 4–6

4½ lb (2.25 kg) assorted chicken pieces, preferably drumsticks and thighs

Salt and freshly ground pepper

3 Tbsp olive oil

6–8 shallots, chopped

3 cloves garlic, chopped

1 bottle (750 ml) full-bodied white wine

3 Tbsp small pieces dried mushrooms, such as chanterelle or porcini

2 cups (16 fl oz/500 ml) chicken broth

2 Tbsp coarsely chopped fresh tarragon

¾ cup (6 fl oz/180 ml) heavy cream

A few drops fresh lemon juice (optional)

2 Tbsp chopped fresh chives

1–2 Tbsp chopped fresh chervil or flat-leaf parsley

Shallots break ground in spring. The purple-hued bulbs have a flavor somewhere between onion and garlic, and they braise to a delectable sweetness. White wine and tarragon enliven the pot, and dried mushrooms provide an earthy undertone.

Preheat the oven to 350°F (180°C). Season the chicken pieces with salt and pepper, then rub with the oil. Heat a large, heavy frying pan over medium-high heat. Working in batches, sear the chicken, turning occasionally, until brown, 10–15 minutes. Transfer to a platter.

Pour off all but 1 Tbsp fat from the pan and place over medium heat. Add the shallots and garlic and sauté until softened, about 5 minutes. Add the wine, raise the heat to high, bring to a boil, and cook until reduced by half, 10–15 minutes. Stir in the mushrooms, broth, and half of the tarragon. Pour the sauce into a deep roasting pan large enough to hold the chicken in a single layer. Arrange the chicken in the sauce. Cook in the oven until the chicken is opaque throughout, 35–40 minutes.

Raise the heat to 400°F (200°C) and cook until the edges of the skin are crisp, about 5 minutes. Transfer to a deep platter and tent with foil.

Skim the fat from the surface of the sauce. Place the pan over high heat, bring the sauce to a boil, and cook, stirring, until reduced by about half, 7–8 minutes. Stir in the cream. Adjust the seasoning with salt and pepper and with lemon juice, if using. Pour the sauce over the chicken. Sprinkle with the chives, chervil, and remaining tarragon, and serve.

24

RISOTTO WITH LEEKS & SUN-DRIED TOMATOES

serves 6

7–8 cups (56–64 fl oz/1.75–2 l) chicken or vegetable broth

¼ cup (2 fl oz/60 ml) olive oil

3 leeks, white part only, thinly sliced crosswise

1 yellow bell pepper, seeded and cut into ½-inch (12-mm) chunks

3 cups (21 oz/655 g) Arborio or Carnaroli rice

1 cup (8 fl oz/250 ml) dry white wine

½ cup (3 oz/90 g) oil-packed sun-dried tomatoes, drained and cut into slivers

2 Tbsp unsalted butter

Salt and freshly ground pepper

Sweet and mild, leeks give this risotto a base of flavor that differs slightly from that of onions, which are more typically used. To clean leeks, trim off the roots and tough green tops and cut the stalks in half lengthwise. Rinse under running cold water, spreading the layers apart to wash away any grit. For this recipe, thinly slice the leeks crosswise.

In a saucepan, bring the broth to a gentle simmer over medium heat. Reduce the heat to low and maintain a simmer.

In a large, heavy saucepan, heat the oil over medium heat. Add the leeks and bell pepper and sauté until softened, about 4 minutes. Using a slotted spoon, transfer the leek mixture to a bowl and set aside.

Add the rice to the pan and stir until well coated with oil and translucent, about 3 minutes. Add the wine and stir until completely absorbed. Add the simmering broth a ladleful at a time, stirring frequently after each addition. Wait until the broth is almost completely absorbed (but the rice is never dry on top) before adding the next ladleful. Reserve ¼ cup (2 fl oz/60 ml) broth to add at the end.

When the rice is tender to the bite but slightly firm in the center and is creamy, after about 20 minutes, stir in the leek mixture and sun-dried tomatoes. Cook to heat through, about 30 seconds. Remove from the heat and stir in the butter and reserved ¼ cup broth. Season with salt and pepper and serve.

29

This tomato- and fennel-flecked fish stew originated on the Mediterranean coast of France, and classically contains up to a dozen different kinds of fish and shellfish. For this recipe, choose what looks best in your local fish market. Clams, mussels, snapper and striped bass fillets, cleaned squid, and shrimp, in any combination, would make a good assortment. Pastis can be substituted for the Pernod.

BOUILLABAISSE
serves 4–6

FOR THE ROUILLE

1 egg

1 clove garlic, chopped

1 Tbsp tomato paste

½ tsp fresh lemon juice

½ tsp sweet paprika

¼ tsp cayenne pepper

Salt

⅔ cup (5 fl oz/160 ml) olive oil

3 lb (1.5 kg) assorted fish and shellfish

2 Tbsp olive oil, plus oil for brushing

1 yellow onion, chopped

½ cup (2 oz/60 g) thinly sliced fennel bulb

6 cloves garlic, 4 minced and 2 peeled but left whole

½ cup (4 fl oz/125 ml) dry white wine

5 cups (40 fl oz/1.25 ml) fish broth

1½ lb (750 g) tomatoes, peeled, seeded, and chopped

2 Tbsp Pernod

½ tsp saffron threads

½ tsp grated orange zest

½ tsp dried thyme

Salt and freshly ground black pepper

1 baguette, cut on the diagonal into slices ½ inch (12 mm) thick

To make the rouille, combine the egg, garlic, tomato paste, lemon juice, paprika, and cayenne in a blender or food processor. Add ¼ tsp salt and process until well combined. With the motor running, pour in the oil in a slow, steady stream and process until the mixture thickens to the consistency of mayonnaise. Spoon into a bowl, cover, and set aside.

If using clams and/or mussels, scrub them well and debeard the mussels. Place in a bowl of water and refrigerate. Cut any fish fillets into 1½-inch (4-cm) chunks. If using squid, cut the bodies into 1-inch (2.5-cm) rings and the tentacles into bite-sized pieces. If using shrimp, peel them, leaving the tail segments intact, and then devein. Put the fillets, squid, and shrimp in a bowl and refrigerate.

In a large, heavy pot, warm the 2 Tbsp olive oil over medium heat. Add the onion, fennel, and minced garlic and cook, stirring ⟶

often, until softened, 6–8 minutes. Add the wine and cook until mostly evaporated, about 2 minutes. Stir in the broth, tomatoes, Pernod, saffron, orange zest, and thyme. Season generously with salt and black pepper. Simmer uncovered for 10 minutes to blend the flavors. Preheat the oven to 400°F (200°C).

Drain the clams and mussels, if using, and add to the pot, discarding any that do not close to the touch. Add the fish, cover, and simmer for about 5 minutes. Add the shrimp and squid, re-cover, and cook until the clams and mussels have opened and the fish and other shellfish are opaque throughout, about 5 minutes longer. Discard any unopened clams or mussels.

Meanwhile, arrange the baguette slices on a baking sheet and brush the tops lightly with olive oil. Toast until golden, about 5 minutes. Remove from the oven and rub the tops with the whole garlic cloves.

Spread the garlic toasts with the rouille and serve alongside the stew.

30

Smothering fish fillets in summer's tomatoes and leeks creates an easy seasonal meal in one pan. If desired, cut fresh basil into thin strips (julienne), and use it to garnish the halibut.

HALIBUT WITH TOMATOES & LEEKS
serves 4

3 lb (1.5 kg) leeks, white and pale green parts, halved lengthwise and thinly sliced

3 Tbsp olive oil

Salt and freshly ground pepper

2 cups (12 oz/375 g) cherry tomatoes, halved

4 halibut fillets, about 6 oz (185 g) each

Preheat the oven to 450°F (230°C).

In a large roasting pan, toss the leeks with 2 Tbsp of the oil and season with salt and pepper. Spread in a single layer and roast until just tender, about 10 minutes. Remove the pan from the oven and add the tomatoes. Preheat the broiler.

Season the halibut with salt and pepper, and lay the fillets over the leeks and tomatoes. Drizzle with the remaining 1 Tbsp oil. Broil just until the fillets are barely opaque throughout, about 8 minutes. Serve.

Al fresco dinners and afternoon barbecues are good ways to showcase summer's delectable ingredients in made-for-sharing one-pot meals. Dishes like barbecue-style brisket, a one-pot clambake, creamy corn chowder, and braised chicken with summer beans and tomatoes are great choices for casual get-togethers. Warm-weather stews—like a light coq au vin—olive oil–braises, stir-frys, and grains offer ample opportunity for making the most of the season's vegetables at their prime.

july

1

STUFFED POBLANO CHILES WITH BLACK BEANS & SQUASH

serves 4–6

Broiling chiles until their skins blacken imparts an alluring smokiness. Here, zucchini, yellow squash, and roasted chiles are added to the hearty black bean and rice filling, which is stuffed into whole chiles for a flavorful, summery dish. Tangy crème fraîche and nutty Parmesan add refreshing accents.

8 poblano chiles, 2 roasted (page 131) and chopped and 6 uncooked and whole

2 Tbsp olive oil

½ white onion, finely chopped

Salt and freshly ground black pepper

1 zucchini, chopped

2 yellow summer squash, chopped

1 tomato, chopped

¼ tsp cayenne pepper

1 can (15 oz/470 g) black beans, rinsed and drained

Leaves from ¼ bunch fresh cilantro, coarsely chopped

1 cup (5 oz/155 g) cooked white rice

½ cup (4 oz/125 g) crème fraîche or sour cream

Parmesan cheese for grating

Preheat the oven to 400°F (200°C).

Cut a slit 2 inches (5 cm) long in each of the 6 unroasted chiles. Carefully scrape out the seeds from the insides of the chiles.

In a frying pan, heat the oil over medium heat. Add the onion and a pinch of salt and sauté until the onion is soft and translucent, 5–6 minutes. Add the zucchini and summer squash and sauté until just tender, about 5 minutes. Add the chopped roasted chiles, the tomato, cayenne, and a pinch each of salt and black pepper and sauté for 2 minutes. Remove from the heat and let the vegetables cool slightly.

Add the beans, cilantro, rice, and crème fraîche to the pan and mix well. Spoon the bean mixture into the 6 uncooked chiles, dividing it evenly. Place the stuffed chiles, cut side up, in a baking dish, and add enough water to come ½ inch (12 mm) up the sides of the dish. Cover tightly with foil and bake until the stuffing is heated through and the water has evaporated, about 20 minutes. Remove the foil, grate some Parmesan over the chiles, and bake until the cheese melts, 4–5 minutes. Remove from the oven and serve.

2

ONE-POT CLAMBAKE

serves 4

Leave the sand at the beach and serve this brimming pot for a fun, casual gathering. Diners can pick out hunks of corn, potatoes, sausages, a clam here, and a lobster claw there. Just provide plenty of napkins, a bowl for the discards, and a loaf of crusty bread.

2 Tbsp olive oil

1 yellow onion, chopped

3 cloves garlic, minced

1 small fennel bulb, chopped, any fronds reserved for garnish

3 sprigs fresh thyme

Salt and freshly ground pepper

1½ cups (12 fl oz/375 ml) white wine

3 cups (24 fl oz/750 ml) chicken broth

1 lb (500 g) red-skinned potatoes, quartered

1 lb (500 g) kielbasa or other smoked sausage, thickly sliced

1 or 2 lobsters (1½ lb/750 g total weight)

2 ears of corn, each cut into 3 pieces

24 mussels, scrubbed and debearded

24 clams, scrubbed

12 large shrimp in the shell

1 lemon, cut into wedges

In a large (16- to 20-qt/15- to 18-l) heavy-bottomed stockpot, heat the oil over medium-high heat. Add the onion, garlic, chopped fennel bulb, and thyme sprigs and season with salt and pepper. Saute until the fennel is soft, about 8 minutes. Add the wine and cook until reduced by half, about 5 minutes. Add the broth and then layer the other ingredients on top in this order: the potatoes, the kielbasa, and the lobster(s). Cover the pot tightly and cook for 10 minutes. Remove the lid and nestle in the corn, mussels and clams (discarding any that do not close to the touch), and shrimp and cover tightly. Cook for another 10 minutes. Discard any unopened mussels or clams.

Using a slotted spoon, transfer the potatoes, corn, kielbasa, and seafood to a large platter. Season the broth in the stockpot to taste with salt and pepper and spoon it over the top of the seafood. Garnish with fennel fronds and lemon wedges, and serve.

JULY

3

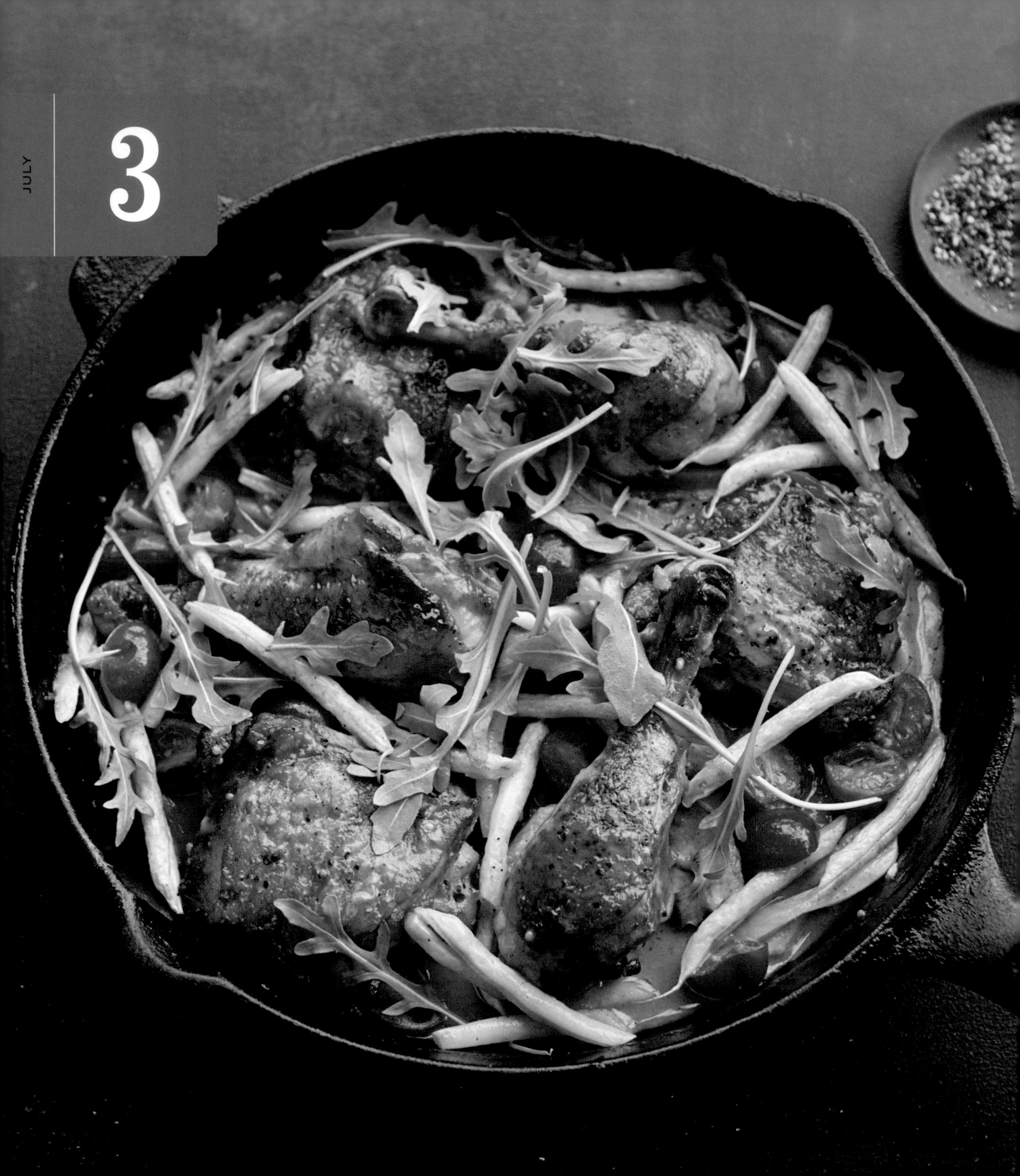

3

SUMMER CHICKEN BRAISE
WITH WAX BEANS & TOMATOES

serves 4

The colors of burnished chicken, yellow beans, red tomatoes, and green arugula make for a show-stopping presentation. Use a skillet or Dutch oven that you can bring straight to the table, and serve the chicken in shallow bowls to include the mustardy pan sauce. Offer plenty of warm crusty bread, and encourage guests to soak up every last drop.

2 Tbsp olive oil

2 lb (1 kg) skin-on, bone-in chicken thighs and drumsticks

Salt and freshly ground pepper

1 yellow onion, chopped

1 carrot, chopped

6 cloves garlic, minced

1¼ cups (10 fl oz/310 ml) dry white wine

3 cups (24 fl oz/750 ml) chicken broth

3 sprigs fresh thyme

¼ cup (2 fl oz/60 ml) heavy cream

3 Tbsp Dijon mustard

1 cup (6 oz/185 g) cherry tomatoes

4 oz (125 g) small yellow wax beans

2 cups (3 oz/90 g) arugula leaves

Preheat the oven to 350°F (180°C).

In a large, heavy pot or a deep skillet, warm the oil over medium-high heat. Season the chicken with salt and pepper. Working in batches, sear the chicken, turning as needed, until browned, about 8 minutes. Transfer to a plate.

Add the onion, carrot, and garlic to the pot and season with salt and pepper. Sauté over medium-high heat until the vegetables soften, about 5 minutes. Add the wine, bring to a simmer, and cook until reduced by half, about 5 minutes. Add the broth and bring to a boil. Return the chicken to the pot, add the thyme, cover, and cook in the oven until the chicken is opaque throughout, about 55 minutes.

Transfer the chicken to a plate. Strain the braising liquid and return to the pot. Bring the liquid to a boil over high heat and cook until reduced by half, about 8 minutes. Reduce the heat to medium-high, stir in the cream and mustard, and cook until the sauce thickens, about 5 minutes. Season with salt and pepper. Arrange the chicken pieces in the pot, cover, and cook over low heat for 15 minutes to develop the flavors. Add the tomatoes and wax beans and cook, covered, until softened, about 5 minutes. Uncover, add the arugula, stir into the sauce, and cook just until wilted, about 1 minute. Serve directly from the pan.

4

FRESH CORN PUDDING

serves 4

Fresh sweet corn straight from the stands is an unrivaled summer treat. If you ever tire of nibbling on ears, try this simple, savory baked dish. Similar to a soufflé, the pudding puffs up, then sinks a little as it cools. It makes a stunning light main course when paired with sliced heirloom tomatoes or a green salad.

Butter for dish

¼ cup (½ oz/15 g) fresh bread crumbs

½ cup (2 oz/60 g) shredded Cheddar cheese

3 shallots, minced

1 cup (8 fl oz/250 ml) heavy cream, lukewarm

3 dashes hot-pepper sauce, such as Tabasco

4 cups (1½ lb/750 g) fresh corn kernels (from 8–10 large ears)

Salt and freshly ground pepper

6 eggs, lightly beaten

2 tsp chopped fresh thyme

Boiling water

Preheat the oven to 350°F (180°C). Butter a 2-qt (2-l) soufflé dish or baking dish. Coat the bottom and sides with the bread crumbs and 2 Tbsp of the cheese.

In a food processor, combine the shallots, cream, and hot-pepper sauce. Add 1 cup (6 oz/190 g) of the corn, 1 tsp salt, and ¼ tsp pepper. Process until creamy. Transfer the corn mixture to a large bowl and stir in the eggs, the remaining 3 cups (18 oz/560 g) corn, the thyme, and the remaining cheese. Pour into the prepared dish. Coat one side of a piece of foil generously with butter and place, butter side down, over the dish. Put the dish in a baking pan and fill the pan with boiling water to reach two-thirds of the way up the sides of the baking dish.

Bake for 45 minutes. Remove the foil and continue baking until the pudding is lightly browned on top and a knife inserted into the center comes out clean, about 15 minutes. Remove from the oven and serve.

5

BEEF STIR-FRY WITH BLACK BEAN SAUCE

serves 4

1 lb (500 g) tri-tip, sliced thinly and cut into 1-inch (2.5-cm) chunks

Salt and freshly ground black pepper

4 Tbsp peanut oil

1 large red bell pepper, seeded and thinly sliced

1 cup (3 oz/90 g) snow peas, trimmed

1 yellow onion, thinly sliced

½ lb (150 g) shiitake mushrooms, stemmed and sliced

¼ tsp red pepper flakes

⅓ cup (3 fl oz/80 ml) black bean sauce

Cooked rice for serving

Black bean sauce and red pepper flakes underscore this pungent and spicy stir-fry. Tri-tip is one of the most flavorful cuts of beef, and an ideal choice for these bold flavors, but should be sliced thinly to keep it tender. Snow peas and bell pepper add some fresh crunch.

Generously season the beef with salt and black pepper.

In a wok or large, deep frying pan, heat 1 Tbsp of the oil over high heat. Add the beef and cook, stirring often, until browned on both sides, about 4 minutes. Transfer to a bowl. Add the remaining 3 Tbsp oil to the wok. When it is hot, add the bell pepper, snow peas, onion, mushrooms, and red pepper flakes and stir-fry until the vegetables are tender-crisp and lightly browned, 4–5 minutes.

Stir in the black bean sauce and 3 Tbsp water, reduce the heat to medium-low, and simmer for 2 minutes.

Stir in the beef and simmer until heated through, 1–2 minutes. Season with salt and pepper and serve over rice.

6

RISOTTO WITH SHRIMP & PESTO

serves 6

7–8 cups (56–64 fl oz/1.75–2 l) shellfish broth or bottled clam juice

¼ cup (2 fl oz/60 ml) olive oil

½ cup (2½ oz/75 g) finely chopped yellow onion

½ lb (250 g) shrimp, peeled and deveined

3 cups (21 oz/655 g) Arborio or Carnaroli rice

1 cup (8 fl oz/250 ml) dry white wine

2–4 Tbsp pesto, store-bought or homemade

Salt and freshly ground pepper

Sweetly scented basil leaves thrive in the hottest months of the year. Let them star in vibrantly green pesto, which is always convenient to have on hand, whether you're tossing it in pasta, spreading it on panini, swirling it into minestrone, or whisking up a salad dressing. Here, just a few spoonfuls infuse a taste of summer into a creamy bowl of rice and shrimp for an easy meal.

In a saucepan, bring the broth to a gentle simmer over medium heat and maintain over low heat.

In a large, heavy saucepan, heat the oil over medium heat. Add the onion and sauté until softened, about 4 minutes. Add the shrimp and sauté until firm and pink, 4–5 minutes. Transfer the mixture to a bowl.

Add the rice to the pan and stir until well coated with oil and translucent, about 3 minutes. Add the wine and stir until completely absorbed. Add the simmering broth a ladleful at a time, stirring frequently after each addition. Wait until the broth is almost completely absorbed (but the rice is never dry on top) before adding the next ladleful. Reserve ¼ cup (2 fl oz/60 ml) broth to add at the end.

When the rice is tender to the bite and looks creamy, after about 20 minutes, stir in the shrimp. Cook to heat through, about 1 minute. Remove from the heat and stir in 2–4 Tbsp pesto, or to taste, and the reserved ¼ cup broth. Season with salt and pepper and serve.

7

CORN & CHILE STRATA WITH MEXICAN CHORIZO

serves 8–10

1 Tbsp olive oil, plus more for greasing

1 lb (500 g) fresh Mexican-style chorizo sausage, casings removed

1 white onion, chopped

3 poblano chiles, roasted and peeled (page 131), seeded, and chopped

1½ cups (9 oz/280 g) fresh or thawed frozen corn kernels

2 cups (16 fl oz/500 ml) milk

8 eggs

½ tsp hot-pepper sauce

Salt

12 slices day-old baguette, each ½–¾ inch (12 mm–2 cm) thick

2 cups (8 oz/250 g) shredded Cheddar cheese

Strata, a casserole of eggs, bread, cheese, and other ingredients, is a busy cook's secret weapon: The dish can be assembled the night before, then baked the next morning to golden perfection. Use fresh Mexican-style chorizo, not the smoked Spanish variety, for this southwestern version, which is studded with mild green chiles and sweet corn.

In a large frying pan, heat the oil over medium heat. Add the chorizo and cook, stirring to break up the meat, until it begins to brown, about 8 minutes. Add the onion and cook, stirring occasionally, until it softens, about 3 minutes. Using a slotted spoon, transfer the sausage mixture to paper towels to drain. Pour off the fat from the pan.

Lightly oil a 3-qt (3-l) baking dish. In a bowl, combine the chiles and corn.

In a large bowl, whisk together the milk, the eggs, the hot-pepper sauce, and ¾ tsp salt. Arrange 6 of the bread slices in a single layer on the bottom of the prepared dish, tearing the slices to fit, if needed. Top evenly with half of the chorizo mixture, half of the chile mixture, and half of the cheese. Repeat the layers a second time.

Slowly pour the milk mixture over the layers. Wrap securely in plastic wrap. Press gently on the plastic to submerge the layers in the milk mixture. Refrigerate for at least 2 hours or up to overnight.

Preheat the oven to 350°F (180°C). Uncover the dish and bake until the strata puffs and becomes golden brown, about 1 hour. Transfer to a wire rack and let cool for about 5 minutes, then serve.

8

GINGER CHICKEN WITH GREEN ONIONS

serves 4

1½ lb (750 g) skinless, boneless chicken breast halves, cut into thin strips

Salt and freshly ground pepper

3 Tbsp peanut or canola oil

4 cloves garlic, minced

3 Tbsp peeled and grated ginger

2 Tbsp finely chopped lemongrass, center white part only *(left)*

4 green onions, thinly sliced

⅔ cup (5 fl oz/160 ml) chicken broth

2 Tbsp Asian fish sauce

2 Tbsp chopped fresh mint

Cooked rice for serving

Lemongrass is a popular Asian ingredient that is available in most well-stocked markets. Use only the bulb portion of the stalk, and remove the tough outer layers before chopping. If you can't find lemongrass, you can substitute 1 Tbsp lemon juice and 2 tsp grated lemon zest. Add them along with the garlic and ginger in the first step.

Season the chicken generously with salt and pepper. In a wok or large frying pan, heat the oil over high heat. Add the chicken and stir-fry until golden and nearly cooked through, 3–4 minutes. Add the garlic, ginger, lemongrass, and half of the green onions and stir-fry just until fragrant, about 30 seconds.

Add the broth and fish sauce to the pan, reduce the heat to medium, and simmer until the chicken is opaque throughout and the sauce is slightly reduced, 2–3 minutes. Sprinkle with the remaining green onions and the mint, and serve with rice.

9

BARBECUE-STYLE BRISKET

serves 6–8

¼ cup (2 oz/60 g) firmly packed dark brown sugar

¼ cup (2 fl oz/60 ml) cider vinegar

2 tomatoes, seeded and chopped

2 cups (16 fl oz/500 ml) beef broth

3 lb (1.5 kg) beef brisket

Salt and freshly ground pepper

2 Tbsp canola oil

2 yellow onions, thinly sliced

2 cloves garlic, minced

½ tsp ground allspice

2 Tbsp all-purpose flour

Brisket is one of the glories of grilling season, but even if you own a smoker it can be a labor of love. Slow cooking it in the oven renders equally tender results, and is much easier. Beef brisket is sold without the bone and is divided into two sections, the flat cut and the point cut. At the meat counter, ask for the flat cut if possible. It has less fat and is easier to slice.

In a small bowl, stir together the sugar, vinegar, tomatoes, and broth. Set aside.

Season the brisket generously with salt and pepper. In a large, heavy pot, heat the oil over medium-high heat. Add the brisket, fat side down, and cook, turning once, until browned on both sides, about 10 minutes. Transfer to a plate.

Pour off all but 2 Tbsp of the fat from the pot. Add the onions and sauté over medium-high heat until softened, about 3 minutes. Add the garlic and sauté for 1 minute. Stir in the allspice. Sprinkle the flour over the onion mixture, reduce the heat to medium, and cook, stirring frequently, until blended, about 3 minutes. Pour in the reserved broth mixture and stir to combine. Bring to a boil and season with salt and pepper.

Preheat the oven to 300°F (150°C). Return the brisket to the pot, cover, and cook in the oven until the brisket is very tender, 3–4 hours. Skim the fat from the surface of the cooking liquid.

Let the brisket cool in the cooking liquid then transfer the brisket to a cutting board and slice the brisket across the grain. Warm the cooking liquid over medium heat. Arrange the slices on a platter, top with the warm cooking liquid and onions, and serve.

10

SPICY HALIBUT WITH RATATOUILLE

serves 4

½ cup (4 fl oz/120 ml) olive oil

4 yellow onions, chopped

4 cloves garlic, minced

10 plum tomatoes, halved, seeded, and cut into chunks

6 zucchini, cut into chunks

2 eggplants, cut into chunks

3 large red bell peppers, seeded and cut into chunks

½ cup (4 fl oz/120 ml) vegetable broth

1 tsp minced fresh thyme

1 tsp minced fresh oregano

Salt and freshly ground pepper

4 halibut fillets, each about 6 oz (185 g)

¾ tsp hot paprika

Traditional ratatouille is the rustic vegetable stew of France, featuring a bounty of summer vegetables: peppers, eggplants, and tomatoes. Adding halibut fillets makes it an even more robust meal. The fish stays moist thanks to a gentle simmer.

In a large frying pan, warm ¼ cup (2 fl oz/60 ml) of the oil over medium heat. Add the onions and garlic and sauté until tender but not brown, about 10 minutes. Transfer to a slow cooker. Add the tomatoes, zucchini, eggplants, bell peppers, broth, thyme, and oregano. Season with 2 tsp each salt and pepper. Stir to combine. Cover and cook on the high setting for 4 hours or the low setting for 8 hours. Set aside 2 cups (12 oz/375 g) of ratatouille, and store the rest for another use.

Season the halibut fillets on both sides with the paprika and salt and pepper to taste. In a large frying pan, heat the remaining ¼ cup oil over medium-high heat. Add the fillets and cook, turning once, until golden brown, about 4 minutes per side.

Spoon the 2 cups ratatouille around the halibut fillets in the pan. Cover, reduce the heat to medium, and cook, stirring the ratatouille once or twice, until the ratatouille is heated through and the fillets are opaque throughout, about 4 minutes. Serve directly from the pan.

11

ROAST PORK WITH APRICOTS

serves 6

¼ cup (1½ oz/45 g) all-purpose flour

Salt and freshly ground pepper

1 boneless pork loin roast,
about 2½ lb (1.25 kg)

2 Tbsp canola oil

1 yellow onion, thinly sliced

1 clove garlic, minced

1 cup (8 fl oz/250 ml) chicken broth

3 cups (18 oz/560 g) dried apricots

½ cup (4 fl oz/125 ml) fresh orange juice

2 Tbsp chopped fresh thyme

2 Tbsp Dijon mustard

This rich dish tastes as good as it looks. The concentrated essence of dried fruit is a classic complement for almost any pork dish. If you like, use prunes in place of the apricots. If you do, omit the orange juice and add a couple tablespoons of fresh lemon juice.

On a plate, stir together the flour, ½ tsp salt, and ¼ tsp pepper. Turn the pork in the seasoned flour, shaking off any excess. In a large, heavy pot, warm the oil over medium-high heat. Cook the pork, turning frequently, until browned on all sides, about 5 minutes. Transfer to a plate.

Pour off all but 1 Tbsp of the fat in the pot. Add the onion and sauté until softened, 3–5 minutes. Add the garlic and sauté for 1 minute. Add the broth and stir to scrape up any browned bits on the pot bottom.

Return the pork and its juices to the pot. Add the apricots, orange juice, and thyme. Reduce the heat to low, cover, and cook until the pork is very tender and an instant-read thermometer inserted in the center reads 140°F (60°C), about 1½ hours.

Transfer the pork to a cutting board and cover loosely with foil to keep warm. Using a slotted spoon, remove the apricots and set aside. Skim as much fat as possible from the surface of the cooking liquid. Strain the juices, and return to the pot. Bring to a boil over high heat and cook, stirring, until reduced and concentrated, about 10 minutes. Stir the mustard into the sauce and add the apricots. Season to taste with salt and pepper.

Cut the pork loin across the grain into thin slices and arrange on a platter. Drizzle with the sauce and apricots, and serve.

12

SPINACH LASAGNA WITH THREE CHEESES

serves 6–8

Salt

2 lb (1 kg) spinach, tough stems removed

1 lb (500 g) whole-milk ricotta cheese

¼ cup (1½ oz/45 g) minced shallots

2 Tbsp fresh thyme leaves

1 egg

4 Tbsp (2 oz/60 g) unsalted butter

¼ cup (1½ oz/45 g) all-purpose flour

¼ tsp grated nutmeg

⅛ tsp cayenne pepper

3 cups (24 fl oz/750 ml) milk, heated

16 no-boil lasagna noodles

6 oz (185 g) *pecorino romano* cheese, grated

10 oz (315 g) fresh mozzarella cheese, thinly sliced

This white lasagna uses a delicate béchamel as a mild backdrop for the flavorful mix of cheeses. The combination of the soft, sweet ricotta, the firm and mild mozzarella, and the strong, almost meaty pecorino romano gives the dish interesting texture and flavor.

Bring a large saucepan of salted water to a boil over medium-high heat. Cook the spinach until limp and tender but still bright green, about 5 minutes. Drain and rinse with cold water. Squeeze to remove excess moisture and chop coarsely. Squeeze again and set aside.

In a bowl, mix together the ricotta, shallots, thyme, egg, and ½ tsp salt. Set aside.

In the saucepan, melt the butter over medium heat. Add the flour, ½ tsp salt, the nutmeg, and the cayenne and whisk until a smooth paste forms. Slowly whisk in the hot milk, reduce the heat to medium-low, and cook, whisking constantly, until the sauce thickens, about 15 minutes. Remove from the heat.

Preheat the oven to 375°F (190°C). Pour a thin layer of the sauce in the bottom of a 9-by-13-inch (23-by-33-cm) baking dish. Add a single layer of 4 lasagna noodles. Top with one-third of the spinach, a thin layer of the sauce, one-third of the ricotta mixture, one-third of the pecorino, and one-fourth of the mozzarella. Repeat the layers twice, then top with the remaining 4 noodles. Pour the remaining sauce over, slipping a spatula along the edges of the layers to ensure that the sauce runs down into the dish. Top with the remaining mozzarella. Bake until the sauce is bubbling, the top is brown, and the pasta is tender, about 45 minutes. Let stand for 10 minutes before serving.

13

Tuna is one of the leanest types of fish, but the gentle heat from a slow cooker keeps the fish moist and full of flavor. The firm, meaty flesh stands up to bold ingredients, such as this garlic-laden tapenade of briny olives and tangy orange zest.

OLIVE OIL–BRAISED TUNA WITH TAPENADE

serves 4

¼ cup (2 fl oz/60 ml) fish or vegetable broth

5 Tbsp (3 fl oz/80 ml) olive oil, plus more for drizzling

¼ cup (2 fl oz/60 ml) dry white wine or rosé

½ yellow onion, finely chopped

3 bay leaves

Salt and freshly ground pepper

1½ lb (750 g) tuna fillets or steaks, cut into 4 serving pieces

1 cup (5 oz/155 g) pitted mild green olives, such as Picholine or Lucques

1 cup (5 oz/155 g) pitted black olives, such as Niçoise

2 cloves garlic, chopped

1 tsp red or white wine vinegar

Grated zest of 1 orange

4 cups (4 oz/125 g) baby spinach

In a slow cooker, stir together the broth, 4 Tbsp (2 fl oz/60 ml) of the oil, the wine, onion, and bay leaves. Season with ½ tsp salt and several grindings of pepper. Cover and cook on the low setting for 30 minutes to blend the flavors. Add the tuna, re-cover, and cook for 15–20 minutes. The tuna should be firm and opaque throughout.

In a food processor, combine the green and black olives, garlic, vinegar, orange zest, and remaining 1 Tbsp oil. Pulse to form a chunky tapenade.

In a bowl, drizzle the spinach with a little oil, season with salt and pepper, and toss to coat evenly. Transfer the spinach to a platter and spread into an even layer. Top with the tuna. Spoon the tapenade onto the tuna, and serve.

14

Chowder has a long history in America. This thick, often creamy, stew is typically characterized by clams or chunks of meaty fish. This sweet corn version, studded with salty bacon and buttery Yukon gold potatoes, is ideal for the summer months.

CORN & BACON CHOWDER

serves 4–6

3 slices thick-cut bacon, cut into ¼-inch (6-mm) pieces

2 yellow onions, finely chopped

2 celery stalks, finely chopped

1 cup (4 oz/125 g) finely chopped carrots

2 cloves garlic, minced

4 cups (32 fl oz/1 l) chicken broth

1¼ lb (625 g) peeled and finely chopped Yukon gold potatoes

1½ lb (750 g) fresh or frozen corn kernels

Salt and freshly ground pepper

1 cup (8 fl oz/250 ml) half-and-half

½ tsp hot-pepper sauce, such as Tabasco

In a heavy-bottomed saucepan over medium-low heat, cook the bacon until crisp and browned, about 3 minutes. Transfer the bacon to a plate. Add the onions, celery, carrots, and garlic to the bacon fat and sauté until tender, about 12 minutes.

Add the broth and bring to a boil. Add the potatoes, corn, 1 tsp salt, and ¼ tsp freshly ground pepper. Reduce the heat to medium-low, cover, and simmer until the potatoes are tender, 10–12 minutes.

Transfer 3 cups (24 fl oz/750 ml) of the soup to a food processor or blender, let cool slightly, then purée. Return the purée to the pan. Add the half-and-half and hot-pepper sauce and heat through. Adjust the seasonings and serve, sprinkled with the bacon.

JULY

16

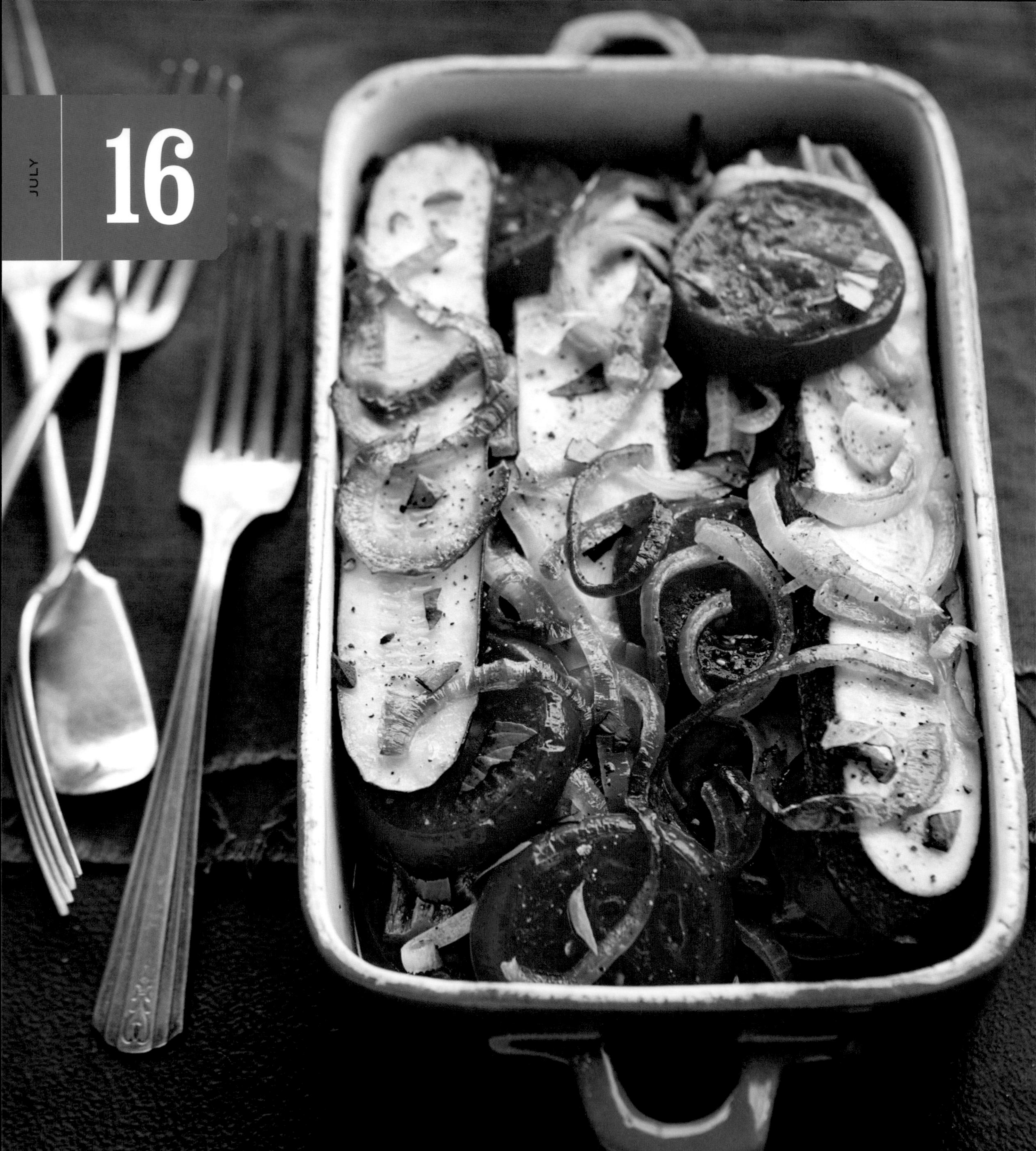

15

SPICY CHICKEN & BASIL STIR-FRY

serves 4

6 Tbsp (3 fl oz/80 ml) chicken broth

2 Tbsp Asian fish sauce

2 tsp firmly packed light brown sugar

1 tsp cornstarch

2 Tbsp canola oil

1 large red bell pepper, seeded and thinly sliced

1 or 2 Thai or jalapeño chiles, cut crosswise into very thin rounds

2 cloves garlic, minced

4 skinless, boneless chicken breast halves, about 1 lb (500 g) total, cut across the grain into thin strips

¾ cup (1 oz/30 g) thinly sliced fresh basil, preferably Thai

3 green onions, white and tender green parts, cut into 3-inch (7.5-cm) lengths

Cooked short-grain or jasmine rice for serving

Sweet peppers juxtapose with chile peppers in this chicken stir-fry. For a more authentic version of this dish, seek out Thai basil, which has smaller, narrower leaves than the common Italian variety, a reddish purple cast, and a more pronounced anise flavor. Look for it in Southeast Asian stores or at farmers' markets, or plant seeds outdoors in pots or beds for easy harvests.

In a small bowl, whisk together the broth, fish sauce, and brown sugar. Add the cornstarch and whisk until the cornstarch and sugar are dissolved. Set aside.

In a wok or large frying pan, heat the oil over high heat. Add the bell pepper and stir-fry for 1 minute. Add the chile and the garlic and stir-fry until fragrant, about 20 seconds. Add the chicken strips and stir-fry until the chicken loses its pink color, about 3 minutes. Stir in the basil and green onions and stir-fry until the green onions are barely wilted, about 1 minute.

Whisk the sauce mixture and pour it into the pan. Cook just until the liquid comes to a boil. Serve the chicken and sauce spooned over the rice.

16

BAKED ZUCCHINI & TOMATO TIAN

serves 4–6

2 Tbsp olive oil, plus more for dish

1 red onion, sliced

Salt and freshly ground pepper

¾ lb (375 g) plum tomatoes, sliced

2 small zucchini, about ¾ lb (375 g), sliced

1 Tbsp minced fresh basil

1 Tbsp minced fresh marjoram

¼ cup (2 fl oz/60 ml) chicken broth or water

A tian is a baked vegetable dish originating from Provence. Here, the technique features zucchini and tomatoes, which are at their best during the summer months. Roasting them in alternate layers is not only pretty, but preserves the delicate texture of the vegetables. It makes a charming meatless meal, but you could also serve this alongside grilled chicken or fish.

Preheat the oven to 350°F (180°C). Oil a shallow 2-qt (2-l) baking dish.

In a frying pan, heat the 2 Tbsp oil over medium heat. Add the onion and sauté until soft, about 10 minutes. Transfer the onion to the prepared dish and spread evenly over the bottom. Season with salt and pepper.

Arrange the tomato and zucchini slices over the onion in alternate rows. Sprinkle with the basil and marjoram and season with salt and pepper. Pour the broth evenly over the top.

Cover with foil and bake until the vegetables are bubbling and tender, about 40 minutes. Remove from the oven and serve.

21

STIR-FRIED TOFU WITH GINGER & LEMONGRASS

serves 4–6

2 lemongrass stalks, center white part only, smashed and thinly sliced

1 serrano chile, seeded and minced

2 Tbsp light soy sauce

1 Tbsp Asian fish sauce (optional)

1 Tbsp fresh lime juice

1 tsp chile-garlic sauce, such as Sriracha

1 Tbsp sugar

1 tsp ground turmeric

6 Tbsp (3 fl oz/80 ml) canola oil

14 oz (440 g) firm tofu, drained and cut into 1-inch (2.5-cm) cubes

4 large shallots, thinly sliced

2 Tbsp peeled and grated fresh ginger

3 cloves garlic, minced

1 Tbsp chopped unsalted dry-roasted peanuts

¼ cup (⅓ oz/10 g) thinly sliced fresh basil, preferably Thai

This aromatic tofu dish displays the signature flavors of Vietnamese cooking: turmeric, lemongrass, shallots, and ginger, along with a garnish of Thai basil and peanuts. Stir-frying the tofu in a nonstick pan helps the cubes hold their shape. Cubes of chicken breast can be substituted for the tofu and should be marinated for at least 3 hours before searing.

In a large, nonreactive bowl, whisk together the lemongrass, chile, soy sauce, fish sauce, if using, lime juice, chile-garlic sauce, sugar, turmeric, and 2 Tbsp of the oil. Add the tofu and toss gently to mix well. Let stand for at least 30 minutes or up to 2 hours.

In a large frying pan, heat 2 Tbsp of the oil over medium-high heat. When the oil is hot, add the shallots, ginger, and garlic and stir-fry until fragrant and lightly browned, about 2 minutes. Stir in ¼ cup (2 fl oz/60 ml) water, reduce the heat to medium-low, and simmer until the liquid has evaporated, 1–2 minutes. Transfer the mixture to a bowl.

Drain the tofu in a colander set over a bowl, reserving the marinade. In the same pan, heat the remaining 2 Tbsp oil over medium-high heat. Add the tofu in a single layer and stir-fry until golden brown and crisp around the edges, 5–8 minutes. Reduce the heat to medium-low, add the shallot mixture and the reserved marinade, and stir gently to mix well. Simmer until the sauce thickens, about 1 minute. Transfer the stir-fry to a large serving bowl, garnish with the peanuts and basil, and serve.

22

SUMMER COQ AU VIN

serves 6–8

3 Tbsp all-purpose flour

Salt and ground white pepper

4 lb (2 kg) assorted chicken pieces, skin on and bone in

3 Tbsp olive oil

4 shallots, minced

2 cups (16 fl oz/500 ml) dry white wine

1 cup (8 fl oz/250 ml) chicken broth

3 sprigs fresh flat-leaf parsley

2 sprigs fresh thyme

½ lb (250 g) summer squash, such as yellow crookneck or zucchini, cut into bite-sized pieces

3 carrots, cut into bite-sized pieces

¼ lb (125 g) frozen pearl onions, or 1 yellow onion, chopped

¼ lb (125 g) sugar snap peas, trimmed (optional)

Using white wine instead of the usual red transforms this slowly simmered stew into a lighter, fresher-tasting dish. If you like, garnish each serving with croutons made by sautéing cubes of crustless, good-quality white bread in a little olive oil until golden. Serve the dish with the same white wine you used to cook it.

On a plate, stir together the flour, 1 tsp salt, and ½ tsp white pepper. Turn the chicken pieces in the seasoned flour, shaking off any excess. In a large, heavy pot, warm the oil over medium-high heat. Working in batches, sear the chicken, turning once, until browned, about 10 minutes. Transfer to a plate.

Add the shallots to the pot and cook over medium-high heat for about 30 seconds. Add the wine and stir to scrape up any browned bits on the pot bottom. Pour in the broth and bring to a boil.

Add the chicken to the pot, arranging the dark meat on the bottom and the breasts on top. Tuck the parsley and thyme sprigs among the chicken pieces. Reduce the heat to low, cover, and cook until the chicken is tender and opaque throughout, about 40 minutes. Uncover and add the squash, carrots, onions, and sugar snap peas (if using), pushing them into the cooking liquid around the chicken. Cover and cook until the vegetables are cooked through, about 20 minutes. Serve directly from the pot.

26

BEEF & BASIL STIR-FRY WITH SUMMER VEGETABLES

serves 4

Thai basil, with its beautiful purple stems, adds an incredible flavor and aroma to this dish. But if you can't find Thai basil, you can substitute sweet basil. This stir-fry is wonderful on its own or served over steamed rice or fresh Asian noodles.

¼ cup (2 fl oz/60 ml) soy sauce

3 Tbsp sherry

1 Tbsp honey

1 tsp cornstarch

2 Tbsp canola oil

1 lb (500 g) flank steak, thinly sliced, then cut into 1-inch (2.5-cm) pieces

Salt and freshly ground pepper

2 cloves garlic, minced

1-inch (2.5-cm) piece peeled fresh ginger, grated

1 yellow squash, cut into ½-inch (12-mm) matchsticks

2 carrots, cut into ½-inch (12-mm) matchsticks

4 oz (125 g) sugar snap peas, trimmed and halved

¼ cup (¼ oz/7 g) small fresh basil leaves, preferably Thai

In a small bowl, stir together the soy sauce, sherry, honey, and cornstarch.

In a wok or large frying pan, heat 1 Tbsp of the oil over high heat. Season the steak pieces with salt and pepper. Add to the pan and, tossing to sear on all sides, cook until browned but still rare inside, about 3 minutes. Transfer to a plate. Pour off any fat from the pan.

Return the pan to high heat and warm the remaining 1 Tbsp oil. Add the garlic and ginger and stir-fry until fragrant, about 1 minute, taking care not to let the garlic and ginger brown. Add the squash, carrots, and sugar snap peas and stir-fry for 4 minutes. Add the steak and the soy sauce mixture and stir to combine. Cook, stirring often, until the sauce thickens, about 3 minutes. Top with the basil leaves and serve.

27

SARDINIAN COUSCOUS WITH CLAMS & TOMATOES

serves 4–6

Sardinian couscous, or fregola, is a small, round pasta resembling Israeli couscous. The dried spheres have been toasted, which gives them a firm texture and a savory, nutty flavor when they are cooked. Sardinia is known for its seafood, inspiring this pairing with clams. Serve the pasta in shallow bowls with crusty bread to soak up the broth.

¼ cup (2 fl oz/60 ml) olive oil

¼ cup (1 oz/30 g) minced shallots

2 Tbsp minced garlic

¼–½ tsp red pepper flakes

2 lb (1 kg) tomatoes, peeled, seeded, and coarsely chopped, or 2 cups (12 oz/375 g) canned crushed tomatoes

½ cup (4 fl oz/125 ml) dry white wine

1¼ cups (10 fl oz/310 ml) bottled clam juice

Salt and freshly ground pepper

2 lb (1 kg) small clams, such as Manila, scrubbed

¾ lb (375 g) fregola or Israeli couscous (about 1½ cups)

⅓ cup (½ oz/15 g) chopped fresh flat-leaf parsley

In a large frying pan, heat the oil over medium-high heat. Add the shallots, garlic, and red pepper flakes and sauté until the shallots are soft and translucent, 3–5 minutes. Add the tomatoes and cook, stirring occasionally, until they begin to break down, about 2 minutes. Add the wine, clam juice, and ¼ tsp salt and simmer for 5 minutes to blend the flavors. Season with pepper and adjust the seasoning with salt. Add the clams, discarding any that do not close to the touch. Cover and cook over medium-high heat until the clams open, 5–7 minutes.

Meanwhile, bring a large pot of salted water to a boil. Add the fregola, stir well, and cook, stirring occasionally, until al dente, or according to the package directions. Drain and then pour into a large serving bowl.

Pour the clams and their sauce over the fregola, discarding any unopened clams. Sprinkle with the parsley and serve.

Summer days call for easy-to-prepare dishes that don't distract from vacation fun and highlight the season's crops—eggplant, zucchini, summer squash, beans, peppers, and herbs galore. Make a meal of summer vegetables simply roasted or sautéed, or pan-roast seafood or meat with garden goodies in a provençal-style sauce or ratatouille. Fit-for-a-crowd favorites include spanakopita, eggplant jambalaya, and vegetable curries. Tomatoes are at their juicy peak and delicious any which way, from herbed strata to Italian tomato-bread soup.

1
CUBAN-STYLE PAELLA
page 176

2
BEEF, ONION & TOMATO GRATIN
page 178

3
CRAB FRIED RICE
page 178

8
VEGETABLE STIR-FRY WITH TOFU
page 182

9
CHICKEN STUFFED WITH SPINACH & CHEESE
page 182

10
PAN-ROASTED PORK MEDALLIONS WITH SUMMER VEGETABLES
page 184

15
SPICY STEAMED CLAMS
page 187

16
CHICKEN LASAGNA WITH THREE CHEESES
page 188

17
VIETNAMESE EGGPLANT CURRY
page 188

22
HERBED TOMATO STRATA
page 192

23
SPANISH SEAFOOD NOODLES
page 192

24
BRAISED BEEF TIPS WITH CRANBERRY BEANS, CHERRY TOMATOES & BASIL
page 193

29
TUNA WITH HERBED WHITE BEANS
page 196

30
BAKED RIGATONI WITH CAULIFLOWER, PANCETTA & CARAMELIZED ONIONS
page 197

31
ITALIAN TOMATO & BREAD SOUP
page 197

4

**BRAISED CHICKEN WITH
TOMATOES & OLIVES**
page 179

5

EGGPLANT JAMBALAYA
page 179

6

**PULLED PORK WITH SPICY
PEACH-MUSTARD SAUCE**
page 181

7

RATATOUILLE
page 181

11

CAJUN SHRIMP BOIL
page 184

12

STIR-FRIED LEMONGRASS CHICKEN
page 185

13

PAD THAI
page 185

14

**POLENTA WITH FONTINA
& ROASTED VEGETABLES**
page 187

18

COD WITH TOMATOES & CHICKPEAS
page 189

19

VEAL SALTIMBOCCA
page 189

20

**PORK MEDALLIONS WITH
ROASTED NECTARINES**
page 190

21

HALIBUT PROVENÇAL
page 190

25

**CHICKEN, EGGPLANT &
PORTOBELLO STIR-FRY**
page 193

26

SPANAKOPITA
page 195

27

LEMONGRASS PORK STIR-FRY
page 195

28

GARLICKY CHICKEN THIGHS
page 196

august

CUBAN-STYLE PAELLA

serves 4–6

½ cup (4 fl oz/125 ml) dry white wine

1 tsp saffron threads

3 Tbsp olive oil

8 chicken wing drumettes

Salt

1 white onion, chopped

½ red bell pepper, seeded and chopped

1 tsp dried oregano

1 tsp ground cumin

2 plum tomatoes, chopped

½ tsp red pepper flakes

½ tsp sweet Spanish paprika

1 bay leaf

1½ cups (10½ oz/330 g) long-grain white rice

2½ cups (20 fl oz/625 ml) chicken broth

¾ cup (3 oz/90 g) thinly sliced cured Spanish-style chorizo

4 large cloves garlic, minced

8 medium shrimp, peeled and deveined, with tails intact

1 large lobster tail, about 1 lb (500 g), shell removed, cut into 1-inch (2.5-cm) chunks

4 large sea scallops, tough muscles removed, halved crosswise

8 jarred sliced red pimiento, drained and chopped

1 lemon, cut into 8 wedges

The trick to making the perfect paella is using the right type of rice and the correct pan. Use a good-quality long-grain white rice or imported Spanish short-grain rice. The pan should be wide and shallow, with sloping sides. If you don't have a specialty paella pan, a large, shallow, ovenproof frying pan will do.

In a small saucepan, gently warm the wine (do not let it boil). Add the saffron and remove from the heat. Let steep for 1 hour.

Position a rack in the lower third of the oven and preheat to 350°F (180°C). In a large, ovenproof pan, warm 1 Tbsp of the oil over medium-high heat. Add the chicken and sear, turning as needed, until golden brown on all sides, about 10 minutes. Sprinkle with ¼ tsp salt and transfer to a plate. Reduce the heat to medium.

Add the onion and bell pepper to the pan and cook, stirring frequently, until softened, about 2 minutes. Crumble the oregano over the onion mixture, then stir in the cumin, tomatoes, red pepper flakes, paprika, and bay leaf. Sauté until the spices are fragrant and most of the liquid has evaporated, about 5 minutes. Transfer the mixture to a bowl. ⇥

Add 1 Tbsp of the oil to the pan and set over medium heat. Add the rice and sauté until golden, 3–5 minutes. Stir in 1 cup (8 oz/250 g) of the onion mixture and sauté for 30 seconds. Add the reserved wine and the broth and stir to mix well. Arrange the chicken on top of the rice. Bake, uncovered, for 15 minutes.

Remove the paella from the oven. In a large frying pan, warm the remaining 1 Tbsp oil over medium-high heat. Add the chorizo and garlic and sauté until the oil turns reddish. Add the shrimp, lobster, and scallops and cook, stirring, until the seafood is almost opaque throughout, 3–4 minutes. Stir in the remaining onion mixture.

Remove the chicken from the paella and set aside on a plate. Stir the seafood mixture gently into the rice. Discard the bay leaf. Arrange the chicken on top, fitting it between the lobster pieces. Sprinkle the pimiento over all.

Return the paella to the oven and bake until all the liquid has been absorbed, about 5 minutes. Remove from the oven and cover with a clean kitchen towel. Let stand at room temperature for at least 10 minutes or up to 30 minutes before serving. Serve with the lemon wedges.

2

BEEF, ONION & TOMATO GRATIN

serves 2–3

1 Tbsp unsalted butter, plus 1 Tbsp melted

1 Tbsp olive oil, plus more for greasing

1 large yellow onion, coarsely chopped

1 can (14½ oz/455 g) whole peeled tomatoes, drained, seeded and coarsely chopped

2 tsp all-purpose flour

1 cup (8 fl oz/250 ml) beef broth

½ lb (250 g) roasted beef or grilled steak, cut into ½-inch (12-mm) chunks

1 large clove garlic, minced

1 Tbsp minced fresh flat-leaf parsley

Pinch of grated nutmeg

Salt and freshly ground pepper

¾ cup (1½ oz/45 g) fresh bread crumbs

2 Tbsp grated pecorino cheese

This is the perfect recipe for those times when you have leftover meat from a roast, for instance, the days after a big Sunday dinner. The leftovers are transformed into a sophisticated dish with complex flavors. While the gratin is browning in the broiler, you can make a simple spinach salad.

In a large ovenproof frying pan, warm the 1 Tbsp butter with the oil over medium-low heat. Add the onion and cook, stirring occasionally, until tender, about 10 minutes. Add the tomatoes and stir for 1 minute. Add the flour, stir to form a paste, and cook, stirring, for about 2 minutes. Stir in the broth, raise the heat to medium-high, and bring just to a simmer. Add the beef, garlic, parsley, and nutmeg. Season with ½ tsp salt and several grindings of pepper. Cook, stirring occasionally, until the sauce has thickened, about 5 minutes.

Preheat the broiler to high. In a small bowl, toss together the bread crumbs, pecorino, and the 1 Tbsp melted butter until the crumbs are evenly moistened. Scatter evenly over the beef mixture. Broil until the top is crisp and brown, about 4 minutes. Let stand, uncovered, for about 5 minutes before serving.

3

CRAB FRIED RICE

serves 4

¼ cup (2 fl oz/60 ml) soy sauce

1½ Tbsp rice vinegar

1 tsp toasted sesame oil

Ground white pepper

2 Tbsp corn or peanut oil

1 Tbsp peeled and grated fresh ginger

3 cloves garlic, minced

3 green onions, white and tender green parts, thinly sliced

4 cups (1¼ lb/625 g) cooked white rice, chilled

2 eggs, lightly beaten

½ lb (250 g) fresh lump crabmeat, picked over for shell fragments

1 cup (5 oz/155 g) thawed frozen baby peas

Sweet lump crab-meat and petite peas bring a more refined profile to the takeout classic. Fried rice comes together in a snap when you already have leftover rice in the refrigerator. To save time, steam a double batch of rice one night, reserving half for another meal.

In a small bowl, combine the soy sauce, vinegar, sesame oil, and a pinch of white pepper and stir to combine.

In a wok or large frying pan, heat the corn oil over high heat. Add the ginger, garlic, and green onions and stir-fry until fragrant, about 5 seconds. Add the rice and continue to stir-fry until the rice is hot, about 5 minutes. Create a small well in the middle of the rice, exposing the bottom of the pan. Add the eggs to the well and immediately stir-fry to incorporate them into the rice. Once the eggs are cooked through, add the crabmeat, peas, and soy sauce mixture and stir-fry until well combined and heated through, 2–3 minutes. Transfer to a platter and serve.

4

BRAISED CHICKEN WITH TOMATOES & OLIVES

serves 6–8

6 skin-on, bone-in chicken legs, about 3 lb (1.5 kg) total, separated into drumsticks and thighs

Salt and freshly ground pepper

2 cups (16 fl oz/500 ml) hearty red wine

2 shallots, minced

1 clove garlic, minced

6 peppercorns

3 or 4 sprigs fresh thyme

3 tomatoes, seeded and chopped

1 Tbsp tomato paste

1 Tbsp unsalted butter, cut into small pieces

1 Tbsp all-purpose flour

1 cup (5 oz/155 g) brined black or green olives, pitted and coarsely chopped

Hearty braised chicken thighs and drumsticks lighten up with a dose of fresh summer tomatoes. A robust red wine, one that can stand up to the strong, full flavors of tomatoes and briny black olives, is best for this dish.

Season the chicken all over with salt and pepper and put it in a large, heavy pot.

In a small saucepan, combine the wine, shallots, garlic, peppercorns, and thyme. Bring to a boil over high heat and cook, stirring frequently, until reduced to about ½ cup (4 fl oz/125 ml), about 20 minutes. Add to the chicken along with the chopped tomatoes. Cover and cook the chicken over medium heat, turning frequently, until very tender and opaque throughout, about 40 minutes.

Transfer the chicken to a plate. Strain the cooking juices through a fine-mesh sieve placed over a small bowl. You should have about 1 cup (8 fl oz/250 ml). Whisk in the tomato paste.

Return the juices to the pot and bring to a boil over medium-high heat. In a small bowl, combine the butter and flour. Using your fingers or a fork, mix until a crumbly paste forms. Add the butter mixture to the pan and cook, whisking constantly, until a thick sauce forms, 7–10 minutes. Season with salt and pepper, and stir in the olives. Add the chicken, turn to coat with the sauce, and cook over medium-low heat until warmed through, about 5 minutes.

Arrange the chicken on a platter, spoon the sauce over the top, and serve.

5

EGGPLANT JAMBALAYA

serves 6

¼ cup (2 fl oz/60 ml) olive oil

1 yellow onion, finely chopped

1 red or yellow bell pepper, seeded and finely chopped

2 celery ribs, finely chopped

½ lb (250 g) smoked ham, cut into ½-inch (12-mm) dice (optional)

3 cloves garlic

2 bay leaves

1½ tsp minced fresh oregano

1 tsp minced fresh thyme

¼ tsp cayenne pepper

¾ cup (2 oz/60 g) chopped green onions, white and tender green parts

1 small eggplant, about ½ lb (250 g), peeled and cut into ½-inch (12-mm) dice

1 can (14½ oz/455 g) diced tomatoes, with juice

1½ cups (12 fl oz/375 ml) chicken or vegetable broth

1 cup (7 oz/220 g) long-grain rice

Salt and freshly ground black pepper

A signature dish of Louisiana, jambalaya is usually rich and meaty. In New Orleans and along the coastal bayous, the seasoned rice might contain shrimp and tomatoes. On the prairies of Cajun country, it's more likely to contain chicken and sausage. This nontraditional recipe features eggplant instead, and could easily be made vegetarian if you leave out the ham.

In a large, heavy pot, heat the oil over medium heat. Add the yellow onion, bell pepper, celery, and ham (if using), and sauté until the vegetables are lightly browned and very tender, 10–15 minutes. Add the garlic, bay leaves, oregano, thyme, and cayenne and cook, stirring, just until the garlic releases its fragrance, about 2 minutes.

Add ½ cup (1½ oz/45 g) of the green onions along with the eggplant, tomatoes, broth, and rice. Stir well and season with salt and black pepper. Raise the heat to medium-high, bring to a boil, and then immediately reduce the heat to low. Stir well, scraping the pan bottom to be sure nothing sticks. Cover tightly and cook, without stirring, for 20 minutes. Check to see if the liquid is absorbed and the rice is tender. If not, re-cover and cook for a few minutes longer.

Remove the pan from the heat and let stand, covered, for 5 minutes. Discard the bay leaves and stir lightly with a fork to fluff the rice. Garnish with the remaining green onions and serve.

6

PULLED PORK WITH SPICY PEACH-MUSTARD SAUCE

serves 12

This pulled pork, doused in a sweet-and-sour soaking sauce with a generous helping of peach jam, is perfect picnic fare. Serve it on a platter alongside soft sandwich rolls, sliced dill pickles, and coleslaw, allowing diners to assemble their own sandwiches.

Oil for pan

1 bone-in pork shoulder, about 6 lb (3 kg)

Salt and freshly ground pepper

1 Tbsp mustard seeds

2 cups (16 fl oz/500 ml) cider vinegar

4 yellow onions, sliced, plus 3 onions, chopped

½ cup (4 oz/125 g) unsalted butter

3 cloves garlic, minced

2 cups (16 fl oz/500 ml) canned crushed tomatoes

2 Tbsp tomato paste

1 cup (10 oz/315 g) peach jam

½ cup (4 oz/125 g) Dijon mustard

½ cup (4 fl oz/125 ml) aged Kentucky bourbon

½ cup (6 oz/185 g) honey

¼ cup (2 oz/60 g) firmly packed dark brown sugar

1 Tbsp hot-pepper sauce

12 soft sandwich rolls

Preheat the oven to 300°F (150°C). Lightly oil a large roasting pan.

Put the pork shoulder in the prepared pan and rub with 1 Tbsp salt, 1 Tbsp pepper, and the mustard seeds. Pour 1 cup (8 fl oz/250 ml) of the vinegar and 1 cup (8 fl oz/250 ml) water over and around the pork. Scatter the sliced onions over and around the meat. Cover with foil and roast for 4 hours.

Meanwhile, in a saucepan, melt the butter over medium heat. Add the chopped onions and the garlic and cook, stirring occasionally, until the onions are soft and beginning to brown, about 10 minutes. Add the tomatoes, tomato paste, jam, mustard, bourbon, honey, brown sugar, remaining 1 cup vinegar, and hot-pepper sauce and stir to mix well. Season with salt and pepper. Bring to a boil, reduce the heat to very low, and simmer, uncovered, stirring occasionally, until the sauce is dark and thick, about 2 hours. Let cool for 15 minutes.

Remove the foil and continue to roast until an instant-read thermometer inserted into the thickest part of the pork away from the bone registers 180°F (82°C) and the juices ⟫

run clear, about 1 hour. Remove the pork from the pan and let stand for 1 hour. Using 2 forks, shred the pork, discarding any fat. Put the pork in a bowl. Using a slotted spoon, lift the roasted onions from the pan and add to the pork. Mix well to combine.

Mix half of the sauce with the shredded pork. Mound the pork on a large platter and place the rolls on a plate. Serve, passing the remaining sauce at the table.

7

RATATOUILLE

serves 10

As soon as tomatoes, zucchini, eggplants, and peppers are ripe in summer, ratatouille is served in homes and restaurants throughout Provence. Some versions call for cooking each vegetable separately, then combining them to finish cooking. However, to save time, home cooks have adapted the dish by cooking all of the vegetables together, as in this recipe.

1 Tbsp olive oil

2 small yellow or white onions, chopped

2 eggplants, cut into 1-inch (2.5-cm) cubes

4 cloves garlic, minced

2 zucchini, cut into 1-inch (2.5-cm) cubes

2 large red, green, or yellow bell peppers, seeded and cut into 1-inch (2.5-cm) pieces

8–10 large tomatoes, 6–7½ lb (3–3.75 kg) total, peeled, seeded, and coarsely chopped

3 sprigs fresh thyme

1 sprig fresh rosemary

1 bay leaf

Salt and freshly ground pepper

¼ cup (⅓ oz/10 g) minced fresh basil

In a large, heavy saucepan, warm the oil over medium heat. Reduce the heat to medium-low, add the onions, and sauté until slightly softened, about 2 minutes. Add the eggplant and garlic and cook, stirring frequently, until the eggplant is slightly softened, 3–4 minutes. Add the zucchini and bell peppers and sauté for 4–5 minutes. Add the tomatoes, thyme, rosemary, and bay leaf. Season with 1 tsp each salt and pepper. Cook, stirring and turning, for 2–3 minutes.

Cover, reduce the heat to low, and cook, stirring occasionally, until the vegetables are soft and have somewhat blended together, about 40 minutes. Stir in the basil, remove from the heat, and serve.

8

Hotter-than-hot days can quell appetites. Keep it light with tofu and fresh vegetables, seasoned with a slew of Asian pantry staples. Serve with a chilled glass of ginger- or jasmine-infused lemonade.

VEGETABLE STIR-FRY WITH TOFU

serves 4

¾ lb (375 g) firm tofu, cut into 1-inch (2.5-cm) cubes

Cornstarch for dusting

3 Tbsp canola oil

2–4 cloves garlic, minced

1 Tbsp peeled and grated fresh ginger

1 carrot, sliced on the diagonal

1 red bell pepper, seeded and chopped

1 yellow onion, cut lengthwise into slices

1 head napa cabbage, about 1½ lb (750 g), cored and coarsely chopped

Salt

¼–½ tsp Chinese five-spice powder

3–4 Tbsp chicken broth

1 tsp sugar

3–4 Tbsp hoisin sauce

Few dashes of soy sauce

Few dashes of chile oil

Few dashes of rice vinegar

½ tsp toasted sesame oil

Cooked white rice for serving

Blot the tofu cubes dry with paper towels, dust with the cornstarch, and blot again. In a wok or large frying pan, heat 1 Tbsp of the canola oil over medium-high heat. Add the tofu and cook until lightly browned on the first side, 2½–4 minutes. Turn the tofu cubes, being careful not to break them up, and cook until browned on the opposite side, 2½–4 minutes. Transfer to a plate.

Wipe the pan clean, heat over high heat, and add 1 Tbsp of the oil. Add the garlic, ginger, carrot, and bell pepper and stir-fry for 1 minute. Add to the tofu.

Return the pan to high heat and warm the remaining 1 Tbsp oil. Add the onion and stir-fry for 1 minute. Add the cabbage and a pinch of salt and stir and toss to coat with the oil. Mix in the five-spice powder and 3 Tbsp broth and stir-fry until the cabbage has begun to soften, 5–6 minutes. Add the sugar, hoisin sauce, soy sauce, and chile oil and stir. Add another Tbsp of broth if the mixture seems dry. Cover and cook over high heat until the cabbage is almost tender-crisp, about 5 minutes. »→

Uncover and add the vegetables and tofu. Stir to blend and heat through, about 3 minutes. The liquid should be almost fully evaporated. Season with the vinegar.

Mound the vegetables on a platter and sprinkle with the sesame oil. Serve with the rice.

9

Butterflied chicken breasts turn into a simple yet elegant meal when stuffed with a filling of tangy goat cheese and earthy spinach. Paper-thin strips of prosciutto help to package it all together and crisp up into a deliciously salty exterior. These bundles are delicious on their own or alongside a simple orzo and cherry tomato salad.

CHICKEN STUFFED WITH SPINACH & CHEESE

serves 4

Oil for baking dish

2 cups (2 oz/60 g) baby spinach, chopped

¼ lb (125 g) fresh goat cheese, crumbled

½ cup (2 oz/60 g) grated Parmesan cheese

Salt and freshly ground pepper

4 skinless, boneless chicken breast halves, about 1½ lb (750 g) total

4 large, thin slices prosciutto or cooked ham

Preheat the oven to 400°F (200°C). Oil a shallow baking dish just large enough to hold the chicken breasts in a single layer. In a bowl, mix together the spinach, goat cheese, and Parmesan. Season with salt and pepper.

Place each chicken breast on a work surface. Holding a sharp knife parallel to the work surface, cut each breast in half lengthwise almost all the way through. Spread one-fourth of the spinach-cheese mixture in the center of each breast. Fold the chicken breast closed and season with salt and pepper. Wrap 1 prosciutto slice tightly around each chicken breast and place in the prepared dish.

Bake until the prosciutto is crisp and the chicken is opaque throughout, about 20 minutes. Serve directly from the dish.

14

POLENTA WITH FONTINA & ROASTED VEGETABLES

serves 6

Bake a pan of polenta until it gets crispy at the edges, and then top it with anything your heart desires. Here, roasted summer vegetables pair with fontina, a mild melting cheese. But this is a fantastic recipe all year long: try it in the fall or winter with butternut squash, mushrooms, and Gorgonzola. Serve this dish with a salad of field greens.

3 Tbsp olive oil, plus more for pans

1 small eggplant, cut into ¾-inch (2-cm) pieces

2 small zucchini, cut into ¾-inch (2-cm) pieces

2 small yellow summer squash, cut into ¾-inch (2-cm) pieces

½ red onion, cut into ¾-inch (2-cm) pieces

1 orange bell pepper, seeded and cut into ¾-inch (2-cm) pieces

Salt and freshly ground pepper

1 cup (7 oz/220 g) stone-ground polenta

2 Tbsp unsalted butter

1 cup (4 oz/125 g) grated Parmesan cheese

2 cups (8 oz/250 g) shredded fontina cheese

Preheat the oven to 450°F (230°C). Oil a rimmed baking sheet and an 8-inch (20-cm) baking dish.

In a large bowl, combine the eggplant, zucchini, summer squash, red onion, and bell pepper. Drizzle with the 3 Tbsp oil, season with salt and pepper, and toss to combine. Arrange in a single layer on the prepared baking sheet. Roast, tossing once, until the vegetables are caramelized, 20–25 minutes. Set aside. Reduce the oven temperature to 350°F (180°C).

Meanwhile, in a heavy saucepan, bring 4 cups (32 fl oz/1 l) salted water to a boil over medium heat. Stirring constantly, very slowly add the polenta. Cook, stirring constantly, until the polenta begins to thicken, about 5 minutes. Reduce the heat to low and continue to cook the polenta, stirring frequently, until the polenta is soft, about 25 minutes. Add the butter, Parmesan, and fontina and stir until the cheeses melt. Pour the polenta into the prepared baking dish and smooth the top.

Bake just until the polenta begins to set, about 15 minutes. Remove from the oven and top evenly with the roasted vegetables. Continue to bake until the vegetables are heated through, about 15 minutes. Serve the polenta directly from the dish.

15

SPICY STEAMED CLAMS

serves 4

A heaping bowlful of clams is a summer treat, whether you make it to the shore or not. Lots of wine, lots of garlic, and a pinch of red pepper flakes pack in the flavor. Don't forget the crusty bread for dipping.

4 Tbsp (2 oz/60 g) unsalted butter

¼ cup (2 fl oz/60 ml) olive oil

1 yellow onion, halved and thinly sliced

½ tsp red pepper flakes

Salt

2 cloves garlic, minced

1 can (14½ oz/455 g) whole peeled tomatoes, with juice

1 cup (8 fl oz/250 ml) dry white wine

2–3 lb (1–1.5 kg) small clams, such as littleneck or Manila, scrubbed and soaked

½ cup (¾ oz/20 g) thinly sliced fresh basil

In a large saucepan, melt the butter with the oil over medium-high heat. Add the onion and red pepper flakes, season with salt, and sauté until the onion is translucent, about 10 minutes. Add the garlic and sauté until fragrant, about 30 seconds. Add the tomatoes with their juices and cook, stirring, to blend the flavors, about 2 minutes.

Raise the heat to high and stir in the wine. Add the clams, discarding any that do not close to the touch. Cover and cook, shaking the pan occasionally, until the clams open, 4–5 minutes.

Discard any empty shells or unopened clams. Spoon the clams into a large shallow serving bowl, top with the cooking liquid, sprinkle with the basil, and serve.

20

Lean pork tenderloin cooks quickly when sliced across the grain into neat rounds. Match the inherent sweetness of the meat with juicy, late-summer nectarines, which caramelize in the heat of the pan. This recipe would also be delicious with peaches or in autumn with fresh figs.

PORK MEDALLIONS WITH ROASTED NECTARINES

serves 4

1 pork tenderloin, about 1½ lb (750 g), cut crosswise into 4–6 medallions

Salt and freshly ground pepper

1 Tbsp olive oil

1 cup (8 fl oz/250 ml) hard apple cider

1 sprig fresh rosemary

2 tsp grainy mustard

2 nectarines or peaches, halved, pitted, and cut into wedges, or 6 figs, halved lengthwise

1 Tbsp unsalted butter

Preheat the oven to 400°F (200°C).

Season the pork with salt and pepper. In an ovenproof frying pan, heat the oil over medium-high heat. Add the pork medallions and cook, turning once, until browned, 4–5 minutes. Transfer to a plate.

Add the cider, rosemary, and mustard to the pan, bring to a boil, and stir to scrape up any browned bits on the pan bottom. Cook until the liquid is reduced by half, 3–4 minutes. Return the pork to the pan, place in the oven, and cook for about 6 minutes. Remove from the oven, turn the pork, and add the sliced nectarines. Return to the oven and cook until the pork is tender and registers 145°F (63°C) on an instant-read thermometer, 6–8 minutes.

Transfer the pork and nectarines to a platter. Place the pan over medium heat and whisk in the butter to make a sauce. Spoon the sauce over the pork and nectarines and serve.

21

Firm white halibut fillets bake up beautifully with tomatoes and white wine. Sprinkle the whole pan with bread crumbs, garlic, and herbs before popping it into the oven. The crunchy topping adds elegance, but it couldn't be easier.

HALIBUT PROVENÇAL

serves 4

3 Tbsp olive oil, plus more for dish

4 halibut fillets, 6–8 oz (185–250 g) each

Salt and freshly ground pepper

2 Tbsp dry white wine

1 lb (500 g) tomatoes, cut into slices ½ inch (12 mm) thick

1 clove garlic, minced

1 Tbsp chopped fresh tarragon

1 Tbsp chopped fresh flat-leaf parsley

¼ tsp fresh thyme leaves

2–3 Tbsp fine dried bread crumbs

Preheat the oven to 375°F (190°C). Lightly oil a baking dish just big enough to hold the fillets snugly in a single layer.

Place the fillets in the prepared dish. Sprinkle with salt and pepper and drizzle with the wine. Arrange the tomato slices in a single layer over the fish, overlapping them slightly if necessary.

In a small bowl, stir together 2 Tbsp of the oil and the garlic, tarragon, parsley, and thyme. Spoon the herb mixture evenly over the tomatoes, season with salt and pepper, and sprinkle with the bread crumbs. Drizzle with the remaining 1 Tbsp oil.

Transfer to the oven and cook until the bread crumbs are browned and the fish is opaque throughout but still moist in the center, 25–30 minutes. Arrange the fish and tomatoes on a platter and serve.

22

*Bright with garden
herbs and tangy
ripe tomatoes, this
savory strata is
wonderful on its
own, or alongside
crisp roasted chicken.
For a simple yet
stylish summer
lunch, top each
serving with lightly
dressed arugula.*

HERBED TOMATO STRATA

serves 6

Butter for greasing

6 eggs

2 cups (16 fl oz/500 ml) milk

1 cup (8 fl oz/250 ml) heavy cream

2 tbsp grated Parmesan cheese

1 tbsp chopped fresh thyme

2 tsp chopped fresh flat-leaf parsley

1 tsp minced fresh sage

Salt and freshly ground pepper

1 loaf country-style bread, cut into slices
½ inch (12 mm) thick

2 cups (8 oz/250 g) shredded mozzarella
cheese

3 large heirloom tomatoes, chopped

Butter a 9-by-13-inch (23-by-33-cm) baking
dish. In a bowl, whisk together the eggs,
milk, cream, Parmesan, thyme, parsley,
and sage. Season with a pinch each of
salt and pepper.

Arrange half of the bread slices on the
bottom of the prepared dish. Top with half
of the egg mixture, half of the mozzarella
cheese, and half of the chopped tomatoes.
Repeat the layers once. Let the strata stand
for 30 minutes, occasionally pressing on
the ingredients with a spatula to keep the
bread well coated.

Preheat the oven to 350°F (180°C).

Bake the strata until golden brown, puffed,
and set, about 1 hour. Halfway through
the cooking time, remove the strata from the
oven and press on the top layer of bread,
keeping it submerged in the custard. After
removing it from the oven, let the strata rest
for 10 minutes. Cut into squares and serve.

23

*This saffron-tinged
noodle dish is a
special type of paella
from Valencia. It
is made with fideos,
short, thin noodles,
in place of rice, but
angel hair pasta
works well too. This
dish is traditionally
served with aioli.*

SPANISH SEAFOOD NOODLES

serves 4

¼ tsp saffron threads

3 Tbsp olive oil

1 yellow onion, finely chopped

½ cup (2½ oz–75 g) chopped green
bell pepper

1 Tbsp minced garlic

3½–4 cups (28–32 fl oz/875 ml–1 l)
fish broth or chicken broth

1 lb (500 g) fresh tomatoes, grated, or 1 cup
(6 oz/185 g) canned crushed tomatoes

½ cup (4 fl oz/125 ml) dry white wine

1½ tsp Spanish smoked paprika

Salt and freshly ground pepper

12 oz (375 g) angel hair pasta, broken in half

¾ lb (375 g) halibut or other white fish fillets,
cut into 1-inch (2.5-cm) chunks

½ lb (250 g) clams, scrubbed and soaked

½ lb (250 g) shrimp, peeled and deveined

3 Tbsp chopped fresh flat-leaf parsley

In a large, deep frying pan, toast the saffron
threads over medium heat, stirring constantly,
until fragrant and a shade darker, about
1 minute. Pour the threads into a bowl and,
when cool, crumble.

In the frying pan, warm the oil over medium-
high heat. Add the onion, bell pepper, and
garlic and sauté until the vegetables are soft,
3–5 minutes. Add 3½ cups (28 fl oz/875 ml)
of the broth and the tomatoes, wine, paprika,
and saffron. Stir to combine and season with
salt and pepper. Stir in the pasta.

Bring to a boil over medium-high heat and
cook, uncovered, for 8 minutes. Adjust the
heat to maintain a gentle simmer and add
½ cup (4 fl oz/125 ml) broth if the mixture
looks dry. Add the halibut and the clams,
discarding any clams that do not close to
the touch. Push the fish down into the liquid.
Cover and cook for 5 minutes. Add the shrimp,
cover, and cook until the clams have opened
(discard any unopened ones), the shrimp
are pink, and most of the liquid is absorbed,
3–5 minutes longer.

Remove from the heat and let stand, covered,
for 10 minutes. Sprinkle with the parsley
and serve directly from the pan.

24

BRAISED BEEF TIPS WITH CRANBERRY BEANS, CHERRY TOMATOES & BASIL

serves 4

Pick up fresh shelling beans at the summer farmers' market. Also called borlotti beans, cranberry beans have a nutty flavor and are beautiful with their red and white spots. Ask your butcher for sirloin tips for slow cooking, as opposed to the more expensive filet mignon tips, which are best cooked quickly and eaten rare. Here, the beef becomes so tender that you can cut it with a fork.

2 Tbsp olive oil

1½ lb (750 g) beef sirloin tips, cut into 1½-inch (4-cm) chunks

Salt and freshly ground pepper

1 large yellow onion, chopped

3 carrots, chopped

2 celery ribs, chopped

4 cloves garlic, minced

1½ cups (12 fl oz/375 ml) red wine

4 cups (32 fl oz/1 l) beef broth

2 Tbsp tomato paste

2 lb (1 kg) fresh cranberry beans, shelled

1 cup (6 oz/185 g) cherry tomatoes

⅓ cup (½ oz/15 g) chopped fresh basil

Preheat the oven to 350°F (180°C).

In a large, heavy pot, heat the oil over medium-high heat. Season the beef with salt and pepper. Add to the pot and sear, turning as needed, until browned on all sides, 6–8 minutes. Transfer to a bowl.

Add the onion, carrots, celery, and garlic to the pot and sauté over medium-high heat until the vegetables are soft, about 8 minutes. Add the wine and stir to scrape up any browned bits on the pot bottom. Cook until the wine is reduced by half, 8–10 minutes. Add the broth and tomato paste and bring to a boil. Add the beef and any juices, cover, and cook in the oven until the meat is very tender, about 2½ hours.

Transfer the beef to a bowl. Strain the braising liquid, discarding the solids, then return the braising liquid and beef to the pot. Add the cranberry beans, tomatoes, and basil, stirring to combine. Cover and cook on the stove top over medium-high heat until the beans are tender, 15–20 minutes. Season with salt and pepper and serve directly from the pot.

25

CHICKEN, EGGPLANT & PORTOBELLO STIR-FRY

serves 4

This hearty stir-fry highlights the big textures of portobello and eggplant, which both pick up smoky flavor from the wok. If you cannot find Asian eggplants, use a globe eggplant of the same weight. It is a good idea to salt larger eggplants to draw out the bitterness. Toss the cubed eggplant with 1 Tbsp salt, place in a colander, and let stand for about 15 minutes. Pat dry before stir-frying.

2 Tbsp soy sauce

2 Tbsp Worcestershire sauce

1 tsp tomato paste or ketchup

1 tsp toasted sesame oil

1 tsp cornstarch

4 Tbsp (2 fl oz/60 ml) corn or peanut oil

½ lb (250 g) skinless, boneless chicken breast halves or thighs, cut into bite-sized chunks

3 Asian eggplants, about 1 lb (500 g) total, cut into bite-sized cubes

1 Tbsp peeled and grated fresh ginger

1 clove garlic, minced

4 oz (125 g) portobello or cremini mushrooms, stemmed and cut into bite-sized pieces

Cooked rice for serving

In a bowl, stir together 2 Tbsp water and the soy sauce, Worcestershire sauce, tomato paste, sesame oil, and cornstarch.

In a wok or large frying pan, heat 2 Tbsp of the corn oil over high heat. Add the chicken and stir-fry until opaque throughout, about 2 minutes. Using a slotted spoon, transfer the chicken to a bowl. Return the pan to high heat and add the remaining 2 Tbsp corn oil. Add the eggplant and stir-fry until crisp and golden brown, about 7 minutes. Add the ginger, garlic, and mushrooms and stir-fry until the mushrooms have released much of their liquid, about 3 minutes. Return the chicken to the pan. Add the soy sauce mixture to the pan and stir until the sauce thickens slightly, 1–2 minutes. Serve with rice.

26

Spanakopita is a marvelous picnic or potluck contender. Layers of flaky filo (found in the freezer aisle) enclose the familiar spinach and feta filling. The whole pan is easy to transport and cut into neat little squares, which will be tasty either warm or at room temperature.

SPANAKOPITA

serves 6

2 lb (1 kg) spinach, tough stems removed

5 Tbsp (3 fl oz/80 ml) olive oil

½ cup (1½ oz/45 g) chopped green onions, white and tender green tops

⅓ cup (2½ oz/75 g) small-curd cottage cheese

½ cup (2 oz/60 g) crumbled feta cheese

¼ cup (⅓ oz/10 g) chopped fresh dill

¼ cup (⅓ oz/10 g) chopped fresh flat-leaf parsley

1 egg, beaten

⅛ tsp grated nutmeg

Salt and freshly ground pepper

16 sheets frozen filo dough, thawed

Preheat the oven to 350°F (180°C). Have ready an 8-inch (20-cm) square baking dish.

Put the spinach in a large sauté pan, cover, and cook over medium heat, stirring several times, until just tender, about 3 minutes. Drain, spread the spinach on a plate to cool, and then squeeze to remove the excess liquid. Finely chop the spinach, put it in a large bowl, and set aside. Wipe out the pan.

Return the pan to medium-high heat, and warm 1 Tbsp of the oil. Add the green onions and sauté until softened, about 3 minutes. Add to the spinach. Add the cottage cheese, feta, dill, parsley, egg, and nutmeg to the bowl. Using a fork, toss to combine well. Season with salt and pepper.

Lay the filo on a dry kitchen towel. Cover with a sheet of plastic wrap, then with a dampened kitchen towel. Place 1 filo sheet on a work surface. Brush lightly with some of the remaining 4 Tbsp (2 fl oz/60 ml) oil, working from the edges to the center. Layer 7 more sheets over the first, lightly oiling each one. Using a sharp knife, trim the stacked sheets into an 8½-inch (21.5-cm) square. Fit the dough stack into the bottom and slightly up the sides of the baking dish.

Spoon the filling into the pan to cover the filo. Using the remaining filo, make another stack of 8 sheets in the same way and trim into an 8-inch (20-cm) square. Place the second stack to cover the spinach filling. Using the knife, cut through the pie, »→

dividing it in half. Turn the pan 90 degrees and cut the pie into thirds to make 6 pieces.

Bake until the filo is crisp and golden, about 45 minutes. Transfer to a wire rack and let cool for about 20 minutes before serving.

27

This light pork dish gets a zing from both lemongrass and lemon juice. Lemongrass is available at Asian markets and well-stocked grocery stores, but if you cannot find it, you can substitute the zest and juice of an additional lemon. Serve the stir-fry over fragrant steamed rice, and scatter with green onions for a verdant finish.

LEMONGRASS PORK STIR-FRY

serves 4–6

4 lemongrass stalks, center white part only, thinly sliced

6 cloves garlic, chopped

¼ cup (⅓ oz/10 g) chopped fresh cilantro

Freshly ground pepper

3 lb (1.5 kg) pork loin, cut into bite-sized chunks

Juice from 1 lemon

2 Tbsp Asian fish sauce

2 tsp firmly packed golden brown sugar

4 Tbsp (2 fl oz/60 ml) corn or peanut oil

6 shallots, thinly sliced

4 green onions, thinly sliced

Steamed rice for serving

In a blender, combine the lemongrass, garlic, and cilantro. Add ½ tsp pepper and ¼ cup (2 fl oz/60 ml) water and process to form a thick paste. Put the pork in a bowl, add the lemongrass mixture, and stir to coat the pork evenly. Set aside for 20 minutes.

In a small bowl, combine 6 Tbsp (3 fl oz/80 ml) water and the lemon juice, fish sauce, and sugar and stir to dissolve the sugar.

In a wok or large frying pan, heat 2 Tbsp of the oil over high heat. Add the pork and cook until browned on all sides, 5–7 minutes. Using a slotted spoon, transfer the pork to a bowl. Place the pan over medium heat and add the remaining 2 Tbsp oil. Add the shallots and stir-fry until translucent, about 2 minutes. Pour the fish sauce mixture into the pan, bring to a boil, and boil for 1 minute. Return the pork to the pan and stir-fry until heated through, about 1 minute. Garnish with the green onions and serve with rice.

28

Garlic can be reliably found in grocers year-round, but its true season peaks at the height of summer. Throw a handful of cloves into the slow cooker, and witness the transformation into a sweet sauce for meaty chicken thighs. Serve over cooked rice or with a simple shaved fennel and arugula salad.

GARLICKY CHICKEN THIGHS

serves 6

3 lb (1.5 kg) skin-on, bone-in chicken thighs

Salt and freshly ground pepper

2 Tbsp olive oil

½ yellow onion, finely chopped

15 cloves garlic

2 sprigs fresh thyme

3 bay leaves

⅓ cup (3 fl oz/80 ml) dry white wine

1 tsp white wine vinegar

Season the chicken thighs generously with salt and pepper. In a large, heavy frying pan, heat the oil over medium-high heat. Working in batches, add the chicken, skin side down, and sear until golden brown, about 4 minutes. Do not turn. Drain the chicken briefly on paper towels, then transfer to a slow cooker.

Pour off most of the fat from the pan and return it to medium-high heat. Add the onion, garlic, thyme. and bay leaves and sauté until the vegetables are just beginning to color, about 4 minutes. Pour in the wine and vinegar and stir to scrape up any browned bits on the pan bottom. Transfer the contents of the pan to the slow cooker. Cover and cook on the low setting for about 3 hours. The chicken should be very tender.

Transfer the chicken thighs to a platter and cover to keep warm. Discard the bay leaves and thyme sprigs.

Strain the braising liquid into a small saucepan, reserving the garlic cloves. Let stand for a few minutes, and then skim the fat from the surface of the braising liquid. Bring to a boil over high heat and boil until slightly reduced and syrupy, about 5 minutes. Spoon the braising liquid and garlic cloves over the chicken, and serve.

29

Tuna and white beans are a classic Mediterranean combination. This crave-worthy version takes the dish to a whole new level. The tender braised fish and creamy beans mix with the sparkling flavors of vinaigrette, fresh herbs, and lemon zest.

TUNA WITH HERBED WHITE BEANS

serves 4

½ cup (4 fl oz/125 ml) vegetable broth

½ cup (4 fl oz/125 ml) dry white wine

4 Tbsp olive oil

1 lb (500 g) plum tomatoes, peeled, seeded, and chopped

½ small yellow onion, finely chopped

3 sprigs fresh thyme

6 cloves garlic, minced

Salt and freshly ground pepper

¾ lb (375 g) ahi tuna

1 can (15 oz/470 g) white beans, rinsed and drained

1 Tbsp red wine vinegar

¼ red onion, thinly sliced

2 Tbsp chopped fresh flat-leaf parsley

Grated zest of 1 lemon

In a slow cooker, stir together the broth, wine, 1 Tbsp of the oil, the tomatoes, the yellow onion, thyme, garlic, ½ tsp salt, and several grindings of pepper. Cover and cook on the low setting for 30 minutes. Add the tuna, re-cover, and cook until firm and done to your liking. After about 15 minutes, it will still be slightly pink at the center; by 20 minutes, it will be opaque throughout.

In a bowl, combine the beans, the remaining 3 Tbsp oil, the vinegar, the red onion, half of the parsley, half of the lemon zest, ¼ tsp salt, and several grindings of pepper. Stir well and adjust the seasoning with salt and pepper if needed. Transfer to a serving platter.

Using a slotted spatula, transfer the tuna and vegetables to a plate. Discard the cooking liquid. Using 2 forks, pull the tuna apart into flakes.

Top the white bean mixture with the flaked tuna and vegetables, garnish with the remaining parsley and lemon zest, and serve.

30

BAKED RIGATONI WITH CAULIFLOWER, PANCETTA & CARAMELIZED ONIONS

serves 8

This baked pasta requires some assembly time, but the intense flavors of caramelized onions and smoky pancetta make those steps well worth the effort. Toasted bread crumbs add a crunchy topping. Fresh bread crumbs are best, but if you are buying dried, be sure to get them unseasoned.

2 Tbsp unsalted butter

4 Tbsp (2 fl oz/60 ml) olive oil, plus more as needed

1 large yellow onion, cut into quarters and thinly sliced

Salt and freshly ground pepper

1 head cauliflower, cut into florets

12 oz (375 g) rigatoni

6 oz (185 g) pancetta, chopped

2 cloves garlic, minced

1 Tbsp all-purpose flour

2 cups (16 fl oz/500 ml) milk

2 cups (4 oz/125 g) fresh bread crumbs

4 oz (125 g) mozzarella cheese, shredded

In a large frying pan, melt the butter with 2 Tbsp of the oil over medium-high heat. Add the onion and sauté until translucent, about 5 minutes. Reduce the heat to low and season with salt and pepper. Cook the onion, stirring occasionally, until it caramelizes and turn dark brown, about 30 minutes. Transfer to a bowl.

While the onion is cooking, bring a large pot of salted water to a boil over medium-high heat. Add the cauliflower and cook for 7 minutes. Using a strainer or slotted spoon, scoop the cauliflower from the water and set aside. Return the water to a boil and add the rigatoni. Cook until al dente, according to package directions. Drain, toss with a splash of oil to prevent sticking, and set aside.

Set a rack in the upper third of the oven and preheat oven to 375°F (190°C). Lightly oil a 9-by-13-inch (23-by-33-cm) baking dish.

In the pan, sauté the pancetta over medium-high heat until it is crisp, 6 minutes. Using a slotted spoon, remove the pancetta from the pan and set aside, leaving the fat in the pan. Add the remaining 2 Tbsp olive oil, the cauliflower, and the garlic to the pan and toss well. Sauté the cauliflower until it is browned, and then reduce the heat to medium-low. If the cauliflower absorbs all the oil, add more oil as needed. Cook the ⟫⟫

cauliflower until it is very soft, using a wooden spoon to break up the florets until you are left with very small pieces, about 15 minutes. Add the flour and cook, stirring continuously, for another 2 minutes. Add the milk and raise the heat to high, bringing the mixture to a boil. Reduce the heat to medium-low and let thicken, about 3 minutes. Pour the sauce over the reserved pasta and mix well. Add the reserved caramelized onions and the pancetta and toss.

Transfer the pasta to the prepared baking dish, spreading it evenly. In a small bowl, combine the bread crumbs and mozzarella, and then sprinkle evenly over the top of the pasta. Bake on the top rack of the oven until the pasta is warmed through, the cheese melts, and the bread crumbs are golden brown, about 20 minutes. Serve.

31

ITALIAN TOMATO & BREAD SOUP

serves 4

Tomato season is tauntingly short, so don't let it fly by without making tomato soup. Pappa al pomodoro is a frugal soup from Tuscany, thickened with cubes of day-old bread. Here, whole-wheat bread crumbs do the job, soaking up the juices from the sun-ripened plum tomatoes.

¼ cup (2 fl oz/60 ml) olive oil

1 yellow onion, chopped

1 celery rib, chopped

3 cloves garlic, minced

1 cup (8 fl oz/250 ml) vegetable or chicken broth

Salt

1½ lb (750 g) plum tomatoes, peeled and cored

2½ cups (10 oz/315 g) dried coarse whole-wheat or white bread crumbs

¼ cup (⅓ oz/10 g) torn fresh basil

In a heavy saucepan, warm the oil over medium-low heat. Add the onion, celery, and garlic and sauté until softened, about 12 minutes. Add the broth, 1 tsp salt, and the tomatoes. Bring to a boil, then reduce the heat to low and simmer until the tomatoes are very soft, about 25 minutes. Let cool to lukewarm.

Purée the soup in a blender or food processor. Return to the pan. Stir in the bread crumbs and reheat gently. Stir in the basil, adjust the seasoning, and serve.

When the air starts to chill, classic comfort foods begin to beckon: chicken pot pie, meat loaf and meatballs, 3-bean chili, eggplant Parmesan, macaroni and cheese, baked ziti with sausage—all one-pot fare fit for autumn. Pumpkin is delicious roasted with sweet potatoes, cherry tomatoes, and garlic; added to slow-simmering beef stew; or stuffed with sage into cannelloni. Vegetarian dishes—like stuffed tomatoes or risottos with wild mushrooms or golden beets and blue cheese—make the most of the late summer and early fall harvest.

4

SPICY PORK &
EGGPLANT STIR-FRY
page 203

5

PUMPKIN-SAGE CANNELLONI
page 204

6

CHICKEN, WALNUT
& BASIL STIR-FRY
page 204

7

PORK, QUINOA &
CHILE CASSEROLE
page 205

11

POLENTA WITH CHEESE,
GARLIC & CHARD
page 208

12

BEEF & PUMPKIN STEW
page 208

13

TUNA WITH TOMATOES & OLIVES
page 209

14

CLASSIC MACARONI & CHEESE
page 209

18

GOLDEN BEET & BLUE
CHEESE RISOTTO
page 212

19

SAUSAGE, RICOTTA &
EGGPLANT ROLL-UPS
page 214

20

TOFU STIR-FRY WITH
BLACK BEAN SAUCE
page 214

21

BEEF & MUSHROOM
STROGANOFF
page 215

25

BAKED ZITI WITH
RICOTTA & SAUSAGE
page 218

26

JAPANESE BRAISED SALMON
page 218

27

CLAYPOT CHICKEN WITH
SHIITAKES & BROCCOLI
page 219

28

CHICKPEA, SQUASH
& EGGPLANT TAGINE
page 219

september

1

PROVENÇAL CHICKEN

serves 6

3½ lb (1.75 kg) assorted chicken pieces, skin on and bone in (breasts cut in half crosswise)

Salt and freshly ground pepper

2 Tbsp olive oil, plus more for drizzling

½ large yellow onion, finely chopped

3 bay leaves

5 cloves garlic, minced

2 tsp chopped fresh tarragon

½ cup (4 fl oz/125 ml) dry white wine

½ cup (4 fl oz/125 ml) chicken broth

4 cups (4 oz/125 g) baby arugula

Prepared tapenade for serving

This classic chicken dish features the flavors of southern France: white wine, garlic, and tarragon. Top the braised chicken with dollops of tapenade and peppery arugula leaves. It makes a charming presentation and a perfect one-pot meal.

Season the chicken pieces well with salt and pepper. In a large frying pan, heat the 2 Tbsp oil over medium-high heat. Working in batches, sear the chicken, turning as needed, until golden brown, about 8 minutes. Transfer to a plate.

Pour off most of the fat from the pan and return it to medium-high heat. Add the onion and bay leaves and sauté until the onion is golden, about 5 minutes. Add the garlic and cook for 1 minute. Stir in the tarragon, ½ tsp salt, and several grindings of pepper. Pour in the wine and broth and stir to scrape up any browned bits on the pan bottom. Transfer the contents of the pan to a slow cooker and arrange the chicken on top. Cover and cook on the low setting for 3 hours. The chicken should be tender.

Transfer the chicken to a platter and tent with foil. Discard the bay leaves. Strain the braising liquid into a small saucepan, let stand for a few minutes, and then skim the fat from the surface. Bring to a boil over high heat and boil until reduced by about half, about 10 minutes.

In a bowl, drizzle the arugula with a little olive oil, season with salt and pepper, and toss. Drizzle the braising liquid over the chicken, then top with spoonfuls of tapenade and the dressed arugula. Serve.

2

ROASTED PUMPKIN WITH GARLIC, SWEET POTATOES & CHERRY TOMATOES

serves 4

1 small sugar pumpkin or other winter squash

2 sweet potatoes

2 red onions

⅔ cup (5 fl oz/16 ml) olive oil

5 sprigs fresh thyme

1 head garlic, halved crosswise

2 Tbsp fresh lemon juice

2 tsp maple syrup

Salt and freshly ground pepper

1 pint grape or cherry tomatoes

This medley of roasted vegetables transitions between the seasons with summer's last tomatoes and autumn's first root vegetables and firm squashes. If you've never combined maple syrup and olive oil before, you're in for a pleasant surprise. Garnish the dish with toasted pumpkin seeds and serve over farro if you like. There is plenty of extra jus to moisten the grains.

Preheat the oven to 400°F (200°C). Cut the pumpkin into quarters and remove and discard the pulp and seeds (alternately, rinse and roast the seeds separately and use to garnish the dish later). Cut each pumpkin quarter into 3 wedges. Quarter the sweet potatoes lengthwise. Peel the onions and cut into wedges.

Place the pumpkin, sweet potatoes, and onions in a large mixing bowl. Add the oil, thyme, garlic, lemon juice, maple syrup, 1 tsp salt, and ½ tsp pepper. Toss to mix well and then spread out in a large roasting pan or on a baking sheet lined with parchment paper. Roast for 40–45 minutes, until all the vegetables are cooked through and golden brown, about 45 minutes.

Add the cherry tomatoes to the roasting pan, toss to coat with olive oil, and return the roasting pan to the oven for about 15 minutes more or until the tomatoes just begin to soften and release their juices. Sprinkle with salt and serve directly from the pan.

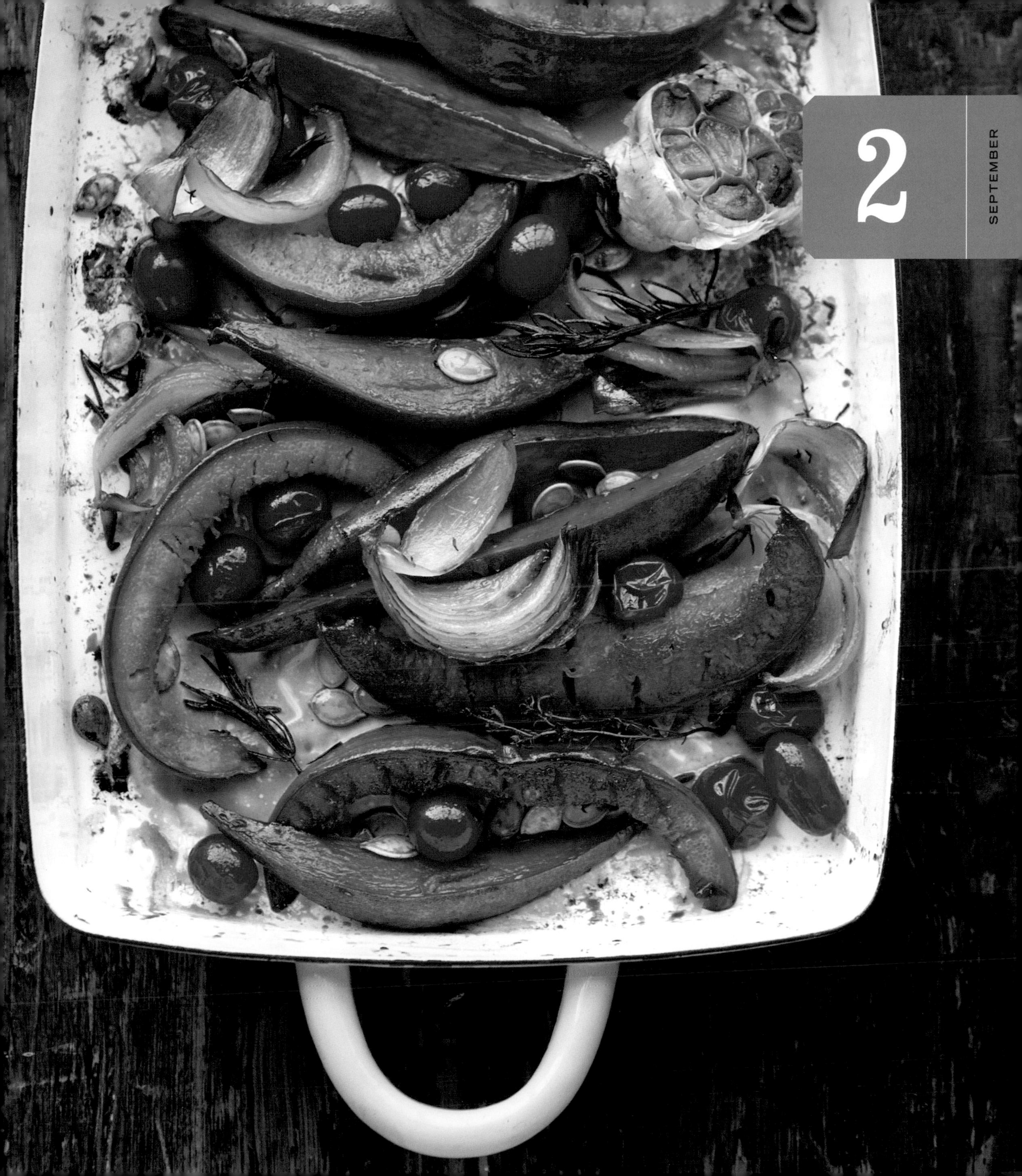

3

WILD MUSHROOM RISOTTO

serves 4

⅔ cup (⅔ oz/20 g) dried porcini mushrooms

4 cups (32 fl oz/1 l) chicken broth or water

2 Tbsp olive oil

2 Tbsp finely chopped shallot

1½ cups (10½ oz/330 g) Arborio
or Carnaroli rice

½ cup (4 fl oz/125 ml) dry white wine

¼ cup (1 oz/30 g) grated Parmesan cheese

Salt and freshly ground pepper

It takes only a small amount of dried porcini to make this intensely flavored risotto. Traditionally made with chicken broth, this risotto is so rich that vegetarians can use water instead. (Water is preferable to vegetable broth because most of the prepared versions have flavors that do not combine well with wild mushrooms.)

In a bowl, combine the mushrooms with 1½ cups (12 fl oz/375 ml) lukewarm water and soak for 20–30 minutes. Drain well, reserving the soaking liquid. Squeeze the mushrooms to remove excess liquid and roughly chop the mushrooms. Strain the soaking liquid through a fine-mesh sieve lined with cheesecloth. Reserve ½ cup (4 fl oz/125 ml).

In a saucepan, bring the broth to a gentle simmer over medium heat and maintain over low heat.

In a large, heavy saucepan, warm 1 Tbsp of the oil over medium-high heat. Add the shallot and sauté until translucent, about 2 minutes. Add the remaining 1 Tbsp oil and the rice, reduce the heat to medium, and stir until the rice is well coated with the oil and translucent, about 1 minute. Pour in the wine and stir until it is absorbed, 2–3 minutes.

Add the simmering broth to the rice a ladleful at a time, stirring frequently after each addition. Wait until the broth is almost completely absorbed (but the rice is never dry on top) before adding the next ladleful. After about half of the broth has been added, stir in the reserved mushroom soaking liquid and the chopped mushrooms. When the liquid is almost fully absorbed, resume adding the broth. The risotto is ready when the rice is tender to the bite and creamy, about 35 minutes total. Remove from the heat.

Stir in the Parmesan and ¼ tsp salt, season with pepper, and serve.

4

SPICY PORK & EGGPLANT STIR-FRY

serves 4

1 pork tenderloin, about 1 lb (500 g), silverskin removed

Salt and freshly ground pepper

1 eggplant, about 1 lb (500 g)

2 Tbsp chile-garlic sauce, such as Sriracha

1½ tsp toasted sesame oil

1½ tsp rice vinegar

3 Tbsp peanut or canola oil

1 Tbsp peeled and grated fresh ginger

6 green onions, white and tender green parts, 4 halved lengthwise and cut into ¾-inch (2-cm) pieces, 2 finely chopped

Indian summer signals the finale of deeply purple eggplants at the market. Toss cubes with tender pieces of pork in a fiery chile sauce. The eggplant flesh emerges from the wok seared on the outside but silken at heart.

Put the pork in the freezer for 20 minutes to firm it up for slicing. Cut into strips about ½ inch (12 mm) thick, 2 inches (5 cm) long, and ¾ inch (2 cm) wide. Season generously with salt and pepper. Cut the eggplant into strips of the same size.

In a small bowl, whisk together the chile-garlic sauce, sesame oil, and vinegar until smooth. Set aside.

In a wok or large frying pan, heat 2 Tbsp of the peanut oil over high heat until very hot. Add the eggplant and stir-fry until slightly softened, 3–4 minutes. Add the ginger and the green onion pieces and stir fry for 1 minute. Transfer the vegetables to a platter.

Add the remaining 1 Tbsp peanut oil to the pan over high heat and swirl to coat. Add the pork, distributing it evenly, and cook without moving it for about 20 seconds. With a metal spatula, toss and stir the pork every 15–20 seconds until browned, about 3 minutes. Return the vegetables to the pan and add the chile-garlic mixture. Reduce the heat to medium and stir-fry for 1–2 minutes to blend the flavors and warm through. Scatter with the chopped green onions and serve.

9

As the weather cools and the days begin to shorten, hunker down with comfort foods. Kids and adults alike are unable to resist the charms of flaky pastry and chicken in a creamy sauce studded with peas and carrots.

CHICKEN POT PIE

serves 4–6

FOR THE PIE DOUGH

1½ cups (7½ oz/235 g) all-purpose flour

Salt

6 Tbsp (3 oz/90 g) cold vegetable shortening

2 Tbsp cold unsalted butter

About ⅓ cup (3 fl oz/80 ml) cold water

Salt and freshly ground pepper

1 cup (4 oz/125 g) sliced carrots (¼-inch/6-mm slices)

1 cup (5 oz/155 g) fresh or frozen peas

1 cup (6 oz/185 g) corn kernels (from 2–3 ears)

2 Tbsp unsalted butter

4 skinless, boneless chicken thighs, about 1¼ lb (625 g) total, cut into bite-sized chunks

2 Tbsp chopped shallot

¼ cup (1½ oz/45 g) all-purpose flour

1½ cups (12 fl oz/375 ml) chicken broth

½ cup (4 fl oz/125 ml) dry white wine

½ cup (4 fl oz/125 ml) half-and-half

1 Tbsp chopped fresh flat-leaf parsley

1 egg yolk beaten with 1 tsp water

To make the dough, stir together the flour and ½ tsp salt. Using a pastry blender, cut in the shortening and butter until a coarse meal forms. Toss with a fork while adding enough of the water for the dough to clump together. Form into a disk, wrap in plastic wrap, and refrigerate for 30 minutes.

Meanwhile, preheat the oven to 400°F (200°C). Bring a saucepan of salted water to a boil. Add the carrots and peas and cook until tender-crisp, 3–5 minutes. Using a slotted spoon, transfer to a colander and drain, then transfer to a bowl. Repeat with the corn, cooking it for 1 minute.

In a large frying pan, melt the butter over medium-high heat. Add the chicken and cook, stirring occasionally, until browned on all sides, about 8 minutes. Add the shallot and cook, stirring, until softened, about 2 minutes. Sprinkle in the flour and stir well. Stir in the broth, wine, half-and-half, and parsley and bring to a simmer. Cover, reduce the heat to low, and simmer for 10 minutes. Stir in the carrots, peas, and corn. Season with salt and pepper. Transfer to a 9-inch (23-cm) pie dish. ⟩⟩→

On a floured work surface, roll out the dough into a round about ⅛ inch (3 mm) thick and large enough to fit over the pie dish. Brush some of the egg yolk mixture in a 1-inch (2.5-cm) border around the edge of the round. Place the round, egg side down, over the filling, and press the dough to the rim of the dish. Crimp or trim off any overhanging dough and brush the surface lightly with the remaining egg yolk mixture. Cut a few slits in the center of the top.

Place the pie dish on a baking sheet. Bake until the crust is golden brown, about 30 minutes. Remove from the oven and serve.

10

Welcome family home from school or work with a big pot of beans on the stove. This spicy chili, made mostly from pantry staples, can be doubled easily to feed a crowd. A splash of rice vinegar gives it an unexpectedly bright and zesty quality. Garnish with grated sharp Cheddar cheese and fresh cilantro leaves, if you like.

SPICY THREE-BEAN CHILI

serves 6–8

2 Tbsp olive or canola oil

1 yellow onion, chopped

2 cloves garlic, minced

1 Tbsp chili powder

1 Tbsp ground cumin

1 tsp dried oregano

Salt

1 can (28 oz/875 g) diced tomatoes, with juice

1 can *each* pinto beans, white beans, and black beans, (15 oz/470 g each), rinsed and drained

2 tsp rice vinegar

¼ cup (⅓ oz/10 g) chopped fresh cilantro

1–2 tsp puréed chipotle chiles in adobo sauce

16 corn tortillas for serving

Preheat the oven to 350°F (180°C).

In a large pot, warm the oil over medium-high heat. Add the onion and garlic and cook, stirring frequently, until the onion softens, about 5 minutes. Stir in the chili powder, cumin, and oregano. Season with ¼ tsp salt and cook, stirring, for 1 minute.

Add the tomatoes and beans. Pour in 2 cups (16 fl oz/500 ml) water and bring to a boil. Cover, reduce the heat to medium-low, and simmer, stirring occasionally, for 20 minutes. Stir in the vinegar, cilantro, and chipotle purée.

Meanwhile, wrap the tortillas in foil and warm in the oven. Serve with the chili.

11

POLENTA WITH CHEESE, GARLIC & CHARD

serves 4–6

4 cups (32 fl oz/1 l) chicken broth

1 cup (7 oz/220 g) stone-ground polenta

Salt and freshly ground pepper

1 bunch Swiss chard

2 Tbsp olive oil

3 cloves garlic, minced

1 cup (6 oz/185 g) cherry tomatoes, halved

½ cup (2 oz/60 g) grated Parmesan cheese

¼ lb (125 g) fontina cheese, cut into cubes

3 Tbsp pine nuts, toasted

If you've never cooked polenta because you are put off by the constant stirring required, this slow-cooker version solves the problem. Topping the polenta with a sautéed mixture of chard and cherry tomatoes delivers fresh flavors and transforms it into a comforting one-bowl meal.

In a slow cooker, stir together the broth, polenta, 1 tsp salt, and several grindings of pepper. Cover and cook on the low setting for 3 to 3½ hours, stirring two or three times if possible. The liquid should be absorbed and the polenta should be thick and soft and no longer gritty.

About 20 minutes before the polenta is ready, remove the stems from the chard leaves. Chop the stems crosswise into small pieces. Cut the leaves crosswise into strips about 1 inch (2.5 cm) wide. In a large, heavy saucepan, heat the oil over medium heat. Add the chard stems and cook, stirring occasionally, until beginning to soften, about 8 minutes. Add the garlic, cherry tomatoes, and chard leaves and season well with salt and pepper. Stir well, cover the pan, and cook until the leaves are wilted and tender, 4–5 minutes more.

About 5 minutes before the polenta is ready, stir in the Parmesan and dot the top with the fontina, then re-cover. Stir the fontina into the polenta, then spoon the polenta onto a platter and top with the chard mixture. Garnish with the pine nuts and serve.

12

BEEF & PUMPKIN STEW

serves 6

3 lb (1.5 kg) beef bottom round, cut into 1¼-inch (3-cm) chunks

Salt and freshly ground pepper

2 Tbsp olive oil

1 yellow onion, finely chopped

2 sprigs fresh thyme

3 bay leaves

4 cloves garlic, minced

1 cinnamon stick

⅓ cup (3 fl oz/80 ml) dry red wine

2 Tbsp plus 1 tsp red wine vinegar

2 carrots, cut into ¾-inch (2-cm) chunks

1 can (14½ oz/455 g) diced tomatoes, drained

⅓ cup (3 fl oz/80 ml) beef or chicken broth

1 lb (500 g) baking pumpkin or butternut squash, peeled, seeded, and cut into ¾-inch (2-cm) chunks

2 green onions, thinly sliced

1 Tbsp chopped fresh mint

In this flavorful and healthful take on a traditional autumn dish, the addition of a light vinaigrette laced with green onions and peppery mint just before serving infuses the stew with bright, fresh flavors. If you like, serve this hearty stew over steamed couscous.

Season the beef well with salt and pepper. In a large, heavy frying pan, warm 1 Tbsp of the oil over medium-high heat. Working in batches, add the beef and sauté until golden brown on all sides, about 8 minutes. Using a slotted spoon, transfer to a plate.

Pour off most of the fat from the pan and return to medium-high heat. Add the onion, thyme sprigs, and bay leaves and sauté until the onion begins to brown, about 6 minutes. Add the garlic and cinnamon and cook for 1 minute. Pour in the wine and the 2 Tbsp vinegar and stir to scrape up any browned bits on the pan bottom. Transfer the contents of the pan to a slow cooker and stir in the carrots, tomatoes, and broth. Add the beef, cover, and cook on the low setting for 5 hours.

Scatter the pumpkin over the top of the beef, re-cover, and continue to cook for 3 hours. The beef and pumpkin should be very tender.

Remove and discard the cinnamon stick, thyme sprigs, and bay leaves. Let the stew stand 5 minutes, then skim the fat from the cooking liquid.

In a bowl, whisk together the 1 Tbsp olive oil and 1 tsp vinegar, ¼ tsp salt, and several grindings of pepper. Stir in the green onions and mint. Spoon over the stew, and serve.

13

TUNA WITH TOMATOES & OLIVES

serves 4

4 Tbsp (2 fl oz/60 ml) olive oil

4 tuna steaks, each about 6 oz (185 g) and ¾ inch (2 cm) thick

Salt and freshly ground pepper

1 yellow onion, thinly sliced

3 large cloves garlic, minced

1 can (14½ oz/455 g) diced tomatoes, drained

½ cup (4 fl oz/125 ml) full-bodied red wine

⅛ tsp red pepper flakes

⅓ cup (2 oz/60 g) pitted small green or black olives, or a combination

1 Tbsp small capers, rinsed and drained

2 Tbsp pine nuts, toasted

2 Tbsp finely shredded fresh basil

Tuna has enough flavor and texture to stand up to an assertive braising sauce, replete with pepper flakes and briny olives and capers. If you have ripe summer tomatoes, substitute them for the canned ones and add an extra ¼ cup (2 fl oz/ 60 ml) wine.

In a large frying pan, warm 2 Tbsp of the oil over high heat. Season the tuna with salt and pepper. Add to the pan and sear, turning once, just until golden, about 3 minutes. Transfer to a plate.

Add the remaining 2 Tbsp oil to the pan and reduce the heat to medium-high. Add the onion and sauté until softened, 3–4 minutes. Add the garlic and sauté for 30 seconds. Stir in the tomatoes, wine, red pepper flakes, olives, and capers. Cover and simmer for about 5 minutes to blend the flavors. Uncover and stir in the pine nuts.

Return the tuna to the pan and spoon the sauce over the steaks. Cook the tuna, occasionally spooning the sauce over the steaks, until the tuna is opaque throughout and the sauce is slightly reduced, about 8 minutes.

Transfer the tuna and sauce to a platter. Sprinkle with the basil and serve.

14

CLASSIC MACARONI & CHEESE

serves 4–6

6 Tbsp (3 oz/90 g) unsalted butter, plus more for dish

Salt

1 lb (500 g) elbow macaroni

¼ cup (1½ oz/45 g) all-purpose flour

3 cups (24 fl oz/750 ml) milk, heated

½ lb (250 g) extra-sharp Cheddar cheese, shredded

½ lb (250 g) Monterey jack cheese, shredded

Hot-pepper sauce

¾ cup (1½ oz/45 g) fresh bread crumbs *(left)*

Back-to-school season calls for comforting, kid-friendly casseroles. Instead of stove-top macaroni, bake this creamy casserole with a crunchy topping of bread crumbs. To make fresh bread crumbs, tear firm white sandwich bread into 1-inch (2.5-cm) pieces. Process the bread in a food processor or blender to make crumbs. Store in the freezer for up to 2 months.

Preheat the oven to 350°F (180°C). Lightly butter a 2½-qt (2.5-l) baking dish.

Bring a large pot of salted water to a boil. Add the macaroni, stir well, and cook for about 6 minutes. The macaroni will still be quite al dente. Do not overcook. Drain thoroughly.

In the same pot, melt 4 Tbsp (2 oz/60 g) of the butter over medium heat. Add the flour and whisk until a smooth paste forms. Reduce the heat to low and let the flour mixture bubble, whisking occasionally, without browning, for 2 minutes. Slowly whisk in the hot milk, raise the heat to medium, and bring to a boil. Remove from the heat, add the cheeses, and stir until melted. Return the macaroni to the pot and stir well. Season with salt and hot-pepper sauce.

In a small saucepan, melt the remaining 2 Tbsp butter over medium heat. Spread the macaroni evenly in the prepared baking dish. Sprinkle the top with the bread crumbs. Drizzle the melted butter evenly over the crumbs. Bake until the sauce is bubbling and the top is browned, about 40 minutes. Remove from the oven and serve.

SEPTEMBER 15

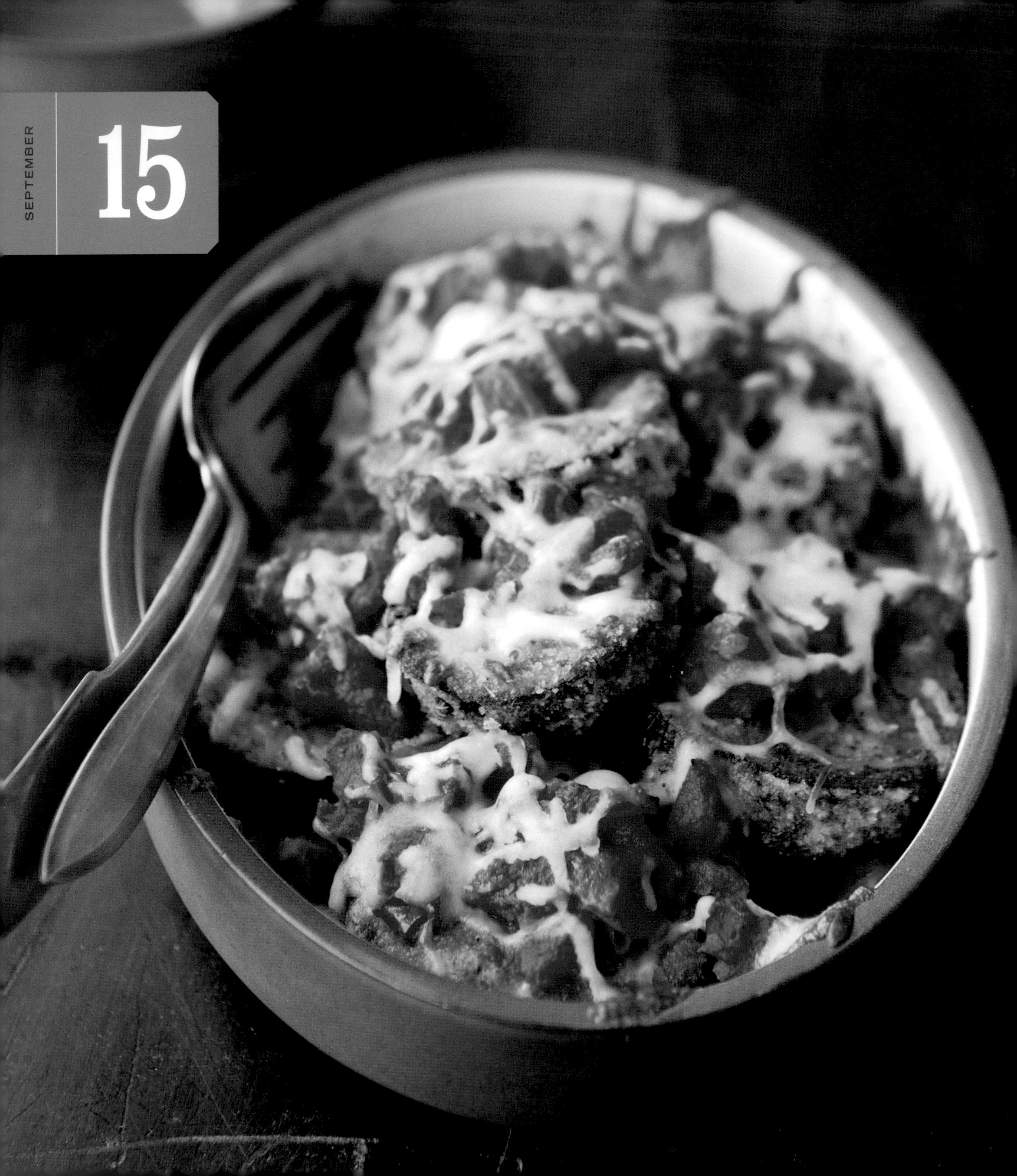

15

Replace chicken or veal with fleshy eggplant for a satisfying meatless meal. Dredging and panfrying the eggplant slices adds crunch and flavor, before smothering them in the pan with spicy marinara sauce. Serve with a big green salad.

BAKED EGGPLANT PARMESAN

serves 4

FOR THE SPICY TOMATO SAUCE

2 Tbsp olive oil

4 large cloves garlic, chopped

4 cans (28 oz/875 g each) diced tomatoes, drained

1 tsp red pepper flakes

Salt and freshly ground pepper

2 Tbsp olive oil, plus more for dish

1 egg, beaten with 1 Tbsp water

½ cup (2 oz/60 g) dried bread crumbs

½ tsp dried oregano

2 Tbsp grated Parmesan cheese

Salt and freshly ground pepper

2 small eggplants, about 1½ lb (750 g) total, each cut crosswise into 8 slices

1 cup (4 oz/125 g) shredded mozzarella cheese

To make the spicy tomato sauce, in a large saucepan, heat the oil over medium heat. Add the garlic and sauté for 1 minute. Add the tomatoes and red pepper flakes, raise the heat to high, and bring to a boil. Reduce the heat to medium-low and simmer, uncovered, until the sauce is thick, about 40 minutes. Season with salt and pepper. Let cool slightly. Measure out 2 cups (16 fl oz/500 ml) of the sauce and set aside. Save the remaining sauce for another use.

Preheat the oven to 400°F (200°C). Lightly oil a 9-by-13-inch (23-by-33-cm) baking dish.

Put the egg mixture in a wide, shallow dish. Put the bread crumbs in another dish and stir in the oregano, Parmesan, ½ tsp salt, and ⅛ tsp pepper.

In a large frying pan, warm 1 Tbsp of the oil over medium-high heat. Working with 4 eggplant slices at a time, dip each slice in the egg mixture, letting the excess drip back into the bowl. Coat both sides with the bread crumbs and cook, turning once, until browned, about 6 minutes. Repeat with the remaining 1 Tbsp oil and remaining eggplant. Transfer to a plate.

Spoon one-third of the reserved sauce over the bottom of the prepared dish. Arrange half of the eggplant slices in a single layer on the sauce. Spoon one-third of the sauce ⟶

onto the slices and sprinkle with half of the mozzarella. Top with the remaining eggplant slices and cover with the remaining sauce and mozzarella.

Bake until the eggplant is tender and the cheese is lightly browned and melted, about 15 minutes. Divide among plates and serve.

16

Shallots are most often used minced, in salad dressings, marinades, or sauces, but the purple-hued bulb is slow-cooked whole in this recipe. Don't let the quantity alarm you, as the shallots will sweeten with long cooking. Red wine and balsamic vinegar enliven the braising liquid for tender-to-the-bone chicken.

BALSAMIC BRAISED CHICKEN

serves 4–6

2 lb (1 kg) shallots

2 lb (1 kg) assorted chicken pieces, skin on and bone in

Salt and freshly ground pepper

2 Tbsp unsalted butter

2 Tbsp canola oil

¼ cup (2 fl oz/60 ml) dry red wine

½ cup (4 fl oz/125 ml) chicken broth

¼ cup (2 fl oz/60 ml) balsamic vinegar

Using a paring knife, cut a shallow X in the root end of each shallot. Season the chicken all over with salt and pepper.

In a large, heavy pot, melt the butter with the oil over medium-high heat. Working in batches, sear the chicken, turning as needed, until browned, about 5 minutes. Transfer to a plate.

Pour off all but 2 Tbsp fat from the pot and return it to medium-high heat. Add the shallots and sauté until lightly browned, about 5 minutes. Add the wine, broth, and vinegar. Raise the heat to high, bring to a boil, and stir to scrape up any browned bits on the pot bottom. Return the chicken to the pot, cover, and cook over medium-low heat until the chicken is tender and opaque throughout, about 40 minutes. Uncover, raise the heat to high, bring to a boil, and cook, turning the chicken and the shallots occasionally to prevent scorching, until the liquid has thickened slightly, 5–10 minutes.

Transfer the chicken and shallots to a platter, top with the sauce, and serve.

17

BRAISED LAMB CHOPS WITH TOMATOES & ROSEMARY

serves 4

4 lamb shoulder chops, each 10–12 oz (315–375 g) and about ¾ inch (2 cm) thick

Salt and freshly ground pepper

2 Tbsp olive oil

2 large shallots, finely chopped

3 cloves garlic, minced

1 Tbsp minced fresh rosemary

⅓ cup (3 fl oz/80 ml) dry red wine

5 canned whole peeled tomatoes, with some of their juices, coarsely chopped

10–12 pitted Kalamata olives, coarsely chopped

1½ Tbsp fresh flat-leaf parsley leaves

Lamb shoulder chops, which develop an irresistible richness after simmering in a rich red-wine broth, are much less expensive than loin or rib chops, and because they have more bones, they are far more flavorful as well.

Season both sides of the chops generously with salt and pepper. In a large sauté pan, heat 1 Tbsp of the oil over medium-high heat. Add the chops and sear, turning once, until well browned, about 5 minutes total. Transfer to a plate.

Pour off the fat from the pan. Reduce the heat to medium-low and add the remaining 1 Tbsp oil. Add the shallots and sauté until softened, about 5 minutes. Add the garlic and rosemary and cook, stirring, for 1 minute. Add the wine and stir to scrape up any browned bits on the pan bottom. Simmer the liquid until reduced by about half, about 2 minutes.

Stir in the tomatoes and their juices and the olives. Return the chops to the pan, reduce the heat to low, cover, and simmer gently until the chops are tender but still slightly pink at the center and an instant-read thermometer inserted into a chop away from the bone registers 135°–145°F (57°–63°C), about 15 minutes. Turn the chops halfway through the cooking. Transfer the chops to a platter.

Raise the heat to high and simmer briskly until the braising juices are slightly thickened, 3–4 minutes. Adjust the seasoning and stir in the parsley. Spoon the sauce over the chops and serve.

18

GOLDEN BEET & BLUE CHEESE RISOTTO

serves 4

¾ lb (375 g) golden or pink beets

Salt and freshly ground pepper

5 cups (40 fl oz/1.25 l) chicken or vegetable broth

3 Tbsp unsalted butter

1 small yellow onion, finely chopped

1½ cups (10½ oz/330 g) Arborio or Carnaroli rice

½ cup (4 fl oz/125 ml) dry white wine

⅓ cup (1 oz/30 g) grated Parmesan cheese

¼ cup (1½ oz/45 g) crumbled blue cheese

When root vegetables start to pile high at the farmers' market, seek out golden beets. Exceptionally sweet, they won't stain as much as their dark garnet cousins, which helps to preserve the pretty color of this risotto. Blue cheese complements the earthiness of this dish.

Preheat the oven to 400°F (200°C). Put the beets in a baking dish with water to cover the bottom of the dish. Cover tightly with foil and bake until the beets are tender when pierced with a fork, 40–60 minutes. Uncover and let cool. Cut off the beet tops and root ends. Peel the beets and cut into bite-sized pieces. Season with salt.

In a saucepan, bring the broth to a gentle simmer over medium heat and maintain over low heat.

In a large, heavy pot, melt 2 Tbsp of the butter over medium heat. Add the onion and a pinch of salt and sauté until the onion is soft, about 8 minutes. Add the rice and stir until translucent and coated with butter, about 3 minutes. Add the wine and stir until completely absorbed. Add a ladleful of the broth and simmer vigorously, stirring often, until the liquid is almost absorbed. Add another ladleful of broth. Continue simmering, stirring, and adding more broth until the rice is tender, about 25 minutes.

Stir in the beets and heat through, about 1 minute. Stir in the remaining 1 Tbsp butter and the cheeses. Let stand for 2 minutes. Season with salt and pepper and serve.

23

BRAISED DUCK LEGS WITH PORT & FIGS

serves 6

Dried figs pair exceptionally well with port and duck meat. Trim away any visible fat from the duck during prep, and skim off the fat after cooking. The duck can be prepared a day in advance and stored in the braising liquid. Before serving, remove the solidified fat and reheat the duck in a Dutch oven, adding the figs and honey and continuing with the final step of reducing the sauce before serving.

1½ tsp ground coriander

½ tsp ground allspice

Salt and freshly ground pepper

6 duck legs

¼ cup (2 fl oz/60 ml) olive oil

1½ cups (12 fl oz/375 ml) ruby port

1 cup (8 fl oz/250 ml) chicken broth

1 yellow onion, quartered and each quarter stuck with 1 clove

2 bay leaves

2 cloves garlic, crushed

6 juniper berries, slightly crushed

3 strips orange zest, each about 4 inches (10 cm) long

2 tsp fresh rosemary leaves

2 tsp fresh thyme leaves

18 dried figs, halved

2 Tbsp honey

2 Tbsp chopped fresh chives

In a small bowl, stir together the coriander, the allspice, 1½ tsp salt, and ¾ tsp pepper. Rub the spice mixture all over the duck legs. In a large, heavy pot, heat the oil over high heat. Working in batches, sear the duck legs, skin side down, until brown, about 5 minutes per side. Transfer to a plate.

Pour off most of the fat from the pot. Add the port, taking care to avoid splattering, and stir to scrape up any browned bits on the pot bottom. Bring to a boil and cook until reduced by about half, about 10 minutes. Stir in the broth and bring to a boil.

Preheat the oven to 325°F (165°C). Return the duck legs to the pot. Spoon the port mixture over the duck. Add the onion quarters, bay leaves, garlic, juniper berries, orange zest, rosemary, and thyme. Reduce the heat to low, cover, and cook for 1½ hours. Uncover and skim as much of the fat as possible from the surface. Immerse the figs in the cooking liquid around the duck legs and drizzle with the honey. Cover and cook until the duck is tender, about 30 minutes. ⟶

Transfer the duck and figs to a serving platter and cover loosely with foil. Simmer the cooking liquid briskly over medium-high heat until reduced to a light syrupy consistency, 10–12 minutes. Spoon the sauce over the duck legs, garnish with the chives, and serve.

24

PAN-ROASTED CLAMS WITH POTATOES & FENNEL

serves 4

Nothing could be easier and tastier than this one-pan meal of tender red potatoes, anise-tinged fennel, toasty garlic, and briny littleneck clams. Red pepper flakes and dry white wine finish the dish, mixing with the clams' juices to create a sauce with just a hint of heat.

2 lb (1 kg) baby red potatoes, quartered

1 fennel bulb, cut into slices ¼ inch (6 mm) thick, any fronds reserved for garnish

5 cloves garlic, roughly chopped

¼ cup (2 fl oz/60 ml) olive oil

Salt and freshly ground pepper

4 lb (2 kg) littleneck clams, scrubbed and soaked

½ tsp red pepper flakes

¼ cup (2 fl oz/60 ml) dry white wine

Preheat the oven to 475°F (245°C).

Heat a large roasting pan over medium-high heat, add the potatoes, fennel slices, garlic, and oil. Season with 1 tsp salt and ¼ tsp pepper. Cook, stirring, for about 5 minutes. Transfer the pan to the oven and roast until the potatoes have browned, about 20 minutes.

Add the clams, discarding any that do not close to the touch, and the red pepper flakes. Cover the pan and roast, stirring the clams once, until most of the clams have opened, about 15 minutes. Remove the pan from the oven, pour in the wine, cover, and let stand for 1 minute. Discard any unopened clams. Garnish with fennel fronds and serve.

25

BAKED ZITI WITH RICOTTA & SAUSAGE

serves 8–10

Sturdy ziti pasta tubes love a meaty sauce. As you mix in the sauce and sausages they not only coat the pasta, but are also trapped inside the hollows, delivering a burst of flavor with each bite. The ricotta and mozzarella cheeses give this rustic, substantial dish a pleasing creamy quality.

MARINARA SAUCE

½ cup (4 fl oz/125 ml) olive oil

4 cloves garlic, minced

2 cans (28 oz/875 g each) diced tomatoes, drained

Salt and freshly ground pepper

1 lb (500 g) sweet Italian pork sausages

Salt

1 lb (500 g) ziti

1 cup (4 oz/125 g) grated Parmesan cheese

2 cups (1 lb/500 g) ricotta cheese

¾ lb (375 g) fresh mozzarella cheese, shredded

To make the marinara sauce, in a large frying pan over medium heat, heat the oil. Add the garlic and sauté until lightly golden, about 2 minutes. Add the tomatoes, 1 tsp salt, and ¼ tsp pepper and stir to combine. Bring to a simmer, reduce the heat to low, and cook until thickened, about 20 minutes. Transfer to a bowl and wipe out the pan.

Arrange the sausages in a single layer in the pan and add water to reach halfway up their sides. Heat over medium heat until the water bubbles gently, and cook until the water evaporates, about 5 minutes. Continue cooking the sausages, turning frequently, until nicely browned on all sides, about 10 minutes. Cut crosswise into slices ¼ inch (6 mm) thick.

Preheat the oven to 350°F (180°C). Bring a large pot of salted water to a boil. Add the pasta and cook, stirring occasionally, until almost al dente, about 2 minutes less than package directions. Drain the pasta and return to the pot. Add the sausages, half of the marinara sauce, and half of the Parmesan. Stir to mix evenly.

Spread half of the pasta mixture in a 9-by-13-by-2-inch (23-by-33-by-5-cm) baking dish. Drop spoonfuls of the ricotta evenly over the top. Sprinkle evenly with the mozzarella. Pour about 1 cup (8 fl oz/250 ml) of the remaining sauce evenly over the mozzarella. Top with the remaining pasta mixture and then »→

the remaining sauce. Sprinkle with the remaining Parmesan.

Cover with foil and bake for 45 minutes. Uncover and continue to bake until the sauce is bubbling around the edges, about 15 minutes longer. If the top is browning too fast, re-cover loosely with foil and continue to bake. Remove from the oven, cover loosely with foil, and let rest on a wire rack for about 15 minutes before serving.

26

JAPANESE BRAISED SALMON

serves 4

Miso, mirin, and sake are a natural trio for flavorful salmon. Part of the cooking liquid is reserved for use as a warm vinaigrette, which gently wilts an assortment of bitter greens. The result is a bold and complex main-course salad.

3 Tbsp canola oil

½ cup (4 fl oz/125 ml) vegetable broth

⅓ cup (3 fl oz/80 ml) mirin

¼ cup (2 fl oz/60 ml) sake

2 Tbsp white miso

2 Tbsp soy sauce

1 Tbsp peeled and grated fresh ginger

2 green onions, white and tender green parts, thinly sliced

4 salmon fillets, each about 6 oz (185 g) and 1 inch (2.5 cm) thick

1 Tbsp rice vinegar

8 cups (5 oz/155 g) mixed greens such as frisée, arugula, and spinach

2 Tbsp chopped fresh cilantro

In a large frying pan, warm 1 Tbsp of the oil over low heat. Add the broth, mirin, sake, miso, soy sauce, and remaining 2 Tbsp oil and stir to combine. Stir in the ginger and green onions. Add the salmon and turn to coat.

Raise the heat to medium, cover, and cook until the salmon is opaque throughout, 12–15 minutes. Transfer to a plate and keep warm. Measure out 4 Tbsp (2 fl oz/60 ml) of the cooking liquid and set aside. Raise the heat to high and cook the remaining liquid until it reduces to about ¾ cup (6 fl oz/180 ml). Stir in the vinegar.

In a bowl, toss the greens with the reserved cooking liquid. Transfer to a platter and top with the salmon. Drizzle with the reduced cooking liquid, sprinkle with the cilantro, and serve.

27

*This classic
Vietnamese dish
is unusual in its
liberal use of sugar.
The sugar is cooked
into a deep-amber
caramel that brings
a sweet-and-savory
juxtaposition
as well as a rich
reddish-brown
hue to the sauce.
Dried shiitakes and
broccoli florets bring
in some vegetables,
making it a well-
rounded meal.*

CLAYPOT CHICKEN WITH SHIITAKES & BROCCOLI

serves 4

12 dried shiitake mushrooms

½ cup (4 oz/125 g) sugar

¾ cup (6 fl oz/180 ml) chicken broth

2 Tbsp Asian fish sauce

2 Tbsp peanut or grapeseed oil

5 skinless, boneless chicken thighs, about 1¾ lb (875 g) total, cut into 1-inch (2.5-cm) chunks

3 shallots, cut crosswise into thin rings

1-inch (2.5-cm) piece peeled fresh ginger, grated

3 cloves garlic, minced

1 Thai or serrano chile, cut into thin rings

Salt

2 cups (4 oz/125 g) broccoli florets

In a bowl, soak the shiitake mushrooms in warm water to cover until softened, about 30 minutes. Drain and rinse with cold water. Cut off and discard the tough stems, then cut each cap in half.

In a heavy saucepan, combine the sugar and 2 Tbsp water and cook over medium-high heat, stirring constantly, until the sugar dissolves. Continue to cook without stirring, occasionally swirling the pan, until the mixture turns a deep copper-brown, about 3 minutes. Carefully stir in the broth and fish sauce. The caramel will solidify. Continue to cook, stirring constantly, until the caramel melts. Remove from the heat.

In a large, heavy pot, heat 1 Tbsp of the oil over medium-high heat. Working in batches, sear the chicken, stirring occasionally, until lightly browned, about 5 minutes per batch. Transfer to a plate.

Heat the remaining 1 Tbsp oil in the pot over medium-high heat. Add the shallots, ginger, garlic, and chile and stir until fragrant, about 15 seconds. Return the chicken to the pot, stir in the caramel mixture, raise the heat to high, and bring to a boil. Reduce the heat to medium-low, cover, and simmer until the chicken is opaque throughout, about 30 minutes. During the last 5 minutes, add the shiitake mushrooms. ⟫

Meanwhile, bring a saucepan of lightly salted water to a boil. Add the broccoli and blanch until tender-crisp, about 2 minutes. Drain in a colander. Add the broccoli to the pot and stir to mix and heat through. Serve.

28

*A tagine is a gently
simmered North
African stew named
after the conical
cooking vessel used
for simmering meats
and vegetables in
their own juices.
Serve the sweetly
spiced eggplant and
golden squash over
couscous with a
dab of harissa, the
fiery Moroccan
chile paste.*

CHICKPEA, SQUASH & EGGPLANT TAGINE

serves 4

1½ Tbsp olive oil

1 yellow onion, chopped

1 clove garlic, minced

2 Tbsp ras el hanout

½ tsp ground turmeric

Salt and freshly ground pepper

1½ lb (750 g) butternut squash, peeled, halved, seeded, and cut into 1-inch (2.5-cm) chunks

1 lb (500 g) Asian eggplants, cut into 1-inch (2.5-cm) chunks

1 can (15oz/470 g) chickpeas, rinsed and drained

1½ cups (12 fl oz/375 ml) vegetable broth

½ preserved lemon, rinsed and chopped

1½ tsp fresh lemon juice

½ cup (¾ oz/20 g) chopped fresh flat-leaf parsley leaves

½ cup (2 oz/60 g) sliced almonds, toasted

¼ cup (1½ oz/45 g) raisins or currants

Warm the oil in a pot over medium-high heat. Add the onion and garlic and cook, stirring frequently, until the onion is soft, about 5 minutes. Stir in the ras el hanout, the turmeric, and ½ tsp salt and cook for 1 minute. Add the squash, eggplant, chickpeas, broth, and preserved lemon and bring to a boil. Reduce the heat to maintain a simmer, cover, and cook until the squash and eggplant are tender, about 20 minutes. Stir in the lemon juice and season with salt and pepper.

In a small bowl, stir together the parsley, almonds, and raisins. Stir two-thirds of the mixture into the tagine, and sprinkle the remaining over the top. Serve.

29

Using a trio of meats is perfect for these tender meatballs. Beef adds hearty flavor, while pork and veal provide a natural sweetness. It is best to use an equal amount of each for the perfect blend. Unlike most recipes that call for browning the meatballs, this one braises them in an herbed tomato sauce. The meatballs and sauce can be prepared a day ahead, refrigerated, and reheated before serving.

MEATBALLS IN TOMATO SAUCE
serves 4

FOR THE MEATBALLS

2 lb (1 kg) mixed ground beef, pork, and veal

1 egg

1 small yellow onion, finely chopped

½ cup (1 oz/30 g) fresh bread crumbs or panko

¼ cup (1 oz/30 g) pine nuts, toasted

¼ cup (1 oz/30 g) grated Parmesan or Romano cheese

2 Tbsp chopped fresh flat-leaf parsley

1 Tbsp chopped fresh oregano

1 Tbsp chopped fresh basil

Salt and freshly ground pepper

2 Tbsp olive oil

1 yellow onion, chopped

3 cloves garlic, minced

1 can (28 oz/875 g) diced tomatoes with juice

½ cup (4 fl oz/125 ml) dry white wine

2 Tbsp chopped fresh basil (optional)

To make the meatballs, in a large bowl, combine the ground meats, egg, the finely chopped onion, bread crumbs, pine nuts, Parmesan, parsley, oregano, and basil. Season with ¾ tsp salt and ½ tsp pepper. Using your hands, gently but thoroughly blend the ingredients. Form the mixture into meatballs about 2 inches (5 cm) in diameter.

To make the sauce, in a large, heavy saucepan, heat the oil over medium heat. Add the chopped onion and sauté until softened, 4–5 minutes. Add the garlic and sauté for 30 seconds. Stir in the tomatoes and wine and bring to a boil. Lower the meatballs into the sauce, gently spooning the sauce over them. Bring to a simmer, reduce the heat to medium-low, cover, and cook until the meatballs are firm and cooked through, 20–30 minutes.

Remove from the heat and let stand for 5 minutes. Stir in the basil (if using). Transfer the meatballs and tomato sauce to a large shallow bowl and serve.

30

Agrodolce is a traditional Italian sweet (dolce) and sour (agro) sauce. Here, the sweetness comes from honey and orange juice, while lemon juice and balsamic vinegar provide the perfect sour balance. As the dish cooks, the flavors deepen and the sauce thickens and caramelizes. Serve with a medium-bodied red wine, such as Pinot Noir.

CHICKEN AGRODOLCE WITH DELICATA SQUASH
serves 4

½ cup (2½ oz/75 g) all-purpose flour

Salt and freshly ground black pepper

4 chicken drumsticks

4 skin-on, bone-in chicken thighs

4 Tbsp (2 fl oz/60 ml) olive oil

3 bay leaves

10 allspice berries

3 cloves garlic, sliced

1 small delicata squash, peeled and cut into 1-inch (2.5-cm) pieces

1 large red onion, cut into 1-inch (2.5-cm) pieces

¼ cup (3 oz/90 g) honey

¼ cup (2 fl oz/60 ml) balsamic vinegar

½ cup (4 fl oz/125 ml) dry white wine

½ cup (4 fl oz/125 ml) fresh orange juice

¼ cup (2 fl oz/60 ml) fresh lemon juice

¼ tsp cayenne pepper

3 Tbsp pine nuts, toasted

Spread the flour on a plate and season with salt and black pepper. Dredge each of the chicken pieces in the flour.

In a large, heavy pot, warm 3 Tbsp of the oil over medium-high heat. Add the bay leaves, allspice, and chicken pieces and cook, turning the chicken once, until browned, about 7 minutes. Transfer the chicken to a plate.

Add the remaining 1 Tbsp oil to the pot and heat over medium-high heat. Add the garlic, squash, and red onion, and sauté until the vegetables begin to caramelize, about 8 minutes. Add the honey, vinegar, and wine, and cook until liquid is reduced by half, about 6 minutes. Add the orange juice, the lemon juice, 1 tsp salt, ½ tsp black pepper, and the cayenne, and stir to combine. Nestle the chicken in the liquid and bring to a boil. Reduce heat to low, cover, and simmer for 15 minutes. Uncover, turn the chicken, and continue cooking until the sauce is thickened and the chicken is opaque throughout, about 15 minutes. Add the pine nuts and cook just until the nuts begin to soften, 2–3 minutes. Remove from the heat and serve.

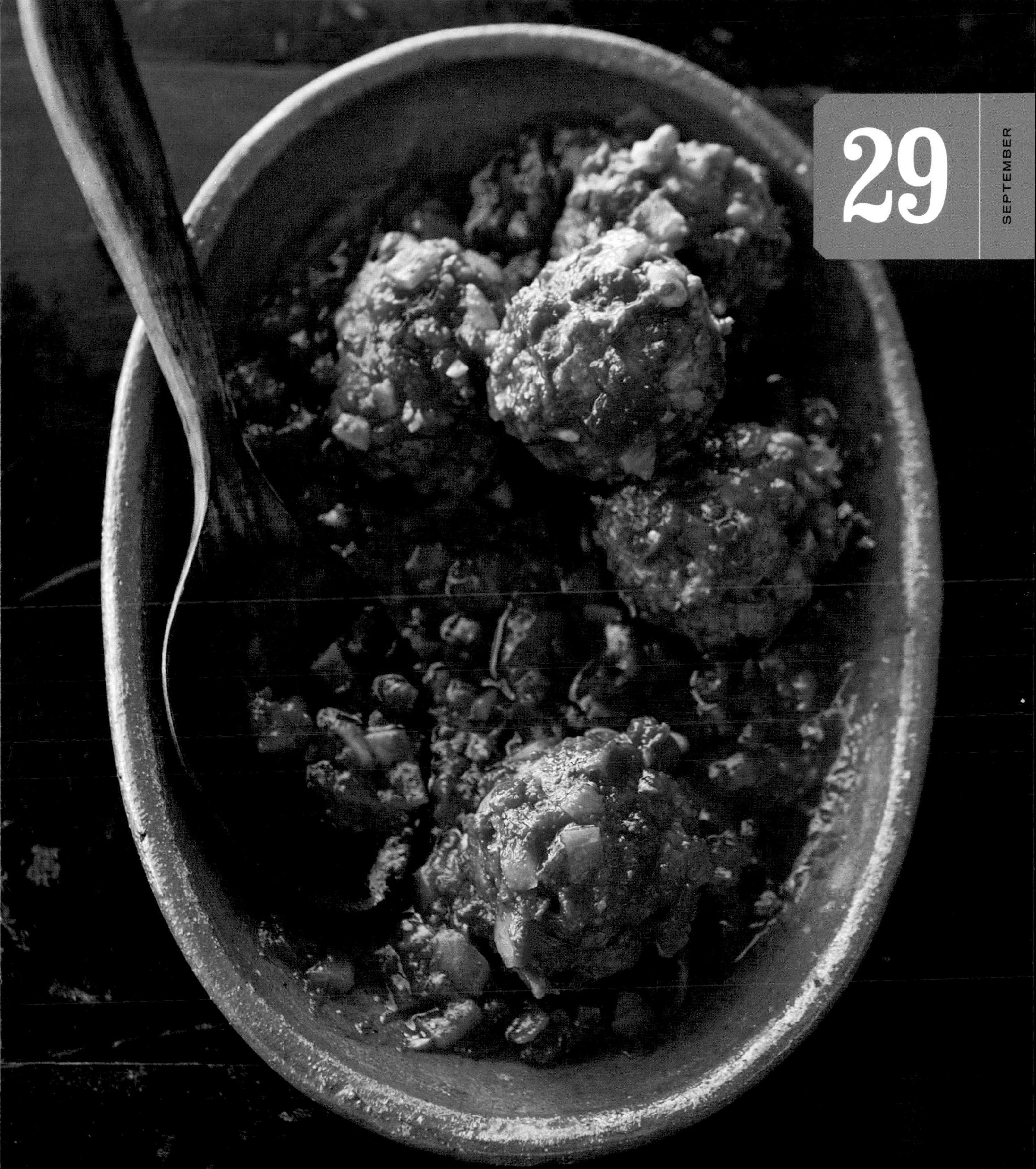

With autumn underway, root vegetables take a leading role in pot roasts, braised meats, rustic tarts, tagines, and savory pies. Take a cue from the season and serve up warming dishes like braised pork chops in apple cider with sautéed apples; ale-braised short ribs; red-wine braised brisket; pumpkin and white bean cassoulet; or succulent shepherd's pie—tender braised lamb stew topped with fluffy mashed potatoes. Latin flavors add depth and warmth to green chicken enchiladas, chicken mole, pozole pork stew, chile verde, and Brazilian seafood stew.

4

CHICKPEA & SWEET
POTATO CURRY
page 226

5

ROASTED SNAPPER
& BELGIAN ENDIVE
page 227

6

CASHEW CHICKEN STIR-FRY
page 227

7

WHITE VEGETARIAN LASAGNA
page 229

11

GREEN CHICKEN ENCHILADAS
page 232

12

BAKED ZITI WITH
THREE CHEESES
page 233

13

ALE-BRAISED SHORT RIBS
page 233

14

CHICKEN, CARAMELIZED
ONION & LEEK RISOTTO
page 235

18

WILD MUSHROOM QUICHE
page 237

19

LAMB SHOULDER WITH
SALSA VERDE
page 237

20

CHILE VERDE
page 238

21

PUMPKIN & CANNELLINI BEAN
CASSOULET WITH ROASTED GARLIC
page 238

25

SHEPHERD'S PIE
page 243

26

POZOLE
page 243

27

ACORN SQUASH & CHORIZO TART
page 244

28

STIR-FRIED PORK IN
BLACK BEAN SAUCE
page 245

october

1

PORTER-BRAISED CHICKEN WITH ROOT VEGETABLES

serves 4

Slightly bitter and with a deep coffee-like flavor, porter, a very dark ale, makes this braise rustic and hearty. Porter's toastiness plus the sweetness of root vegetables and the spiciness of Dijon mustard creates a stew full of contrasting, but harmonious, flavors.

8 skin-on, bone-in chicken thighs, about 3½ lb (1.75 kg) total

Salt and freshly ground pepper

2 Tbsp canola oil

2 Tbsp unsalted butter, plus 5 Tbsp (2½ oz/75 g) at room temperature

1 large yellow onion, chopped

2 carrots, cut into 1-inch (2.5-cm) chunks

2 red potatoes, cut into 1-inch (2.5-cm) chunks

1 celery root, about 14 oz (440 g), peeled, trimmed, halved, and cut into 1-inch (2.5-cm) chunks

2 bottles (12 fl oz/375 ml each) porter

2 cups (16 fl oz/500 ml) chicken broth

2 Tbsp packed light brown sugar

2 Tbsp Dijon mustard

2 tsp tomato paste

1 tsp dried thyme

⅓ cup (2 oz/60 g) all-purpose flour

Season the chicken thighs with salt and pepper. In a large, heavy pot, heat the oil over medium-high heat. Working in batches, sear the chicken thighs, turning once or twice, until lightly browned on both sides, about 5 minutes. Transfer to a plate. Pour off the fat in the pot.

Reduce the heat to medium and melt the 2 Tbsp butter. Add the onion and sauté until golden, about 6 minutes. Add the carrots, potatoes, and celery root, and stir in the porter, broth, sugar, mustard, tomato paste, and thyme. Return the chicken thighs to the pot, submerging them in the liquid, and bring to a simmer. Cover, reduce the heat to medium-low, and simmer, stirring occasionally, for 30 minutes.

In a heatproof bowl, mash together the 5 Tbsp butter and the flour to form a thick paste. Gradually whisk about 2 cups (16 fl oz/500 ml) of the hot cooking liquid into the flour-butter mixture, and then stir this mixture into the pot. Cover and simmer, stirring occasionally, until the chicken is opaque throughout, about 10 minutes. Adjust the seasoning and serve.

2

PEPPER JACK & JALAPEÑO SPOON BREAD

serves 4–6

Spoon bread is a classic Southern invention, somewhere between a grainy cornbread and an eggy soufflé. It is often a side dish to ham, but amped up with fiery jalapeños and gooey cheese, it can easily steal the show. To reduce some of the heat in hot chiles, such as those used here, cut out the membranes, or ribs, and discard the seeds.

Oil for dish

1 cup (5 oz/155 g) yellow cornmeal

3 cups (24 fl oz/750 ml) milk

1 or 2 large jalapeño chiles, seeded and minced

1 Tbsp finely chopped fresh cilantro

½ lb (250 g) pepper jack cheese, cut into ½-inch (12-mm) cubes

4 eggs, separated, at room temperature

Pinch of sugar

Salt

2 Tbsp thinly sliced green onion, tender green parts only

Hot-pepper sauce for serving (optional)

Preheat the oven to 350°F (180°C). Generously oil a 10-inch (25-cm) round or oval baking dish.

In a bowl, whisk together the cornmeal and 1 cup (8 fl oz/250 ml) of the milk. In a saucepan, heat the remaining 2 cups (16 fl oz/500 ml) milk over medium-high heat until small bubbles appear along the edge of the pan. Pour in the cornmeal-milk mixture and bring to a simmer, stirring constantly. Cook until the cornmeal has thickened enough that you can see the bottom of the pan when you stir, about 5 minutes. Remove from the heat and stir in the jalapeño, cilantro, cheese, egg yolks, and sugar. Season with 1 tsp salt.

In a clean bowl, using an electric mixer on high speed, beat the egg whites until stiff peaks form. Fold one-fourth of the egg whites thoroughly into the cornmeal mixture to lighten it, then fold in the remaining whites, being careful not to overmix. Pour into the prepared dish.

Bake until the spoonbread is puffed and golden, and a toothpick inserted in the center comes out clean, about 45 minutes. Serve, sprinkling the green onion and a little hot-pepper sauce, if using, over each serving.

3

Eye of round becomes tender and meltingly moist in this hearty Italian-style roast. Carrots, celery, and mushrooms cook along merrily in the juices. The intense sauce, fragrant with pancetta and fresh rosemary, begs to be served over pasta or creamy polenta.

ITALIAN POT ROAST

serves 6–8

¼ cup (2½ oz/75 g) all-purpose flour

Salt and freshly ground pepper

1 beef eye of round roast, about 4 lb (2 kg)

2 Tbsp unsalted butter

2 Tbsp grapeseed oil

6 oz (185 g) pancetta, finely chopped

2 carrots, finely chopped

1 yellow onion, chopped

1 celery rib, thinly sliced

1 clove garlic, minced

½ lb (250 g) assorted mushrooms, thinly sliced

2 cups (16 fl oz/500 ml) hearty red wine

1 cup (8 fl oz/250 ml) beef broth

2 tomatoes, peeled, seeded, and chopped

1 Tbsp chopped fresh rosemary

Preheat the oven to 325°F (165°C).

On a plate, stir together the flour, 1 tsp salt, and ½ tsp pepper. Turn the roast in the seasoned flour, shaking off any excess. In a large, heavy pot, melt the butter with the oil over medium-high heat. Add the roast and cook, turning occasionally, until evenly browned on all sides, 5–7 minutes. Transfer to a plate.

Add the pancetta to the pot and sauté over medium-high heat until the fat is rendered, about 5 minutes. Drain on paper towels.

Pour off all but 1 Tbsp fat from the pot. Add the carrots, onion, and celery and sauté over medium-high heat until softened, about 5 minutes. Add the garlic and cook for 1 minute. Add the mushrooms, cover, and cook until they begin to release their liquid, about 5 minutes. Reduce the heat to medium, uncover, and cook, stirring frequently, until most of the liquid has evaporated, about 10 minutes. Pour in the wine and stir to scrape up any browned bits on the pot bottom. Stir in the broth, tomatoes, and rosemary and bring to a boil. Stir in the reserved pancetta and season with salt and pepper.

Return the roast to the pot, cover, and cook, turning occasionally, until the roast is tender, about 4 hours. ⟫

Transfer the roast to a cutting board and tent with foil. If the sauce is too thin, bring it to a boil over high heat and cook until thickened, about 10 minutes. Cut the roast into thick slices. Arrange the slices on a platter, top with the sauce, and serve.

4

This robust vegetarian curry is a fusion of sweet and earthy flavors and toothsome textures. Chickpeas are a mainstay of Indian cooking, but sweet potatoes are native to the Americas. When refrigerated, the leftovers will thicken considerably. To reheat, add a little water before re-warming.

CHICKPEA & SWEET POTATO CURRY

serves 4

2 Tbsp canola oil

1 small yellow onion, chopped

2 cloves garlic, minced

1 Tbsp peeled and grated fresh ginger

1 Thai or jalapeño chile, seeded and minced

1 Tbsp curry powder

Salt and freshly ground pepper

1 large sweet potato, peeled and cut into ½-inch (12-mm) cubes

1 can (15 oz/470 g) chickpeas, rinsed and drained

1 can (13½ fl oz/420 ml) coconut milk, well shaken

½ cup (2½ oz/ 75 g) frozen peas

½ cup (3 fl oz/80 ml) canned diced tomatoes, drained

Cooked basmati rice for serving (optional)

In a heavy saucepan, heat the oil over medium-low heat. Add the onion, garlic, ginger, and chile and cook, stirring occasionally, until the onion is translucent, about 4 minutes. Stir in the curry powder and cook, stirring constantly, until fragrant, about 30 seconds. Season with salt and pepper.

Add the sweet potato, chickpeas, coconut milk, and 1 cup (8 fl oz/250 ml) water to the pan. Raise the heat to medium-high, bring just to a boil, reduce the heat, and simmer, uncovered, until the sweet potato is tender, about 10 minutes. Add the peas and tomatoes and cook until heated through. Serve over steamed rice, if desired.

5

ROASTED SNAPPER & BELGIAN ENDIVE

serves 4

6–8 heads white or red Belgian endives, or a combination, 12–14 oz (375–440 g) total

2 Tbsp unsalted butter, melted

Salt and freshly ground pepper

¼ cup (2 fl oz/60 ml) chicken broth

1 Tbsp sherry vinegar

½ tsp sugar

2 skinless red snapper fillets, 10–12 oz (315–375 g) each, or 4 small fillets, 5–6 oz (155–185 g) each

Olive oil for brushing

Sweet paprika

As the frost sets in, bitter greens such as endive cultivate a crisp and pleasing texture. Their slight bitterness, which softens during cooking, complements the mild snapper. Many species of saltwater fish are sold as snapper, but true red snapper has a rosy pink skin and red eyes. Rockfish, also known as Pacific snapper, is a good substitute in this recipe, as is sea bass or halibut.

Preheat the oven to 450°F (230°C).

Cut the endives in half lengthwise, then cut out the hard core and discard. Cut the halves lengthwise into strips about ½ inch (12 mm) wide. Pour the melted butter into a shallow baking dish just large enough to hold the fish in a single layer. Add the endive strips and toss to coat with the butter. Sprinkle with salt and pepper.

Place the dish in the oven and roast the endives for 10 minutes. Remove from the oven and turn the endive strips with a spatula. Add the broth, vinegar, and sugar. Continue to roast for another 10 minutes.

Meanwhile, lightly brush both sides of the fillets with olive oil, then season both sides with salt and pepper. Lightly sprinkle one side with paprika.

Remove the dish from the oven and place the fillets, paprika side up, on top of the endive strips. Roast the fish until opaque throughout, 8–10 minutes. Serve directly from the dish.

6

CASHEW CHICKEN STIR-FRY

serves 4

1 head iceberg lettuce, quartered

2 Tbsp hoisin sauce

1 Tbsp soy sauce

1 tsp rice vinegar

¼ cup (2 fl oz/60 ml) chicken broth

1 Tbsp cornstarch

¼ tsp toasted sesame oil

2 Tbsp peanut oil

¾ lb (375 g) skinless, boneless chicken breast halves, cut into ½-inch (12-mm) chunks

1 Tbsp minced garlic

4 green onions, white and tender green parts, cut into slices ½ inch (12 mm) thick

1 green bell pepper, seeded and chopped

1 red bell pepper, seeded and chopped

1 serrano chile, thinly sliced

½ cup (2 oz/60 g) coarsely chopped raw cashews

Resist the urge to reach for a takeout menu, and try whipping up this easy Chinese-American dish at home. Tender chicken, sweet and spicy chiles, and toasty cashews make it a complete meal in a wok. Take a break from rice, and serve in crunchy lettuce leaves for a light meal eaten out of hand.

With your fingers, separate 3 layers from each of the lettuce quarters, making 4 lettuce cups. Place the cups on a large plate, cover with moist paper towels, and refrigerate.

In a small bowl, stir together the hoisin sauce, soy sauce, vinegar, broth, cornstarch, and sesame oil.

In a wok or large saucepan, heat the peanut oil over medium-high heat. Add the chicken and stir-fry until it changes color, about 2 minutes. Using a slotted spoon, transfer the chicken to a plate. Add the garlic, green onions, bell peppers, and chile and stir-fry until tender-crisp, about 2 minutes. Return the chicken to the pan and add the nuts. Stir the hoisin sauce mixture, add to the pan, and stir-fry until chicken is opaque throughout, 2–3 minutes.

Divide the stir-fry among the chilled lettuce cups and serve.

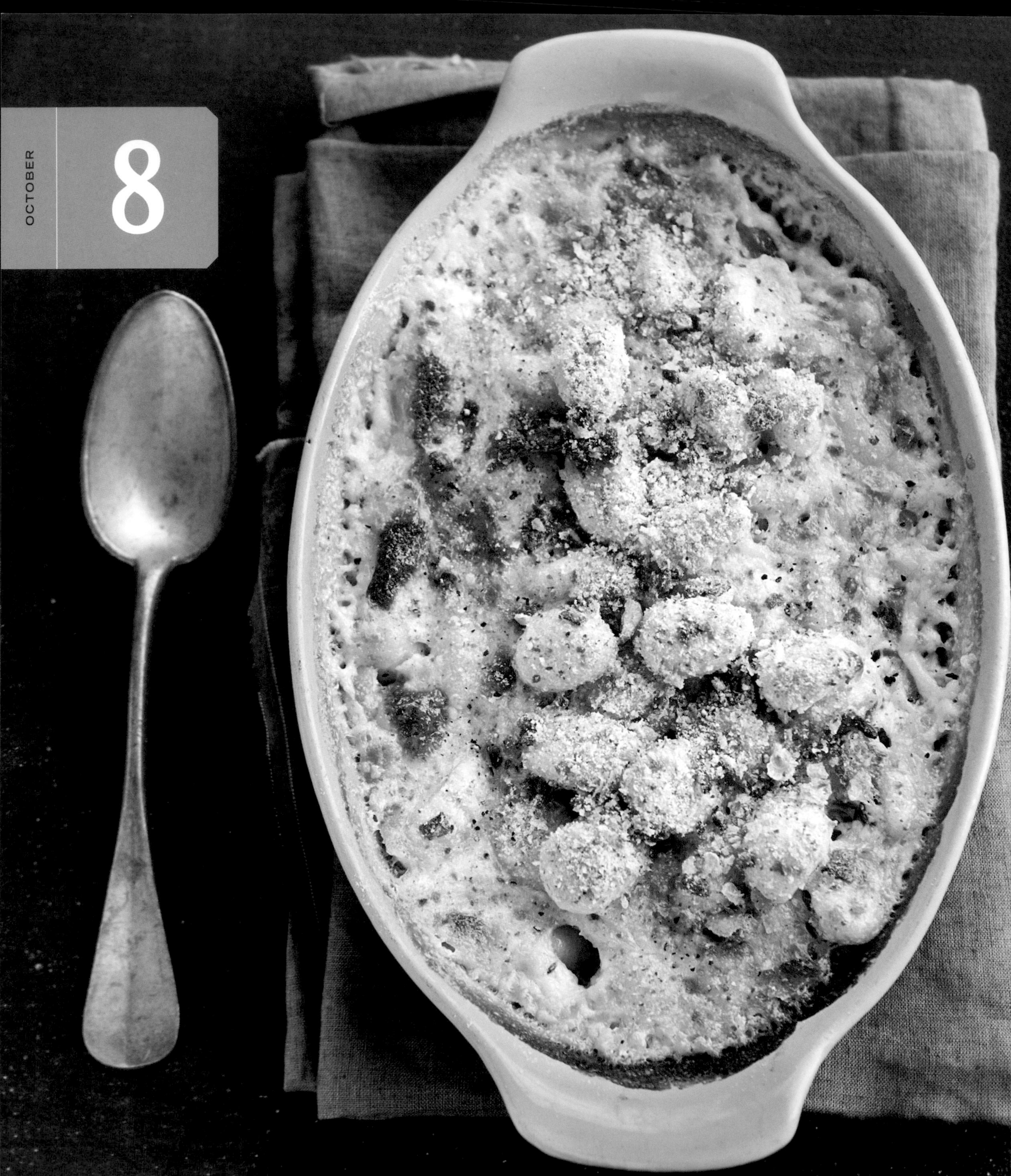

7

OCTOBER

*Cooked dried
lasagna noodles
are layered with
an assortment of
mushrooms and
spinach for this
delicious departure
from the common
tomato-cheese
combination. As in
most baked pasta
dishes, a creamy
sauce plays a crucial
role in binding the
ingredients together
and keeping the
pasta moist.*

WHITE VEGETARIAN LASAGNA

serves 4–6

Salt

9–12 dried lasagna noodles

2 tsp olive oil

6 Tbsp (3 oz/90 g) unsalted butter

¼ cup (1½ oz/45 g) all-purpose flour

2 cups (16 fl oz/500 ml) milk, heated

4 cups (32 fl oz/1 l) vegetable broth

4 large carrots, shredded

10 oz (315 g) mixed mushrooms,
stemmed and chopped

2 Tbsp minced fresh thyme

10 oz (315 g) baby spinach

1½ cups (1½ oz/45 g) fresh basil leaves

1 lb (500 g) fresh mozzarella cheese, shredded

1 cup (4 oz/125 g) grated Parmesan cheese

Bring a large pot of salted water to a boil. Add
the lasagna noodles, stir well, and cook, stirring
occasionally, until half cooked. Drain and
rinse with cold water. Toss the noodles with
the oil and set aside on damp kitchen towels.

In a saucepan, melt 4 Tbsp (2 oz/60 g) of the
butter over low heat. Add the flour and ½ tsp
salt and whisk to remove any lumps. Cook,
stirring frequently, for 4 minutes. Stirring
constantly, gradually add the hot milk.
Continue cooking, stirring often, until the
sauce is smooth and thick enough to coat
the back of a spoon, about 5 minutes. Add
2 cups (16 fl oz/500 ml) of the broth and cook,
stirring, until heated through. Remove the
sauce from the heat.

In another saucepan, bring the remaining
2 cups broth to a boil. Add the carrots, cover,
and cook until just tender, about 4 minutes.
Strain over a large heatproof bowl, reserving
the carrots and broth separately.

Melt the remaining 2 Tbsp butter in the
saucepan over medium heat. Sauté the
mushrooms until nearly tender, 2–3 minutes.
Stir in the thyme and remove from the heat.

Preheat the oven to 350°F (180°C). Gently
reheat the sauce over low heat. Ladle ¼ cup
(2 fl oz/60 ml) of the sauce onto the bottom
of a 9-by-13-inch (23-by-33-cm) baking dish.
Lay 3 or 4 noodles side by side on top of
the sauce. Scatter half of the spinach over ⇥

the noodles. Top with half of the basil leaves.
Distribute half of the carrots over the basil.
Arrange another layer of noodles over the
carrots. Distribute the mushroom mixture
over the noodles. Ladle a scant 2 cups (16 fl oz/
500 ml) of the sauce over the mushrooms.
Top with half of the mozzarella and then
with half of the Parmesan. Arrange another
layer of the noodles on top of the cheese, and
top with the remaining spinach and then the
remaining basil. Distribute the remaining
carrots over the basil. Ladle the remaining
sauce over the top, and then sprinkle with
the remaining mozzarella, followed by the
remaining Parmesan. Pour the reserved
2 cups broth along the sides of the dish,
being careful not to disturb the topping.

Bake until the lasagna is cooked through
and the topping is bubbling, 40–45 minutes.
Let stand for 15 minutes before serving.

8

OCTOBER

*Pick up packs
of fresh gnocchi,
the little potato
dumplings, to create
easy—but filling—
dinners in a pinch.
They are lovely
boiled until tender
and simply sauced,
but easily dressed
up in a gratin,
featuring decadent
Italian bacon and
cheeses. You can
also make this recipe
using 1 lb (500 g)
penne or rigatoni
instead of gnocchi.*

BAKED GNOCCHI WITH TALEGGIO, PANCETTA & SAGE

serves 4

2 packages (13 oz/410 g each) prepared gnocchi

¼ lb (125 g) pancetta, cut into ½-inch
(12-mm) pieces

2 Tbsp chopped fresh sage

1½ cups (12 fl oz/375 ml) half-and-half

½ lb (250 g) Taleggio cheese, rind removed,
cut into ¼-inch (6-mm) cubes

¼ cup (1 oz/30 g) bread crumbs, toasted

Freshly ground pepper

Preheat the oven to 375°F (190°C). Butter four
7-inch (18-cm) shallow oval baking dishes.

Cook the gnocchi according to the package
directions. Drain and set aside.

In a large frying pan, sauté the pancetta over
medium heat until it starts to brown, about
4 minutes. Remove from the heat and stir in
the sage, half-and-half, Taleggio, and gnocchi.

Divide the gnocchi mixture among the
prepared dishes. Sprinkle with the bread
crumbs and season with pepper.

Bake the gnocchi until golden brown, about
15 minutes. Remove from the oven and serve.

9

RED WINE–BRAISED BRISKET
serves 6

2-lb (1-kg) beef brisket

Salt and freshly ground pepper

2 Tbsp olive oil

1 large yellow onion, coarsely chopped

1 carrot, coarsely chopped

5 cloves garlic, smashed

1 tsp dried oregano

½ cup (4 fl oz/125 ml) dry red wine

½ cup (4 fl oz/125 ml) chicken or beef broth

Chimichurri Sauce for serving
(optional; *see left*)

2 cups (12 oz/375 g) cherry or grape tomatoes, halved, for serving

To make the chimichurri sauce, in a food processor, combine 1½ cups (1½ oz/45 g) packed flat-leaf parsley leaves and cut-up tender stems; 6 cloves garlic, quartered; and 2 tablespoons fresh oregano leaves. Process until finely chopped. Stir in ¾ cup (6 fl oz/ 180 ml) extra-virgin olive oil, 2 teaspoons coarse sea salt, 1 teaspoon freshly ground pepper, and a pinch of red pepper flakes. Use at once, or cover and refrigerate for up to 4 hours. Just before serving, stir in 3 tablespoons white wine vinegar.

Season the brisket generously all over with salt and pepper. In a large, heavy frying pan, heat the oil over medium-high heat. Add the brisket and sear, turning once, until deep golden brown on both sides, about 5 minutes per side. Transfer to a plate.

Pour off most of the fat from the pan and return it to medium-high heat. Add the onion and carrot and sauté until softened, about 5 minutes. Add the garlic and oregano and cook for about 1 minute. Pour in the wine and stir to scrape up any browned bits on the pan bottom. Stir in 1 tsp salt, several grindings of pepper, and the broth. Transfer the contents of the pan to a slow cooker. Place the brisket and any juices on top. Cover and cook on the low setting for 9 hours, turning the brisket once halfway through. The brisket should be very tender.

Transfer the brisket to a cutting board and let rest for a few minutes. Skim the fat from the surface of the braising liquid.

Cut the brisket crosswise across the grain into thick slices. Arrange the slices on a platter and spoon the braising liquid around the slices. Drizzle with the chimichurri sauce, if using. Sprinkle with the cherry tomatoes and serve.

10

SPICED SQUASH TAGINE
serves 6

6–8 saffron threads

2 Tbsp olive oil

1 large yellow onion, finely chopped

1 tsp ground ginger

½ tsp ground cinnamon

½ tsp ground turmeric

1 butternut squash, about 1¼ lb (625 g), peeled, seeded, and cut into 1-inch (2.5-cm) cubes

1 large carrot, cut into slices ½ inch (12 mm) thick

1 large tomato, halved, seeded, and chopped

3 Tbsp dried currants

1 Tbsp honey

Salt and freshly ground pepper

1 large sweet potato, about ½ lb (250 g)

This fragrant Moroccan stew, or tagine, combines winter squash, sweet potato, onion, and carrot with an aromatic blend of spices and the sweetness of dried currants and honey. It is traditionally cooked in a shallow earthenware pot with a conical top, but a Dutch oven or other heavy pot can be substituted. Butternut squash is the ideal winter squash for this dish, as it contains less water than many other types.

In a small bowl, combine the saffron with 1 Tbsp warm water and let soak for about 10 minutes.

In a large, heavy pot, heat the oil over medium-high heat. Add the onion and cook, stirring often, until softened, about 5 minutes. Stir in the ginger, cinnamon, and turmeric and cook, stirring often, until the spices are fragrant, about 30 seconds. Add the squash, carrot, tomato, currants, honey, and saffron with its soaking liquid. Pour in ¾ cup (6 fl oz/180 ml) water. Season with salt and pepper. Bring to a boil, reduce the heat to medium, cover, and simmer for about 10 minutes.

Peel the sweet potato, halve lengthwise, and then cut each half crosswise into slices ¾ inch (2 cm) thick. Add to the pot and cook, covered, until the vegetables are tender but still hold their shape, about 25 minutes. Serve directly from the pot.

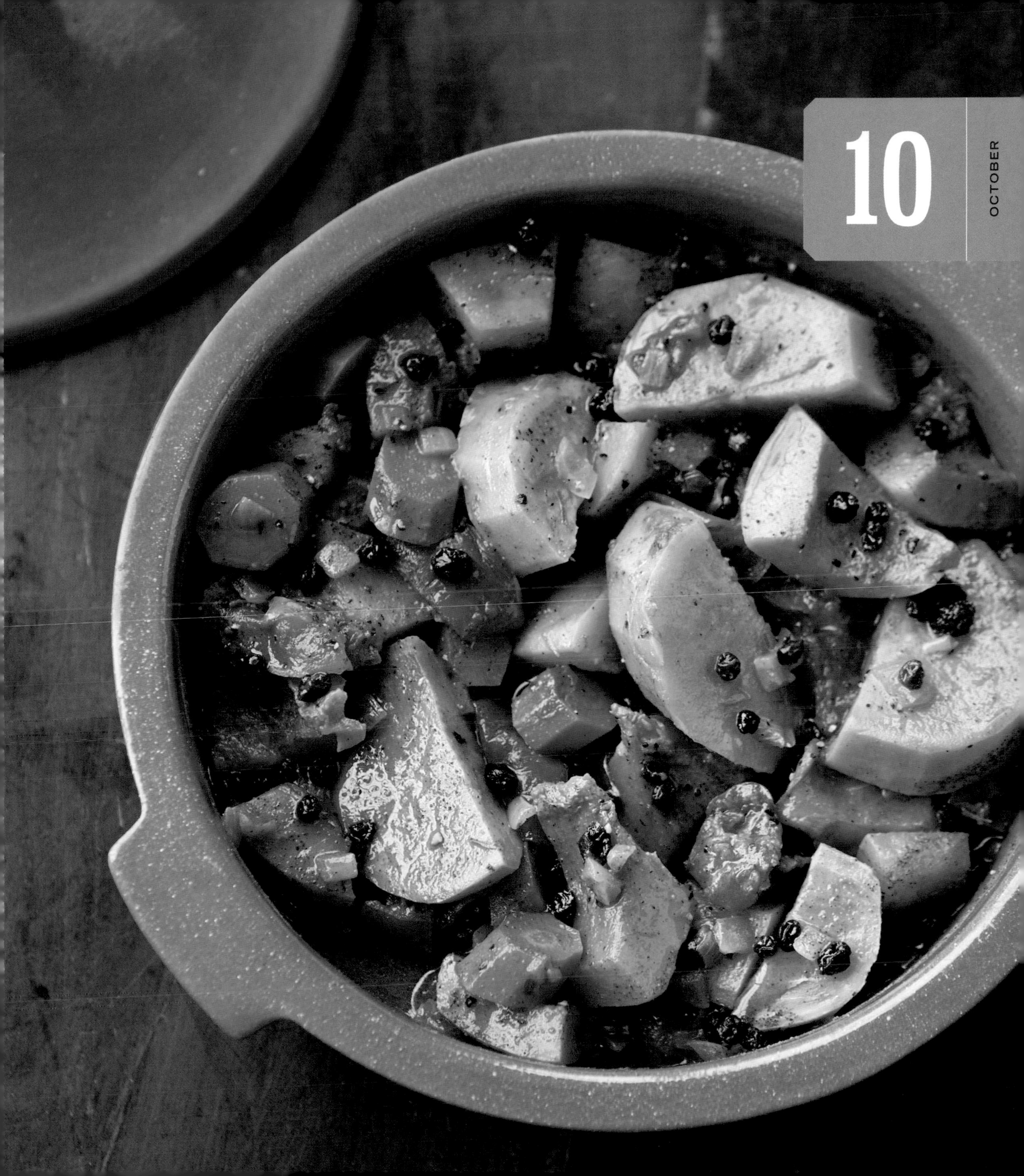

14

CHICKEN, CARAMELIZED ONION & LEEK RISOTTO

serves 6

7–8 cups (56–64 fl oz/1.75–2 l) chicken broth

4 Tbsp olive oil

2 sweet white onions, sliced

1 leek, white and tender green parts only, halved lengthwise and sliced

1 cup (8 fl oz/250 ml) Madeira wine

3 cups (21 oz/655 g) Arborio or Carnaroli rice

2 cups (¾ lb/375 g) chopped cooked chicken

2 Tbsp unsalted butter

Salt and freshly ground pepper

This savory and sweet risotto calls on two vegetable cousins: onions and leeks. Onions are naturally high in sugar, but choose an especially sweet variety, such as California Red, Maui, Vidalia, or Walla Walla for this recipe. When cooked to a golden brown, their natural sugars melt and caramelize, giving them a delicious flavor with no trace of acidity. This is a delicious way to use up leftover roasted chicken.

In a saucepan, bring the broth to a gentle simmer over medium heat and maintain over low heat.

In a large frying pan, heat 2 Tbsp of the oil over medium heat. Add the onions and leek and sauté until the onions turn golden brown, about 15 minutes. Add the Madeira and stir to scrape up any browned bits on the pan bottom. Cook over medium-high heat to reduce the liquid by half. Add 1 cup (8 fl oz/250 ml) of the simmering broth to the onion mixture and continue to cook until the liquid has reduced slightly, about 15 minutes.

In a large, heavy saucepan, warm the remaining 2 Tbsp olive oil over medium heat. Add the rice and stir until well coated and translucent, about 3 minutes. Add the simmering broth a ladleful at a time, stirring frequently after each addition. Wait until the broth is almost completely absorbed (but the rice is never dry on top) before adding the next ladleful. Reserve ¼ cup (2 fl oz/60 ml) broth to add at the end.

When the rice is tender to the bite and looks creamy, after about 20 minutes, stir in the chicken. Cook to heat through, about 1 minute. Remove from the heat and stir in the butter, caramelized onion-leek mixture, and reserved ¼ cup broth. Season with salt and pepper and serve.

15

ROCKFISH BRAISED WITH FENNEL & ONIONS

serves 4

3 Tbsp olive oil

1 yellow onion, sliced

3 ribs celery, sliced

2 carrots, peeled, halved lengthwise, and sliced

1 small fennel bulb, trimmed and thinly sliced *(left)*

2 cloves garlic, minced

2 Tbsp chopped fresh dill, plus sprigs for garnish

Salt and freshly ground pepper

1 rockfish, about 2 lb (1 kg), cleaned

1 cup (8 fl oz/250 ml) dry white wine

Roasting a whole fish creates an impressive one-pot meal. A scattering of thinly slivered vegetables cook quickly in the same pan. To prepare fennel for cooking, first trim the bulb of any browned bits. Cut off the long stalks and use only the bulb, trimming away the base of the core if it is thick and tough. Halve the bulb crosswise then cut into thin lengthwise slices.

Preheat the oven to 400°F (200°C).

In a large frying pan, warm the oil over medium-high heat. Add the onion, celery, carrot, fennel, and garlic and sauté until soft, about 5 minutes. Stir in the chopped dill and season with salt and pepper. Transfer two-thirds of the vegetable mixture to an ovenproof baking dish large enough to hold the fish flat.

Lay the fish on top of the vegetables, then scatter the remaining vegetables on top. Warm the frying pan over medium heat and add the white wine. Bring to a simmer and stir to scrape up any browned bits on the pan bottom. Simmer for 1 minute, and then pour over the fish and vegetables. Cover the dish with foil.

Bake, basting occasionally with the pan juices, until the fish is opaque throughout and an instant-read thermometer inserted into the thickest part of the fish behind the head registers 140°F (60°C), about 30 minutes. Garnish with the dill sprigs and serve directly from the dish.

20

CHILE VERDE

serves 8–10

Literally "green chile," this traditional stew from Mexico and the American Southwest couldn't be simpler to make, combining bite-size pieces of lean pork stew meat with mild green chiles and green tomatillos. Many home cooks add ripe red tomato, which enriches the dish without interfering with the dish's signature color. Serve it tucked into warm corn tortillas.

4 lb (2 kg) boneless pork shoulder, cut into 1-inch (2.5-cm) chunks

Salt and freshly ground pepper

4 cans (7 oz/220 g each) diced fire-roasted green chiles

2 cans (12 oz/375 g each) whole tomatillos, drained and broken up by hand

1 large yellow onion, finely chopped

4 cloves garlic, minced

1 large jalapeño chile, seeded and minced

2 cups (16 fl oz/500 ml) chicken broth

¾ lb (375 g) ripe tomatoes, seeded and finely chopped

1 Tbsp dried oregano

2 tsp ground cumin

Warmed corn tortillas for serving

Sour cream for garnish

Chopped fresh cilantro for garnish

Put the pork in a large, heavy pot and season with 2 tsp salt and 1 tsp pepper. Add the green chiles, tomatillos, onion, garlic, jalapeño, broth, tomatoes, oregano, and cumin and stir briefly to combine. Bring to a boil over high heat, reduce the heat to very low, partially cover, and cook until the pork is very tender and a thick sauce has formed, 2–3 hours.

Ladle the chile verde into a large shallow serving bowl. Pass the tortillas, sour cream, and cilantro at the table.

21

PUMPKIN & CANNELLINI BEAN CASSOULET WITH ROASTED GARLIC

serves 4

White beans, autumn squash, and onions bake under a crisp blanket of garlicky bread crumbs in this spectacular meatless main dish. You can roast the garlic, caramelize the onions, and even assemble the cassoulet the day before you plan to serve it. Feel free to substitute another orange-fleshed squash like kabocha or butternut for the pumpkin.

2 heads garlic

3 Tbsp olive oil

2 yellow onions, halved and thinly sliced

4 cans (15 oz/470 g *each*) cannellini or white kidney beans, rinsed and drained

2 lb (1 kg) Sugar Pie pumpkin, peeled, seeded, and cut into ½-inch (12-mm) cubes

1 cup (8 fl oz/250 ml) vegetable broth

½ tsp dried thyme

Salt and freshly ground pepper

1 cup (2 oz/60 g) fresh bread crumbs

¼ cup (1 oz/30 g) grated Parmesan cheese

Preheat the oven to 375°F (190°C). Cut the garlic heads in half crosswise and wrap together in foil. Bake until the cloves are soft, about 45 minutes. Let cool, then squeeze the cloves from cut halves into a bowl, discarding the papery skins.

In a large, heavy, ovenproof pot, heat 2 Tbsp of the oil over medium-high heat. Add the onions and sauté until they soften. Reduce the heat to medium-low and continue to cook, stirring frequently, until the onions are very soft and browned, 25–30 minutes. Reduce the heat and stir in a splash of water if necessary to keep the onions from sticking. Stir in the beans, pumpkin, broth, thyme, and reserved garlic. Season with ¼ tsp salt and ⅛ tsp pepper.

Cover and bake until the pumpkin is tender, about 1 hour. In a small bowl, stir together the bread crumbs, Parmesan, and remaining 1 Tbsp oil. Sprinkle evenly over the cassoulet and continue to bake, uncovered, until the crumbs are browned, 10–15 minutes. Remove from the oven and serve.

OCTOBER

25

25

The best shepherd's pie starts with a languorously simmered lamb stew, fragrant with rosemary and a hint of garlic. Capped with creamy mashed potatoes, the topping becomes golden brown in the oven. Ask for boneless lamb shoulder at the meat counter, or if you like, substitute beef stew meat for a "cottage" pie.

SHEPHERD'S PIE

serves 6

2 lb (1 kg) boneless lamb shoulder, cut into 1-inch (2.5-cm) chunks

Salt and freshly ground pepper

2 Tbsp olive oil

8 Tbsp (4 oz/125 g) unsalted butter

1 large yellow onion, chopped

3 carrots, chopped

3 celery ribs, chopped

2 small cloves garlic, minced

1/3 cup (2 oz/60 g) all-purpose flour

3 1/3 cups (27 fl oz/840 ml) beef broth

2/3 cup (5 fl oz/160 ml) dry white wine

2 tsp minced fresh rosemary

3 lb (1.5 kg) russet potatoes, peeled and cut into chunks

About 1/3 cup (3 fl oz/80 ml) heavy cream, warmed

1 cup (5 oz/155 g) fresh or thawed frozen peas

Preheat the oven to 325°F (165°C). Season the lamb with salt and pepper. In a large ovenproof pot, heat the oil over medium-high heat. Working in batches, sear the lamb, turning, until browned on all sides, about 5 minutes. Transfer to a plate.

In the same pot, melt 4 Tbsp of the butter over medium heat. Add the onion, carrots, celery, and garlic, cover, and cook, stirring, until the carrots are tender-crisp, about 5 minutes. Uncover, sprinkle with the flour, and stir well. Gradually stir in the broth and wine. Add the rosemary. Bring to a boil over medium heat, stirring to scrape up any browned bits from the pot bottom. Return the lamb to the pot, cover, place in the oven, and cook until the lamb is tender, 1 1/2 hours.

About 30 minutes before the lamb is ready, oil a 3-qt (3-l) baking dish. In a saucepan, combine the potatoes with salted water to cover and bring to a boil. Reduce the heat to medium, and simmer until the potatoes are tender, 20–25 minutes. Drain well. Return the potatoes to the pan and stir over medium-low heat for 2 minutes to evaporate the excess moisture. Cut 3 Tbsp of the butter into pieces and add to the potatoes. Using a potato masher, mash the potatoes while adding enough cream to create a smooth mixture. Season with salt and pepper. ⟶

Season the lamb mixture with salt and pepper, stir in the peas, and pour into the prepared dish. Spread the mashed potatoes evenly on top. Cut the remaining 1 Tbsp butter into bits and use to dot the top. With the oven still at 325°F (165°C), bake until the top is lightly tinged with brown, about 20 minutes. Remove from the oven and let stand for about 5 minutes before serving.

26

Pozole is a rib-sticking Mexican soup containing hominy, a type of dried corn. The soup reaches potency with fire-roasted tomatoes and a jalapeño. To cut down on the heat, remove the membranes and seeds from the chile, which is where most of the chemical capsaicin resides. Wash hands in soap and warm water after working with chiles, and with very spicy varieties, consider wearing a pair of thin rubber gloves.

POZOLE

serves 4

2 Tbsp corn or canola oil

1 lb (500 g) pork tenderloin, cut into 1/2-inch (12-mm) chunks

1 yellow onion, finely chopped

3 cloves garlic, minced

1 1/2 Tbsp chili powder

1/2 tsp ground cumin

1/2 tsp dried oregano

3 cups (24 fl oz/750 ml) chicken broth

1 can (14 1/2 oz/455 g) diced fire-roasted tomatoes

1 can (15 oz/470 g) white hominy, rinsed and drained

1 jalapeño chile, seeded and minced

Salt and freshly ground pepper

Sliced avocado, green onions, lime wedges, and warmed tortillas for serving

In a large, heavy pot, heat the oil over medium heat. Working in batches, sauté the pork until opaque on all sides but not browned, about 3 minutes. Transfer to a plate.

Add the onion to the pot and sauté until softened, 3–5 minutes. Add the garlic, chili powder, cumin, and oregano and cook, stirring to blend the spices, for 1 minute.

Add the broth, tomatoes with their juice, hominy, jalapeño, and sautéed pork with any juices. Season with salt and pepper and bring to a boil over high heat. Reduce the heat to low, cover, and simmer until the pork is cooked through and the soup is fragrant, about 15 minutes.

Serve the soup garnished with the avocado and green onions. Pass the lime wedges and warm tortillas at the table.

30

BRAZILIAN SEAFOOD STEW

serves 6–8

1 lb (500 g) firm white fish fillets, such as black cod or halibut, cut into 1½-inch (4-cm) chunks

1 lb (500 g) large sea scallops, tough muscles removed

1 lime, cut into wedges

2 Tbsp olive oil

1 large yellow onion, finely chopped

3 cloves garlic, minced

2 large tomatoes, chopped

1 yellow bell pepper, seeded and chopped

½ tsp red pepper flakes

Salt and freshly ground pepper

2 large, ripe plantains, peeled and thinly sliced

1 large yam, peeled and cut into ½-inch (1.25-cm) slices

1 can (13½ fl oz/420 ml) unsweetened coconut milk

2 Tbsp firmly packed dark brown sugar

¾ cup (¾ oz/20 g) coarsely chopped fresh cilantro

Assembled in layers, this spicy-and-sweet stew seems like a metaphor for Brazil's medley of cultures. If you prefer, substitute large, ripe-but-firm bananas for the plantains. Serve over steamed white rice or with crusty bread.

Combine the fish and scallops in a nonreactive bowl. Squeeze the juice from the lime wedges over the seafood, add the wedges to the bowl, and toss gently. Cover and marinate in the refrigerator for about 30 minutes.

Meanwhile, in a large, heavy pot, heat the oil over medium-high heat. Add the onion and garlic and sauté until they start to become tender, about 3 minutes. Add the tomatoes, bell pepper, red pepper flakes, 1½ tsp salt, and ½ tsp pepper, and sauté until the tomatoes begin to release their juices and the bell peppers start to soften, 3–5 minutes.

Arrange the fish and scallops on top of the tomato mixture, nestling them into the mixture. Arrange the plantain and yam slices over the seafood, overlapping them. Pour the coconut milk evenly over the top, then sprinkle with the brown sugar and cilantro. Partially cover and cook over low heat until the fish is opaque throughout and the plantains and yams are tender, 45–60 minutes. Serve directly from the pot.

31

CIDER-BRAISED PORK CHOPS WITH APPLES

serves 4

1 tsp dried oregano

½ tsp five-spice powder

½ tsp sweet paprika

Salt and freshly ground pepper

4 thin boneless center-cut pork loin chops, about 1 lb (500 g) total

4 tsp canola oil

1 yellow onion, thinly sliced

⅓ cup (3 fl oz/80 ml) apple cider

2 Tbsp red wine vinegar

1 Fuji apple, peeled, halved, cored, and cut into 8 wedges

1 cup (8 fl oz/250 ml) chicken broth

¼ cup (2 fl oz/60 ml) evaporated milk

While Fuji apples are a good choice here, pair any crisp, slightly tart apple that's in season at your local farmers' market. Braising the spice-coated pork chops in cider enhances the autumnal flavor.

In a small bowl, stir together the oregano, five-spice powder, paprika, ½ tsp salt, and ¼ tsp pepper. Coat the pork chops evenly on both sides with the spice mixture. Set the meat on a plate and let stand for 10 minutes.

In a large, deep frying pan, warm 2 tsp of the oil over medium-high heat. Add the onion and sauté until lightly browned, about 5 minutes. Transfer to a plate.

Add the remaining 2 tsp oil to the pan and return it to medium-high heat. Add the pork chops and sear until lightly browned, about 4 minutes. Turn and brown on the second side, 3–4 minutes. Transfer to the plate holding the onion.

Place the pan over medium heat and pour in the cider and vinegar. Stir to scrape up any browned bits on the pan bottom. Return the pork and onion to the pan and arrange the apple wedges on top of the pork. Pour in the broth, cover, and simmer until the chops are opaque throughout, about 10 minutes, reducing the heat if the liquid begins to boil.

Transfer the chops, apple wedges, and onion to a platter. Pour the milk into the pan, raise the heat to high, and boil until the liquid is reduced by one-third, about 5 minutes. Pour the sauce over the chops and serve.

As winter nears, late-autumn vegetables star in rich and savory dishes like stews, curries, cassoulets, and slow-cooked osso buco with gremolata. White beans and mushrooms add heft and earthy flavor to rib-sticking mains such as chicken baked with marsala and pasta baked with creamy cheese, while maple is the seasonal flavor of choice for braised pork chops. Use leftover holiday turkey in mole enchiladas or a classic tetrazzini casserole.

1
QUICK CASSOULET
page 250

2
CHICKEN BREASTS WITH WILD MUSHROOMS & MARSALA
page 250

3
SPANISH-STYLE COD WITH PEPPERS
page 252

8
POT AU FEU
page 255

9
BRAISED PORK LOIN ROAST
page 256

10
VIETNAMESE CLAY POT FISH
page 256

15
BEEF, BASIL & GOAT CHEESE LASAGNA ROLL-UPS
page 261

16
BRAISED CHICKEN WITH TOMATOES & BACON
page 261

17
APPLE JUICE–BRAISED BEEF
page 262

22
OSSO BUCO WITH GREMOLATA
page 264

23
POLENTA LASAGNA WITH BUTTERNUT SQUASH & SPINACH
page 266

24
TURKEY MOLE ENCHILADAS
page 267

29
THAI PUMPKIN & CHICKEN CURRY
page 271

30
RISOTTO WITH BEEF & BAROLO
page 271

4
BAKED PENNE WITH MUSHROOMS
& COMTÉ CHEESE
page 252

5
BEEF & SWEET POTATO STIR-FRY
page 253

6
BACON, MUSHROOM &
SWEET ONION FRITTATA
page 253

7
BROCCOLI RABE, PESTO &
SMOKED MOZZARELLA STRATA
page 255

11
CUBAN-STYLE STUFFED
FLANK STEAK
page 258

12
TURKEY POBLANO CHILI
page 258

13
BUTTERNUT SQUASH
RISOTTO WITH SAGE
page 259

14
MAPLE-BRAISED PORK CHOPS
page 259

18
WILD RICE PILAF WITH DRIED
CRANBERRIES & PECANS
page 262

19
CHICKEN CACCIATORE
page 263

20
STIR-FRIED PORK WITH GARLIC
page 263

21
STILTON & LEEK TART
page 264

25
ITALIAN MEAT LOAF
page 267

26
TURKEY TETRAZZINI
page 269

27
WINTER VEGETABLE STEW
page 269

28
STUFFED CANNELLONI WITH
BOLOGNESE SAUCE
page 270

november

1

QUICK CASSOULET

serves 4–6

1½ lb (750 g) pork sausages

2 Tbsp olive oil, plus more as needed

5 slices thick-cut bacon, chopped

1 yellow onion, chopped

4 cloves garlic

4 cans (15 oz/470 g each) cannellini or navy beans, rinsed and drained

1 cup (8 fl oz/250 ml) chicken broth

Salt and freshly ground pepper

1 sprig fresh thyme

1 can (14½ oz/455 g) diced tomatoes

1½ tsp sugar

1 cup (2 oz/60 g) fresh bread crumbs (optional)

4 Tbsp (2 oz/60 g) unsalted butter, melted (optional)

Traditional cassoulet is a hearty, rustic dish, combining several types of meat with beans. Most busy home cooks don't have time to slowly poach a duck confit, but you can try this approximation instead. It takes a few well-advised shortcuts with quality pork sausages, bacon, and canned beans.

Slit each sausage diagonally several times on each side. In a large frying pan, warm 1 Tbsp of the oil over medium heat. Add the sausages and cook, turning once, until browned on the outside and cooked through, about 10 minutes. Transfer to a plate.

Add 1 Tbsp oil to the frying pan, add the bacon, and sauté until it starts to brown, about 5 minutes. Transfer to a plate.

Drain off all but 2 Tbsp fat from the pan, adding some olive oil if necessary. Increase the heat to medium-high and add the onion and garlic to the pan. Sauté until the onion is translucent, about 4 minutes. Add the beans and broth and bring to a simmer. Reduce the heat to medium-low and simmer to blend the flavors, about 15 minutes. Stir in the bacon, thyme, tomatoes, and sugar. Bring to a simmer and cook, stirring frequently, until the flavors are blended, about 5 minutes. Season with salt and pepper.

Butter a 3-qt (3-l) baking dish and distribute the sausages evenly in the dish. Spoon the bean mixture over the sausages. If desired, spread the bread crumbs on top and drizzle with the melted butter. Bake until the beans are bubbly and the crumb topping is golden brown, about 20 minutes. Let cool slightly before serving.

2

CHICKEN BREASTS WITH WILD MUSHROOMS & MARSALA

serves 4

4 skinless, boneless chicken breast halves, about 6 oz (185 g) each, lightly pounded to an even thickness

Salt and freshly ground pepper

¼ cup (1½ oz/45 g) all-purpose flour

2 Tbsp canola oil

2 Tbsp unsalted butter

¾ lb (375 g) fresh cremini or white button mushrooms, sliced

2 Tbsp finely chopped shallot

1 Tbsp ground dried porcini mushrooms (optional; see note page 263)

½ cup (4 fl oz/125 ml) dry Marsala

½ cup (4 fl oz/125 ml) chicken broth

The sweetness of Marsala wine marries well with the fresh and dried woodsy mushrooms in this well-loved Italian-American classic. You could swap out the pounded chicken for tender veal cutlets, if you like.

Season the chicken breasts with salt and pepper. Put the flour on a plate. Dredge the chicken in the flour, shaking off any excess.

In a large frying pan, heat the oil over medium-high heat. Add the chicken breasts and cook, turning once, until lightly browned on both sides and barely firm when pressed in the center, 6–8 minutes. Transfer to a plate and cover to keep warm.

In the same pan over medium heat, melt the butter. Add the fresh mushrooms and cook, stirring occasionally, until they release their liquid and it evaporates, about 6 minutes. Stir in the shallot and cook until softened, about 2 minutes. Stir in the dried mushrooms, then add the Marsala. Raise the heat to medium-high and boil for 30 seconds. Add the broth and return to a boil.

Return the chicken to the pan and turn to coat with the sauce. Reduce the heat to low and simmer until the sauce is thickened, about 2 minutes. Season with salt and pepper and serve.

3

SPANISH-STYLE COD WITH PEPPERS

serves 6

Winter citrus and saffron combine the flavors of sunny, Mediterranean climes, even as the days grow colder. Combined with hot-house peppers and tomatoes, they make a chunky, vibrant sauce for mild cod. A true Spaniard wouldn't dream of skimping on the garlic.

Large pinch of saffron threads

¼ cup (2 fl oz/60 ml) plus 3 Tbsp dry white wine

6 Tbsp (3 fl oz/80 ml) olive oil

20 cloves garlic

3 bay leaves

3 plum tomatoes, seeded and coarsely chopped

½ cup (4 fl oz/125 ml) vegetable broth

Salt and freshly ground pepper

1½ lb (750 g) cod fillets

1 orange

1 small red bell pepper, seeded and finely chopped

3 tsp coarsely chopped fresh flat-leaf parsley

1½ Tbsp sherry vinegar

In a small bowl, soak the saffron in the 3 Tbsp white wine for 20 minutes. In a large frying pan, warm 2 Tbsp of the oil over low heat. Add the garlic and cook, stirring occasionally, until fragrant and tender but not browned, about 10 minutes. Add the ¼ cup wine, then transfer the contents of the pan to a slow cooker.

Stir in the bay leaves, tomatoes, and broth. Add the saffron mixture and ¼ tsp salt. Cover and cook on the low setting for 3 hours. Stir the liquid, add the fish, cover, and cook for 30 minutes. The fish should be firm yet very tender.

Meanwhile, grate the zest from the orange. Trim away the remaining rind and pith and cut the orange into segments, removing any seeds. Roughly chop the segments. In a bowl, combine the orange zest, chopped orange segments, bell pepper, parsley, and vinegar. Stir in the remaining 4 Tbsp (2 fl oz/60 ml) oil. Season with ¼ tsp salt and several grindings of pepper, and stir gently to combine.

Transfer the fish to a platter. Discard the bay leaves. Spoon the orange mixture over the fish. Spoon the braised tomatoes and some of the braising liquid over the fish, and serve.

4

BAKED PENNE WITH MUSHROOMS & COMTÉ CHEESE

serves 6–8

Think of this dish as French-style macaroni and cheese. Comté, a mild, nutty cheese, melts quickly into the crème fraîche mixture to form a sophisticated sauce. Japanese bread crumbs, known as panko, form a crunchy crust.

5 Tbsp (2½ oz/75 g) unsalted butter, plus more for greasing

2 Tbsp olive oil

1 lb (500 g) cremini mushrooms, stemmed and quartered

Salt and freshly ground pepper

1 lb (500 g) short tubular pasta, such as penne, ziti, or cavatappi

¼ cup (1½ oz/45 g) all-purpose flour

2 cups (16 fl oz/500 ml) milk, heated

1 cup (8 oz/250 g) crème fraîche or sour cream

3 cups (12 oz/375 g) shredded Comté or Gruyère cheese

½ cup (2 oz/60 g) panko or coarse dried bread crumbs

Preheat the oven to 350°F (180°C). Butter a 9-by-13-inch (23-by-33-cm) baking dish.

In a large frying pan, warm the oil over medium-high heat. Add the mushrooms and cook, stirring occasionally, until lightly browned, about 10 minutes. Season with salt and pepper and remove from the heat.

Bring a large pot of salted water to a boil. Add the pasta, stir well, and cook, stirring occasionally, until the pasta just short of al dente, a little less than package directions. Drain, rinse with cold water, and set aside.

In the same pot, melt 4 Tbsp (2 oz/60 g) of the butter over medium heat. Whisk in the flour, reduce the heat to low, and cook, stirring, for 1 minute, without letting the mixture brown. Gradually whisk in the hot milk and then the crème fraîche. Raise the heat to high and continue to whisk until the mixture comes to a boil and thickens enough to coat the back of a spoon. Add the cheese, stir until melted, and remove from the heat. Stir in the pasta and mushrooms and season with salt and pepper. Transfer to the prepared dish and sprinkle with the bread crumbs. Cut the remaining 1 Tbsp butter into tiny cubes and dot over the top.

Bake until the surface is bubbling and the topping is crisp, about 25 minutes. Let stand for 5 minutes before serving.

5

BEEF & SWEET POTATO STIR-FRY

serves 2–4

½ lb (250 g) flank steak

1½ tsp soy sauce, plus more for serving

1½ tsp plus 4 Tbsp (2 fl oz/60 ml) peanut oil

1½ tsp oyster sauce

1 sweet potato, peeled and cut into matchsticks

2 small dried red chiles

4 green onions, cut diagonally into 1½-inch (4-cm) pieces

2 cloves garlic, thinly sliced

1-inch (2.5-cm) piece peeled fresh ginger, cut into thin slices

Fresh cilantro leaves for garnish

Cooked rice for serving (optional)

Cut the steak in half lengthwise. Cut the halves across the grain into slices about ⅛ inch (3 mm) thick. In a small bowl, toss together the beef, the 1½ tsp soy sauce, the 1½ tsp oil, and the oyster sauce. Cover and refrigerate for 2 hours.

In a large, heavy frying pan, warm 2 Tbsp of the oil over high heat. Add the beef and sear without stirring for 1 minute. Stir-fry the beef until the meat is cooked through, about 2 minutes. Transfer to a plate.

Return the pan to high heat and heat the remaining 2 Tbsp oil. Add the sweet potato and dried chiles, season with salt, and sear without stirring for 1 minute. Add the green onions and stir-fry until the sweet potato is just tender, about 1 minute. Add the garlic and ginger and stir-fry for 1 minute. Return the beef to the pan and stir-fry until heated through, about 2 minutes.

Transfer to a large platter and garnish with cilantro. Serve with rice (if using) and pass the soy sauce at the table.

Sweet potatoes often appear in candied form on the holiday table, but these sweet cold-weather roots are worth enjoying throughout the season in a variety of ways. Cut into matchsticks, they cook quickly in a wok, alongside thin slices of marinated flank steak.

6

BACON, MUSHROOM & SWEET ONION FRITTATA

serves 4–6

½ lb (250 g) bacon, cut crosswise into ½-inch (12-mm) strips

1 Tbsp olive oil

½ sweet onion, chopped

Salt and freshly ground pepper

½ lb (250 g) cremini or button mushrooms, sliced

10 eggs

1 Tbsp heavy cream or milk

1 tsp minced fresh thyme

Preheat the oven to 425°F (220°C).

In a 10-inch (25-cm) ovenproof frying pan, cook the bacon over medium heat, stirring occasionally, until crisp, about 10 minutes. Drain on paper towels. Pour off all but 1 tsp of the bacon fat.

Add the oil to the pan and return it to medium heat. Stir in the onion and a pinch of salt and cook until the onion just begins to soften, about 5 minutes. Stir in the mushrooms and continue cooking, stirring occasionally, until the onion is soft and translucent and the mushrooms are tender, 4–6 minutes.

In a bowl, whisk together the eggs, cream, thyme, and a pinch each of salt and pepper.

When the onion and mushrooms are done, reduce the heat to medium-low. Add the egg mixture and the bacon and cook, stirring gently, until the eggs begin to set but do not begin to scramble. Cook the eggs, undisturbed, until they begin to set around the edges, 2–3 minutes. Transfer the pan to the oven and cook until the eggs are set around the edges and just firm in the center, about 5 minutes.

Loosen the sides of the frittata with a spatula, cut into wedges, and serve.

When you're looking for comfort food, this frittata will satisfy even the most voracious appetite. And, the mouthwatering combination of salty bacon, sweet onions, and earthy mushrooms are items you are likely to have on hand. Serve it with warm bread and a salad of bitter greens.

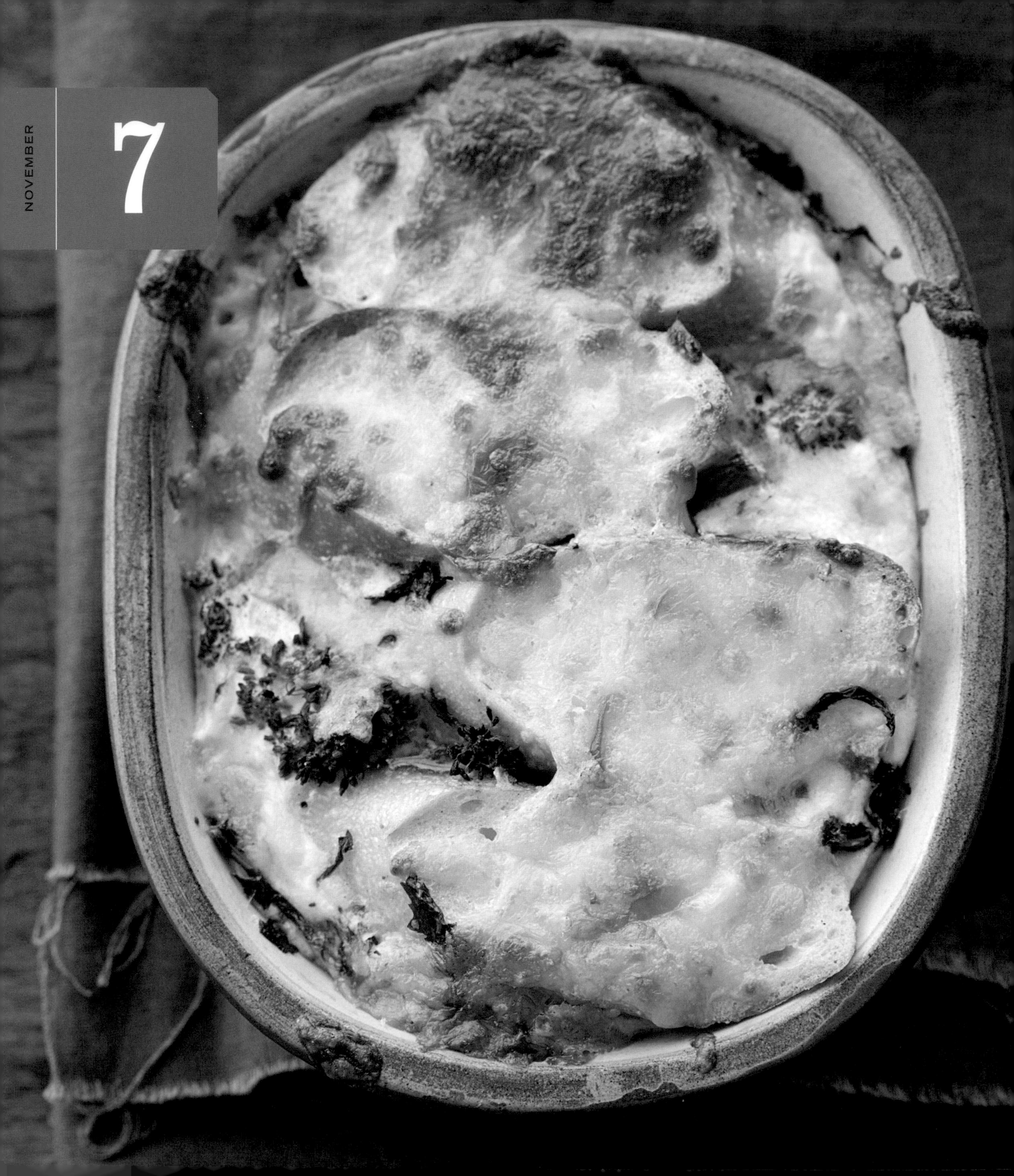

7

Broccoli rabe—also known as broccoli raab, rapini, and Italian broccoli— has slender stalks with small, jagged leaves and florets. It has a slightly bitter taste with overtones of sweet mustard. Layer it with egg-soaked sourdough, pesto, and Italian cheese in this gorgeous winter strata.

BROCCOLI RABE, PESTO & SMOKED MOZZARELLA STRATA

serves 4–6

Salt and freshly ground pepper

¾ lb (375 g) broccoli rabe, thick stems removed

Oil for baking dish

5–7 slices sourdough bread, about ½ inch (12 mm) thick, crusts removed

¼ cup (2 fl oz/60 ml) prepared pesto

1½ cups (6 oz/185 g) shredded smoked mozzarella or fontina cheese

1 cup (8 fl oz/250 ml) milk

¾ cup (6 fl oz/180 ml) heavy cream

4 eggs

2 tsp Dijon mustard

Bring a large saucepan of lightly salted water to a boil. Add the broccoli rabe and cook until almost tender, about 5 minutes. Drain and rinse with cold water, and then squeeze out as much water as possible. Coarsely chop the broccoli rabe.

Generously oil a 7-by-11-inch (18-by-28-cm) baking dish. Place a few slices of the bread in the bottom of the prepared dish, cutting them as necessary to make an even layer. Spread the broccoli rabe evenly over the bread. Dollop the pesto over the broccoli rabe, spacing it evenly. Scatter with half of the smoked mozzarella and top with the remaining bread, again cutting to fit.

In a large bowl, combine the milk, cream, eggs, and mustard. Season with ½ tsp salt and a generous grinding of pepper. Whisk vigorously until smooth. Pour over the bread and use the back of a large spoon to press the bread down into the egg mixture. Cover the dish with plastic wrap and let stand at room temperature for about 30 minutes.

Meanwhile, preheat the oven to 350°F (180°C). Press the bread down into the egg mixture after about 15 minutes and again just before placing in the oven.

Sprinkle the top with the remaining cheese. Bake until puffed, golden, and crisp, about 45 minutes. Let stand for 5 minutes before serving.

8

When the days start to turn cold, pot au feu may appear scribbled on the chalk menus of bistros and brasseries. A long-reigning favorite among French children, it combines beef and garden vegetables in a comforting one-pot meal. Sprinkle liberally with green herbs before serving, if you like. Serve with slices of baguette, so that diners can scoop out the delicate marrow from the center of the shank bones.

POT AU FEU

serves 8

3 qt (3 l) chicken broth

3½ lb (1.75 kg) beef brisket

4 beef shanks, ¾–1 lb (375–500 g) each, with marrow bone

9 small leeks, white and pale green parts only

2 Tbsp peppercorns

2 bay leaves

8 carrots, halved crosswise

8 baby red potatoes

Salt

French bread, Dijon mustard, and Horseradish Cream (page 62) for serving

In a large, heavy pot, combine the broth, the brisket, the beef shanks, and 3 qt (3 l) water. The beef should be well covered with liquid. Slice one of the leeks, bundle the slices with the peppercorns and bay leaves in a piece of cheesecloth, and tie with kitchen string to make a bouquet garni. Add to the pot. Bring to a simmer over medium heat and cook, uncovered, for 20–30 minutes, skimming off the foam that rises to the surface.

Partially cover the pot, reduce the heat to low, and simmer gently until the meat is fork-tender, about 2½ hours. Skim occasionally to remove any foam. Using a fork and a slotted spoon, transfer the brisket and shank meat to a cutting board. Cover loosely with foil to keep warm.

Cut the remaining 8 leeks lengthwise down the middle but leave them intact at the base. Add the leeks, carrots, and potatoes to the pot and season with salt. Return to a simmer over medium-low heat and cook gently until the vegetables are just tender, about 25 minutes. Discard the bouquet garni. Adjust the seasoning.

Thinly slice the brisket across the grain and break up the shank meat into pieces, then arrange the meat and vegetables on a platter. To serve, spoon the meat and vegetables into shallow bowls, ladle the broth over the meat, and pass the bread, Dijon mustard and horseradish cream at the table.

9

Tuck a pork loin into the slow cooker in the morning with a few simple seasonings and you'll have a flavorful pot roast come evening. A splash of vinegar adds a hint of tang. The shape of this cut makes it particularly easy for carving. Serve with a heap of mashed potatoes, if you'd like.

BRAISED PORK LOIN ROAST
serves 6

2 lb (1 kg) boneless pork loin roast, about 4 inches (10 cm) in diameter

Salt and freshly ground pepper

2 Tbsp olive oil

2 large shallots, finely chopped

1 celery rib, finely chopped

4 cloves garlic, smashed

⅓ cup (3 fl oz/80 ml) dry white wine

⅔ cup (5 fl oz/160 ml) chicken broth

1 Tbsp white wine vinegar

Season the pork generously with salt and pepper. In a large, heavy frying pan, heat the oil over medium-high heat. Add the pork and sear, turning as needed, until golden brown on all sides, 8–10 minutes. Transfer to a plate.

Pour off most of the fat from the pan and return it to medium-high heat. Add the shallots and celery and sauté until golden brown, about 6 minutes. Add the garlic and cook for 1 minute. Pour in the wine, broth, and vinegar and stir to scrape up any browned bits on the pan bottom. Transfer the contents of the pan to a slow cooker. Place the pork on the top. Cover and cook on the low setting for 6–7 hours. The meat should be very tender.

Transfer the pork to a platter and let rest for a few minutes. Skim the fat from the surface of the braising liquid. Slice the pork across the grain and arrange on plates. Drizzle with some of the braising liquid and serve.

10

In this Vietnamese classic, two seemingly contradictory flavors—intensely sweet caramel and briny fish sauce—reach an enticing harmony by gently simmering together, along with aromatic seasonings. Fish fillets, added during the final minutes of cooking, not only soak up the flavors but also acquire a deep, glossy mahogany color.

VIETNAMESE CLAY POT FISH
serves 6–8

½ cup (4 oz/125 g) sugar

¼ cup (2 fl oz/60 ml) canola oil

3 cloves garlic, minced

3 shallots, minced

1-inch (2.5-cm) piece peeled fresh ginger, grated

2 small red or green Thai chiles or other small hot chiles, halved lengthwise, seeded, and thinly sliced

¼ cup (2 fl oz/60 ml) Asian fish sauce

¼ cup (2 fl oz/60 ml) soy sauce

2 lb (1 kg) firm, mild white fish fillets such as black cod or halibut, cut into equal-sized pieces

Freshly ground pepper

In a small, heavy-bottomed saucepan, combine the sugar and ¼ cup (2 fl oz/60 ml) water. Cook over medium-high heat, stirring occasionally, until the sugar melts. Bring to a boil, stirring frequently, until the mixture turns caramel brown, about 15 minutes. Watch carefully so that it doesn't burn. Remove from the heat and, taking care to avoid splatters, stir in ¼ cup water until thoroughly blended.

In a large, heavy pot, warm the oil over medium-high heat. Add the garlic, shallots, ginger, and chiles and sauté until just tender, 1–2 minutes. Stir in the fish sauce, soy sauce, caramel, and 1 cup (8 fl oz/250 ml) water. Bring to a boil, stirring occasionally.

Reduce the heat to low, partially cover, and cook until the sauce is syrupy but still very fluid, about 15 minutes. If the sauce becomes too thick, stir in ½ cup (4 fl oz/125 ml) water. Add the fish chunks, gently turning to coat with the sauce. Cover and cook, turning the fish once at the midway point, until opaque throughout, about 15 minutes. Season with pepper. Serve the fish in shallow bowls, drizzled with the sauce.

NOVEMBER

15

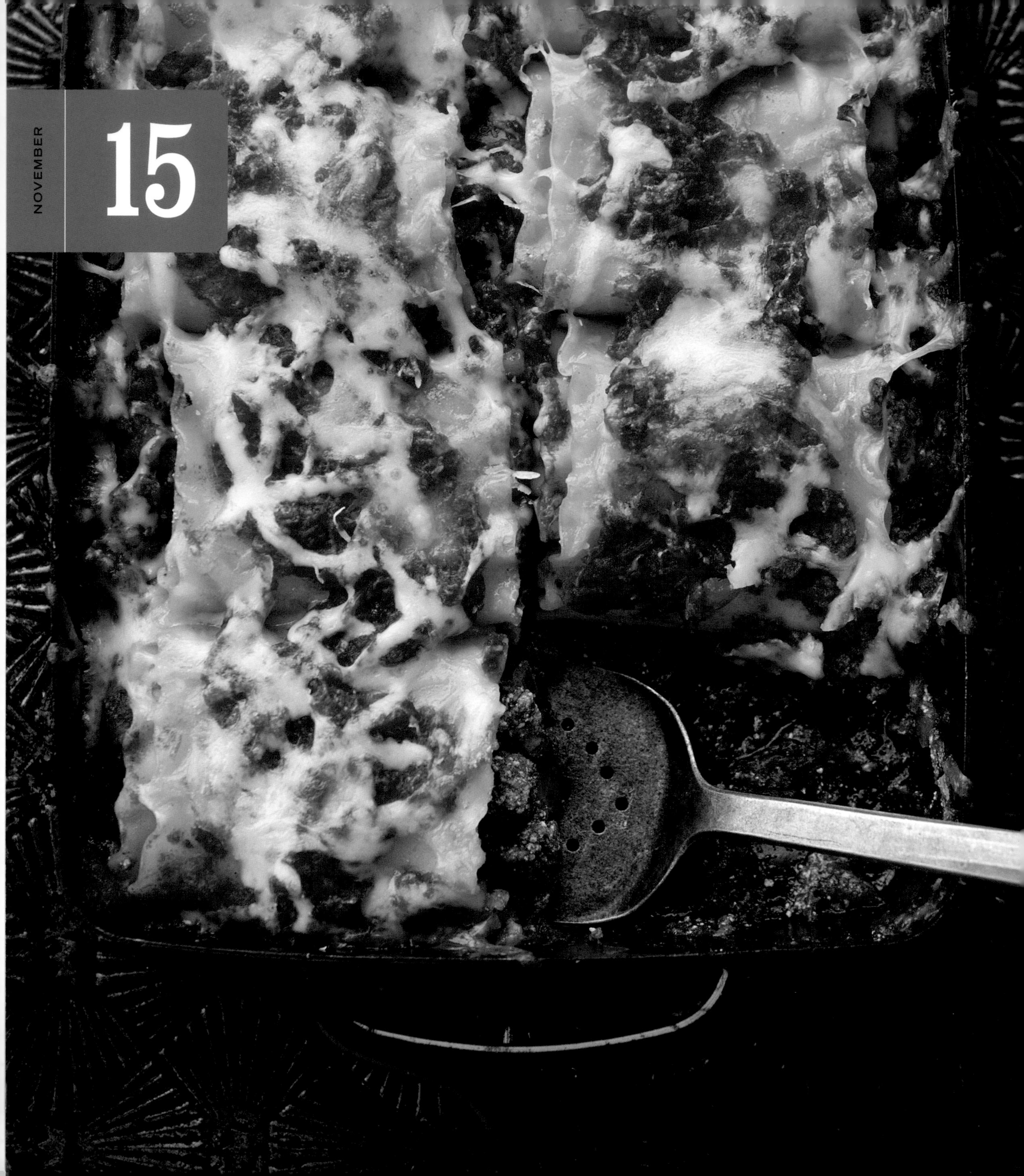

15

Tidy bundles of pasta and filling are easy to dish out to family and friends. Four different cheeses verges on indulgent, but the goat cheese is essential, adding unique flavor and creamy texture. Save any extra meat filling for another use, or simply tuck it in around the rolls. A big green salad, garlic bread, and a dry red wine complete this dinner.

BEEF, BASIL & GOAT CHEESE LASAGNA ROLL-UPS

serves 6–8

3 Tbsp olive oil

1 yellow onion, chopped

3 cloves garlic, minced

¼ tsp red pepper flakes (optional)

Salt and freshly ground pepper

1 can (28 oz/875 g) crushed tomatoes

¾ lb (375 g) dried lasagna noodles

1 lb (500 g) ground beef

½ lb (250 g) ricotta cheese

4 oz (125 g) fresh goat cheese

1 cup (4 oz/125 g) grated Parmesan cheese

1 egg, lightly beaten

⅓ cup (½ oz/15 g) chopped fresh basil

1 cup (4 oz/125 g) shredded mozzarella cheese

In a large saucepan, warm 2 Tbsp oil over medium-high heat. Add the onion and sauté until it begins to soften, about 4 minutes. Stir in the garlic, the red pepper flakes (if using), 2 tsp salt, and 1 tsp pepper and cook for 2 minutes. Add the tomatoes and stir to combine. Bring the sauce to a boil, reduce the heat to low, and simmer to allow the flavors to develop, about 20 minutes. Season again with salt and pepper.

Bring a large pot of salted water to a boil. Add the lasagna noodles and cook until al dente, according to the package directions. Drain the noodles and arrange in a single layer on a baking sheet.

Preheat the oven to 400°F (200°C).

In a frying pan, warm the remaining 1 Tbsp oil over medium-high heat. Add the ground beef and cook, stirring to break it up into small pieces, until browned, about 6 minutes. Season with salt and pepper, transfer to a large bowl, and let cool slightly. Add the ricotta, the goat cheese, half of the Parmesan, the egg, the basil, and ⅓ cup (3 fl oz/80 ml) of the tomato sauce and stir to combine.

Ladle 1½ cups (12 fl oz/375 ml) of the tomato sauce into the bottom of a 9-by-13-inch (23-by-33-cm) baking dish. Lay a noodle on a work surface. Put ⅓ cup of the meat mixture on one end and roll up the noodle. Place ⟶

the roll, seam side down, in the dish. Repeat with the remaining noodles and meat mixture. Cover the roll-ups with the remaining tomato sauce. Sprinkle with the mozzarella and the remaining Parmesan.

Bake until the sauce is bubbling and the cheese is melted, about 20 minutes. Serve.

16

This one-pan chicken recipe calls for only a few pantry staples, most of which you probably already have on hand. Thighs sear and simmer quickly in a combination of tomatoes and white wine, with a little chopped bacon added for flavor. Of the canned tomatoes available, those from San Marzano, Italy are king.

BRAISED CHICKEN WITH TOMATOES & BACON

serves 4–6

4 slices thick-cut bacon, chopped

6 skin-on, bone-in chicken thighs, about 2 lb (1 kg) total

Salt and freshly ground pepper

1 yellow onion, chopped

2 large cloves garlic, minced

¼ cup (2 fl oz/60 ml) dry white wine

1 Tbsp chopped fresh oregano

¼ tsp red pepper flakes

1 can (14½ oz/455 g) diced tomatoes

In a large frying pan, sauté the bacon over medium heat until crisp, 4–5 minutes. Using a slotted spoon, transfer to a small plate. Drain off all but 2 Tbsp fat from the pan.

Season the chicken with salt and pepper. Heat the pan over medium-high heat, add the chicken, and cook, turning once or twice, until golden brown, about 8 minutes. Transfer to a plate. Add the onion and garlic and sauté until softened, about 4 minutes. Pour in the wine and stir to scrape up any browned bits on the pan bottom. Stir in the oregano, red pepper flakes, and the tomatoes and their juices.

Return the chicken and any juices to the pan, cover, reduce the heat to medium-low, and cook until the chicken is opaque throughout, 25–30 minutes. Uncover, raise the heat to medium-high, bring to a simmer, and stir in the bacon. Serve directly from the pan.

21
NOVEMBER

STILTON & LEEK TART
serves 6

1½ cups (6 oz/185 g) all-purpose flour

Salt

½ cup (4 oz/125 g) cold unsalted butter, cut into small pieces

3–4 Tbsp ice water

3 Tbsp canola oil

5 small leeks, white and pale green parts, thinly sliced

3 oz (90 g) Stilton cheese or other strong blue cheese

1 egg, plus 1 egg yolk

½ cup (4 fl oz/125 ml) heavy cream

Salt and freshly ground pepper

Sharp, rich Stilton is a blue-veined cow's milk cheese that hails from England and is a favorite during the colder months, particularly at Christmastime. This simple yet decadent tart pairs the nutty cheese with sweet, tender leeks in a buttery crust.

To make the pastry, put the flour, salt, and butter in a food processor and pulse a few times until the mixture forms coarse crumbs; transfer to a bowl. Using a fork, stir in enough of the water to form a rough dough. Turn the dough out onto a floured work surface and press into a disk. Wrap tightly in plastic wrap, and refrigerate for at least 30 minutes or up to overnight. On a floured work surface, roll out the dough into a disk about 10 inches (25 cm) in diameter. Drape the dough over the rolling pin and ease into a 9-inch (23-cm) tart pan, pressing it into place. If there is an overhang, roll the rolling pin across the rim of the pan to remove it. Prick the dough with a fork in several places, line with parchment paper, and fill with pie weights. Refrigerate for 30 minutes.

Preheat the oven to 400°F (200°C). Bake the tart shell until the pastry looks dry but is not colored, 15–18 minutes. Carefully remove the paper and pie weights. Set the tart shell aside. Reduce the oven temperature to 350°F (180°C).

Meanwhile, make the filling. In a frying pan over medium heat, warm the oil. Add the leeks and cook, stirring occasionally, until wilted, about 4 minutes. Transfer to a small bowl. Place the cheese, whole egg, and egg yolk in a food processor and purée until smooth. Transfer to a bowl and stir in the cream. Add the leeks and stir to combine. Season with salt and pepper. Pour into the tart shell. Bake until the filling is golden brown, about 25 minutes. Serve in wedges.

22
NOVEMBER

OSSO BUCO WITH GREMOLATA
serves 6–8

¾ cup (4 oz/125 g) all-purpose flour

Salt and freshly ground pepper

6 bone-in veal shanks, about 6 lb (3 kg) total, each about 1 inch (2.5 cm) thick

½ cup (4 fl oz/120 ml) olive oil

1 yellow onion, chopped

1 carrot, chopped

1 celery rib, chopped

2 cloves garlic, minced

1½ cups (12 fl oz/375 ml) dry red wine

1 cup (6 oz/185 g) canned diced tomatoes

5 cups (40 fl oz/1.25 l) beef broth

FOR THE GREMOLATA

½ cup (¾ oz/20 g) minced fresh flat-leaf parsley

Grated zest of 1 lemon

2 cloves garlic, minced

Kick off dinner-party season with this rustic yet elegant recipe, in which veal shanks are slowly braised to melting tenderness. The traditional accompaniments are gremolata, a parsley and lemon relish that provides a welcome counterpoint to so much richness, and a golden-hued risotto perfumed with saffron.

Put the flour on a plate and season with salt and pepper. Dust the veal shanks with the seasoned flour, shaking off the excess. In a large, heavy sauté pan with a lid, warm the oil over medium-high heat. Working in batches, sear the shanks, turning once, until well browned on both sides, about 8 minutes. Transfer to a plate.

Return the pan to medium heat, add the onion, carrot, celery, and garlic, and sauté until softened, 3–4 minutes. Add the wine and stir to scrape up any browned bits on the pan bottom. Raise the heat to high and cook until the liquid has thickened and is reduced by half, 3–4 minutes. Add the tomatoes and broth and bring to a boil. Reduce the heat to low, return the veal shanks to the pan, cover, and simmer, turning occasionally, for 1 hour. Uncover and cook until the veal is tender, about 30 minutes.

Meanwhile, to make the gremolata, in a small bowl, stir together the parsley, lemon zest, and garlic.

Divide the veal shanks among plates. Top with the pan sauce, sprinkle with the gremolata, and serve.

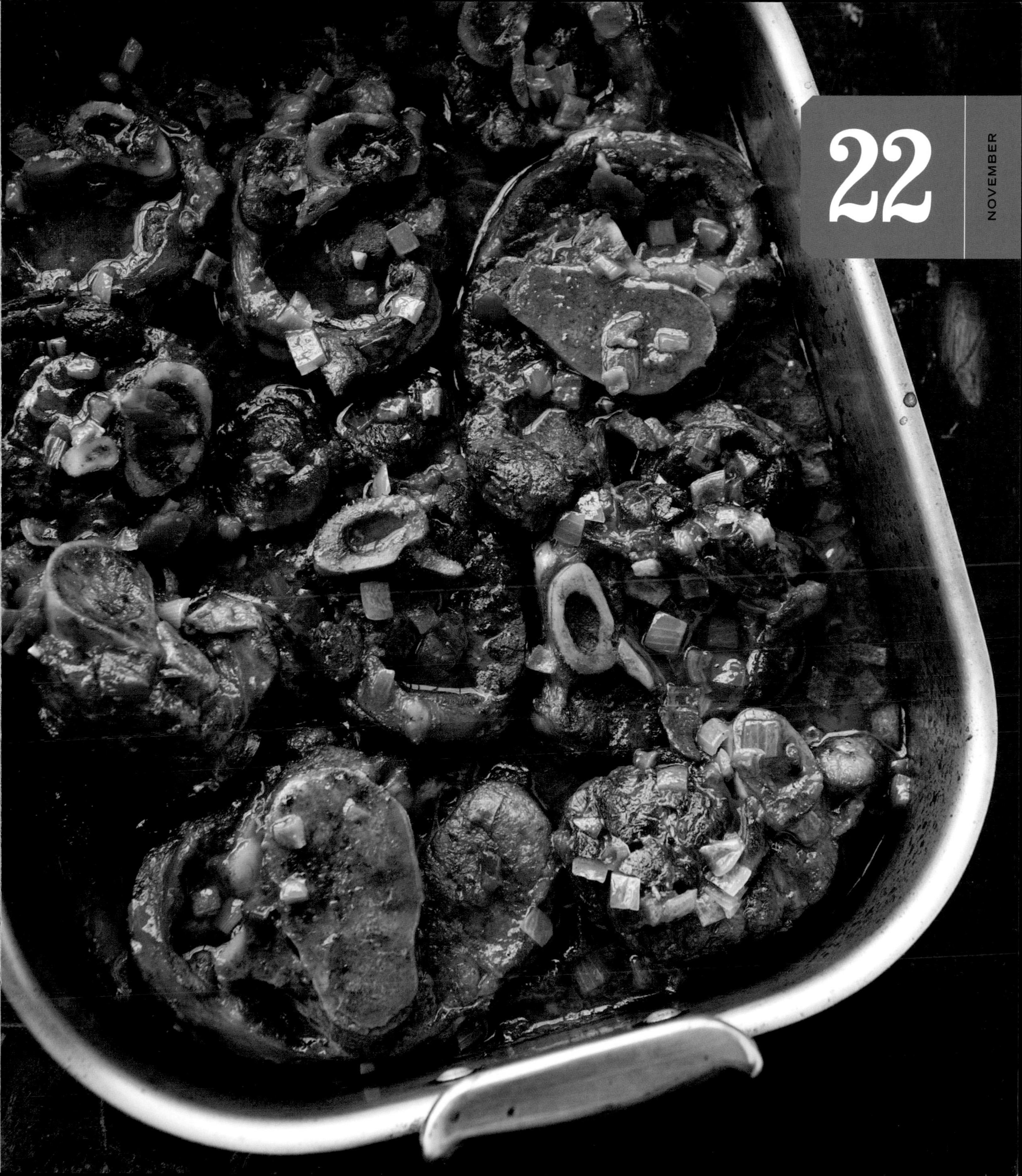

22

NOVEMBER

26

This retro casserole uses up leftover turkey in a tangle of egg noodles, button mushrooms, and cheesy sauce—with delicious results. Baked in one pan, or divided into individual ramekins, it is sure to become an annual post-holiday tradition. Use both white and dark turkey meat, as the dark meat will add moisture.

TURKEY TETRAZZINI

serves 6–8

Olive oil for greasing

7 Tbsp (3½ oz/105 g) unsalted butter

2 shallots, minced

½ lb (250 g) button mushrooms, sliced

⅓ cup (2 oz/60 g) all-purpose flour

3 cups (24 fl oz/750 ml) chicken broth

Salt and ground white pepper

3 cups (18 oz/560 g) shredded cooked turkey

½ lb (250 g) egg noodles, cooked according to package directions

¾ cup (3 oz/90 g) grated Parmesan cheese

2 green onions, white and tender green parts, chopped

1 cup (2 oz/60 g) fresh bread crumbs

Preheat the oven to 450°F (230°C). Oil a 9-by-13-inch (23-by-33-cm) baking dish or 6 individual ramekins or baking dishes.

In a large frying pan, melt 2 Tbsp of the butter over medium-high heat. Add the shallots and mushrooms and sauté until the mushrooms begin to brown, about 5 minutes. Transfer to a large bowl.

Add 4 Tbsp of the butter to the pan and melt over medium-high heat. Add the flour and cook, stirring constantly, for 2 minutes. Add the broth and bring to a boil. Cook, stirring frequently, until the sauce thickens, about 4 minutes. Season with 1 tsp salt and ½ tsp pepper. Pour the sauce into the bowl with the mushrooms and add the turkey, the cooked noodles, ½ cup (2 oz/60g) of the Parmesan, and the green onions and stir to combine.

In a small bowl, mix the bread crumbs with the remaining ¼ cup (1 oz/30 g) Parmesan.

Transfer the turkey mixture to the prepared dish(es). Sprinkle evenly with the bread crumb mixture. Using your fingers, break the remaining 1 Tbsp butter into small pieces and sprinkle over the top.

Bake until the tetrazzini is bubbly around the edges and the bread crumbs are golden brown, about 15 minutes. Serve.

27

This comforting cool-weather dish sparkles with color and appealing flavors. Adding the lemon zest to the warm vegetables imbues citrusy, fresh aroma. Accompany with a green salad and a crusty baguette.

WINTER VEGETABLE STEW

serves 6

2 Tbsp olive oil, plus more for drizzling

1 large yellow onion, finely chopped

2 celery ribs, finely chopped

10 cloves garlic, smashed

2 Tbsp tomato paste

½ cup (4 fl oz/125 ml) medium-dry sherry

½ cup (4 fl oz/125 ml) chicken or vegetable broth

1 tsp sherry vinegar or red wine vinegar

1 butternut squash, about 2½ lb (1.25 kg), peeled, seeded, and cut into chunks

3 parsnips, peeled and cut into chunks

3 large carrots, cut into chunks

1 tsp dried tarragon

Salt and freshly ground pepper

Grated zest and juice of 1 lemon

1 bunch watercress, tough stems removed, leaves chopped

In a large, heavy frying pan, warm 2 Tbsp of the oil over medium-high heat. Add the onion and celery and sauté until softened and beginning to brown, about 6 minutes. Add the garlic and tomato paste and stir for 1 minute. Pour in the sherry, broth, and vinegar and stir to scrape up any browned bits on the pan bottom. Transfer the contents of the pan to a slow cooker.

Add the squash, parsnips, carrots, and tarragon to the slow cooker, season with salt and pepper, and stir to blend evenly. Cover and cook on the low setting for 5 hours. The vegetables should be tender. Stir the lemon juice into the stew.

Serve, garnished with the watercress and lemon zest and drizzled with a little oil.

The holidays call for celebrations, get-togethers, and classic dishes like fall-off-the-bone lamb shanks; slow-simmered beef bourguignon; risottos spiked with rich cheeses or crab; and truffled mac and cheese. Winter citrus brightens slow-cooked short ribs with orange-tarragon cream and braised chicken with tangerine and star anise, while spices like cumin and turmeric add warmth. One-pot meals like shellfish cioppino and creamy fish chowder add variety and interest to this month filled with hearty dishes.

1
CITRUS-BRAISED LAMB SHANKS
page 274

2
CHICKEN STEW WITH DUMPLINGS
page 274

3
MUSHROOM RAGÙ WITH POLENTA
page 276

8
CHICKEN & LEEK PIE
page 279

9
WILD RICE, BEEF & MUSHROOM CASSEROLE
page 280

10
BRAISED BLACK COD WITH SHIITAKE MUSHROOMS
page 280

15
BEEF BOURGUIGNON
page 285

16
BAKED EGGPLANT WITH YOGURT & POMEGRANATE
page 285

17
BROCCOLI-CHEDDAR QUICHE
page 286

22
STIR-FRIED BEEF & BOK CHOY WITH GINGER
page 288

23
BRAISED STUFFED PORK SHOULDER
page 290

24
FOUR-CHEESE RISOTTO
page 290

29
GRATINÉED RICOTTA & SPINACH GNOCCHI
page 294

30
WINE-BRAISED SAUSAGES
page 295

31
DUNGENESS CRAB RISOTTO
page 295

4
**SMOKY WHITEFISH
& POTATO CHOWDER**
page 276

5
BALSAMIC BEEF STEW
page 277

6
**STIR-FRIED CHICKEN WITH
BROCCOLI & MUSHROOMS**
page 277

7
TRUFFLED MAC & CHEESE
page 279

11
LENTIL, SPINACH & BACON STEW
page 281

12
**SPICY STIR FRIED SQUID
WITH VEGETABLES**
page 281

13
**SPICED RICE PILAF WITH
BUTTERNUT SQUASH & PISTACHIOS**
page 282

14
**BRAISED CHICKEN WITH
TANGERINE & STAR ANISE**
page 282

18
**ALE-BRAISED PORK CHOPS
WITH CANADIAN BACON**
page 286

19
BAKED CHICKEN RICE PILAF
page 287

20
**CORN SPOON BREAD WITH
CHEDDAR & BACON**
page 287

21
CHICKEN TIKKA MASALA
page 288

25
**BRAISED SHORT RIBS WITH
ORANGE-TARRAGON CREAM**
page 291

26
CIOPPINO
page 293

27
SAUSAGE & MUSHROOM STRATA
page 293

28
**BEEF & BROCCOLI STIR-FRY
WITH NOODLES**
page 294

december

1

CITRUS-BRAISED LAMB SHANKS

serves 4

2 Tbsp olive oil

4 lamb shanks, about 1 lb (500 g) each

Salt and freshly ground pepper

1 carrot, finely chopped

1 yellow onion, finely chopped

2 celery ribs, finely chopped

3 small sprigs fresh thyme

1 bay leaf

3 cloves garlic, minced

1½ Tbsp tomato paste

2 cups (16 fl oz/500 ml) dry white wine

1 cup (8 fl oz/250 ml) chicken broth

Grated zest and juice of 1 lemon

Grated zest and juice of 1 lime

Grated zest and juice of 1 orange

Lamb shanks meet a bright trio of winter citrus—lemon, lime, and orange—in this dish. The rich braising liquid that results from the slow cooking almost surpasses the lamb shanks themselves. If you want to stretch the recipe to serve six, shred the meat from the bones, divide among shallow bowls, and serve over rice, orzo, or polenta, with the reduced juices drizzled over each serving.

In a large, heavy pot, heat 1 Tbsp of the oil over medium-high heat. Season the shanks with salt and pepper. Working in batches, sear the shanks, turning as needed, until browned on all sides, 6–8 minutes. Transfer to a platter and pour off the fat from the pot.

Preheat the oven to 250°F (120°C). Add the remaining 1 Tbsp oil to the pot and place over medium-low heat. Add the carrot, onion, and celery and sauté until softened, about 5 minutes. Add the thyme, bay leaf, garlic, and tomato paste. Stir in ½ tsp salt, season with pepper, and stir for 1 minute. Add the wine, broth, and lemon and lime zests and juices.

Return the shanks to the pot and bring the liquid to a gentle simmer. Cover and cook in the oven, turning the shanks every hour, until the meat is completely tender, about 2½ hours. Transfer the shanks to a platter and keep warm in the oven.

Pour the juices from the pot into a large, heatproof measuring pitcher and let stand for 1 minute. The fat will rise to the top. Use a bulb baster to transfer the juices underneath the fat to a small saucepan. Simmer to reduce slightly. Stir in the orange zest and juice.

Drizzle the reduced juices over the lamb shanks and serve.

2

CHICKEN STEW WITH DUMPLINGS

serves 4

1½ lb (750 g) skinless, boneless chicken thighs, cut into bite-sized chunks

Salt and freshly ground pepper

½ cup (4 oz/125 g) cold unsalted butter, cut into small pieces, plus 2 Tbsp

3 carrots, thinly sliced

1 yellow onion, chopped

2 celery ribs, thinly sliced

2 cups (10 oz/315 g) plus 2 Tbsp all-purpose flour

4 cups (32 fl oz/1 l) chicken broth

½ cup (2½ oz/75 g) thawed frozen baby peas

2 tsp baking powder

½ cup (4 fl oz/125 ml) milk

2 Tbsp minced fresh flat-leaf parsley

Bitter winter days welcome a warming stew of tender chicken and pillowy dumplings. To add extra punch, make cheese or herb dumplings. Simply stir 1 cup (4 oz/ 125 g) grated Cheddar or asiago cheese or 1 Tbsp finely chopped fresh chives, basil, or parsley into the dry ingredients and proceed with the recipe.

Season the chicken with salt and pepper. In a large, heavy pot, melt the 2 Tbsp butter over medium-high heat. Add the chicken and cook, stirring often, until golden, about 4 minutes. Add the carrots, onion, and celery, season with salt and pepper, and cook until the vegetables begin to soften and the chicken is opaque, 4–5 minutes. Sprinkle with the 2 Tbsp flour and cook, stirring, for about 2 minutes. Gradually pour in the broth, add the peas, and bring to a boil.

Meanwhile, in a bowl, combine the 2 cups flour, the baking powder, and 1 tsp salt. Using a pastry blender or 2 knives, cut in the ½ cup butter until the mixture forms coarse crumbs the size of peas. Add the milk and stir, then knead a few times until a soft dough forms.

Drop heaping tablespoonfuls of the dough over the top of the boiling stew. Reduce the heat to low, cover the pot, and cook until the dumplings have nearly doubled in size, about 8 minutes. Sprinkle with the parsley and serve directly from the pot.

7

TRUFFLED MAC & CHEESE

serves 6

Salt and freshly ground pepper

1 lb (500 g) elbow macaroni

2 tsp truffle oil

4 Tbsp (2 oz/60 g) butter, plus more for greasing

¼ cup (1½ oz/45 g) all-purpose flour

½ tsp sweet paprika

½ tsp Dijon mustard

2 cups (16 fl oz/500 ml) milk

1 cup (8 fl oz/250 ml) half-and-half

1½ cups (6 oz/185 g) shredded Gruyère cheese

1½ cups (6 oz/185 g) shredded white Cheddar cheese

2 Tbsp minced chives

Break out the special-occasion ingredients this time of the year. Comforting macaroni and cheese reaches a new level with a drizzle of sumptuous truffle oil. Try baking individual portions in buttered muffin pans, and pass a tray of mini macs at your next party.

Preheat the oven to 375°F (190°C). Butter a 9-by-13-inch (23-by-33-cm) baking dish.

Bring a large saucepan of salted water to a boil. Add the macaroni and cook, stirring occasionally, until not quite al dente, about 2 minutes less than the package directions. Drain and transfer to a large bowl. While the pasta is still warm, drizzle with the truffle oil and stir well.

Add the butter to the saucepan and melt it over medium-high heat. Add the flour, paprika, and mustard and cook, stirring well, until no visible flour remains, 1–3 minutes. Whisk in the milk, half-and-half, and a generous pinch of salt and bring to a boil. Simmer, whisking frequently to smooth out any lumps, for 4–5 minutes. Remove from the heat. Add a pinch of pepper and 1 cup (4 oz/125 g) each of the Gruyère and Cheddar. Stir until smooth.

Pour the cheese sauce onto the macaroni, add the chives, and mix well. Transfer to the prepared dish and top with the remaining cheeses. Bake until the top is lightly browned and the sauce is bubbly, 25–30 minutes. Let stand for 5 minutes before serving.

8

CHICKEN & LEEK PIE

serves 4–6

9 Tbsp (4½ oz/140 g) unsalted butter

2 large leeks, white and pale green parts, thinly sliced

Salt and freshly ground pepper

2⅓ cup (12 oz/375 g) all-purpose flour

¼ cup (2 fl oz/60 ml) dry white wine

4 cups (32 fl oz/1 l) chicken broth

About 4 cups (1½ lb/750 g) shredded cooked chicken

1 cup (5 oz/155 g) thawed frozen baby peas

4 tsp baking powder

1½ cups (12 fl oz/375 ml) milk

For an alternative to the drop-biscuit topping here, use thawed purchased puff pastry dough. Preheat the oven to 425°F (220°C) and lay the dough on top of the filling in the dish. Trim the dough, leaving a 1-inch (2.5-cm) overhang. Fold the overhang back over itself and press it into the sides of the dish to make a sturdy rim. Prick the dough with a fork to create steam vents and bake until golden brown.

Preheat the oven to 375°F (190°C). In a large ovenproof frying pan, melt 4 Tbsp butter over medium-high heat. Add the leeks, season with salt and pepper, and sauté until softened, about 5 minutes. Add the ⅓ cup (2 oz/60 g) flour and cook, stirring, for 2 minutes. Stir in the wine and broth and bring to a boil. Reduce the heat to low and simmer, stirring occasionally, until the liquid thickens slightly, about 5 minutes. Stir in the chicken and peas and season with salt and pepper.

In a bowl, combine the remaining 2 cups (10 oz/310 g) flour, the baking powder, and ½ tsp salt. Using a pastry blender or 2 knives, cut in the remaining 5 Tbsp butter until the mixture forms coarse crumbs about the size of peas. Add the milk and, using a rubber spatula, stir until evenly moistened. Place heaping spoonfuls of the batter evenly over the chicken filling. Bake until the topping is golden brown and the filling is bubbling, about 25 minutes. Remove from the oven, let stand for 5 minutes, then serve.

9

DECEMBER

This is an unexpected ground beef casserole, verging on upscale with nutty wild rice, fresh mushrooms and spinach, and melted cheese on top. A pinch of cumin imparts earthy spice. Tuck away a pan at the back of the fridge or freezer. After a long day of presents shopping, dinner will be prepped and ready to go straight into the oven.

WILD RICE, BEEF & MUSHROOM CASSEROLE

serves 6

1 cup long-grain and wild rice blend

2 cups (16 fl oz/500 ml) chicken broth

1 Tbsp unsalted butter

1 lb (500 g) ground beef

Salt and freshly ground pepper

4 Tbsp olive oil

1 yellow onion, chopped

3 cloves garlic, minced

2 tsp ground cumin

1 tsp onion salt

½ lb (250 g) button mushrooms, thinly sliced

5 oz (155 g) baby spinach

6 oz (185 g) Muenster cheese, thinly sliced

In a small saucepan with a tight-fitting lid, add the rice, broth, and butter. Bring to a boil over medium-high heat. Reduce heat to low, cover, and cook until all the liquid is absorbed, about 50 minutes. Set aside.

While the rice is cooking, season the beef with salt and pepper. In a frying pan, warm 1 Tbsp of the oil over medium-high heat. Add the meat and cook, stirring, until it is no longer pink. Using a slotted spoon, transfer the beef to a large bowl and set aside. Pour off the fat from the pan. Add 2 Tbsp of the oil and the onion and saute until it begins to soften, about 3 minutes. Add the garlic, cumin, onion salt, a sprinkle of salt and pepper, and continue to sauté until aromatic, about 2 minutes. Add the mushrooms to the pan and toss to coat with oil. Sauté until they have released their liquid and are soft and well browned, about 6 minutes. Transfer the mushroom mixture and the cooked rice to the bowl with the beef and stir to combine.

Preheat the oven to 375°F (190°C) and set a rack in the upper third of the oven.

Add the remaining 1 Tbsp oil to the frying pan and set over medium-high heat. Add the spinach, season with salt and pepper, and sauté until completely wilted. Allow the spinach to cool and drain all the liquid that collects at the bottom of the pan. Transfer the spinach to a cutting board and chop. »→

Spoon half of the beef mixture into an 8-by-11-inch (20-by-28-cm) casserole dish. Top with the spinach and then spread half of the cheese slices over the spinach in a single layer. Spread the remaining beef mixture on top, then finish with the remaining cheese slices.

Put the casserole in the oven and cook just until the cheese is melted, about 10 minutes. Serve at once.

10

DECEMBER

Dark soy sauce, Japanese rice wine, and thinly sliced shiitake mushrooms and green onions lend earthiness and depth to the salty-sweet sauce that laps these tender black cod fillets. Serve this with a steaming bowl of rice on the side to catch every drop of the seductive sauce.

BRAISED BLACK COD WITH SHIITAKE MUSHROOMS

serves 4

1 Tbsp canola oil

4 black cod fillets, skin removed

¼ cup (2 fl oz/60 ml) dark soy sauce

¼ cup (2 fl oz/60 ml) sake

2 Tbsp sugar

2 slices peeled fresh ginger, smashed

2 star anise

1 cinnamon stick

2 tsp cornstarch dissolved in 2 tsp cold water

12 shiitake mushrooms, stemmed and thinly sliced

4 green onions, white and tender green parts, cut into 1-inch (2.5 cm) pieces

In a large frying pan, heat the oil over medium-high heat. Add the fish and sear for 1–2 minutes. Turn and sear on the second side for 1–2 minutes. Transfer to a plate. Drain the oil from the pan.

Add the soy sauce, sake, sugar, ginger, star anise, cinnamon, cornstarch mixture, mushrooms, and green onions to the pan. Pour in ½ cup (4 fl oz/125 ml) water. Bring to a boil and simmer for about 2 minutes. Place the fish in the broth, cover, and simmer until opaque throughout, about 10 minutes. Discard the ginger, star anise, and cinnamon from the broth. Serve directly from the pan.

11

LENTIL, SPINACH & BACON STEW

serves 4–6

A piping-hot bowl of lentils will warm you to the core. Bacon adds a hit of smokiness, but if you have a leftover ham bone from a holiday roast, you could use that instead. Serve the stew simply as is, with a loaf of rustic levain bread.

3 thick-cut slices bacon, chopped

2 carrots, cut into 1-inch (2.5-cm) chunks

½ small yellow onion, finely chopped

1 celery rib, chopped

3 cloves garlic, smashed

Salt and freshly ground pepper

2 cups (14 oz/440 g) small green French lentils, picked over and rinsed

2 cups (16 fl oz/500 ml) chicken broth

1 tsp chopped fresh thyme

1 bay leaf

6 cups (8 oz/250 g) baby spinach leaves

Heat a large saucepan over medium heat. Add the bacon and sauté until most of its fat is rendered and the bacon is golden brown, about 5 minutes. Add the carrots, onion, celery, and garlic and sauté until tender, 2–3 minutes. Season with salt and pepper.

Add the lentils and stir to coat with the fat. Raise the heat to medium-high, add 3 cups (24 fl oz/750 ml) water, the broth, thyme, and bay leaf, and bring to a boil. Reduce the heat to medium-low, add 1 tsp salt, and simmer, uncovered, until the lentils are tender, 35–40 minutes.

Stir the spinach into the lentil mixture and cook until wilted, about 4 minutes. Season with salt and pepper and discard the bay leaf. Serve.

12

SPICY STIR-FRIED SQUID WITH VEGETABLES

serves 4–6

Take a breather from rich holiday fare with a fresh and fast weeknight stir-fry. Tender calamari rings and tentacles meet a slew of tasty vegetables and spice. The squid is one of the last additions; take care to cook it just until tender, and no longer.

3 cloves garlic, minced

1 Tbsp peeled and grated fresh ginger

2 Tbsp light soy sauce

1 Tbsp toasted sesame oil

1 tsp chile bean paste

½ tsp sugar

⅛ tsp chili powder

3 Tbsp canola oil

1 yellow onion, thinly sliced

1 small carrot, cut into matchsticks about 3 inches (7.5 cm) long

½ green bell pepper, seeded and cut into matchsticks about 3 inches (7.5 cm) long

½ cup (2 oz/60 g) canned bamboo shoots, cut into matchsticks about 3 inches (7.5 cm) long

2 lb (1 kg) squid, cleaned, bodies cut into 1-inch (2.5-cm) rings and tentacles left whole

2 green onions, white and tender green parts, cut into matchsticks about 3 inches (7.5 cm) long

1 tsp sesame seeds, toasted

In a bowl, stir together the garlic, ginger, soy sauce, sesame oil, chile bean paste, sugar, and chili powder. Stir in 2 Tbsp water.

In a wok or large frying pan, heat 2 Tbsp of the canola oil over high heat. Add the yellow onion, carrot, and bell pepper and stir-fry until brown around the edges. Stir in the bamboo shoots and stir-fry for 1 minute. Transfer the vegetables to a bowl.

Return the pan to high heat and add the remaining 1 Tbsp canola oil. Add the squid and stir-fry until it just begins to curl and turn opaque, 1–2 minutes. Transfer to a colander and let drain. Return the pan to high heat. Return the vegetables and squid to the pan, add the green onions, and pour in the soy sauce mixture. Stir-fry until the squid and vegetables are heated through and most of the liquid has evaporated, about 1 minute. Transfer to a platter, garnish with the sesame seeds, and serve.

13

SPICED RICE PILAF WITH BUTTERNUT SQUASH & PISTACHIOS

serves 4–6

Fragrant rice or bulgur pilaf, replete with herbs, nuts, and meat or vegetables, is a popular accompaniment on the Turkish table. This golden pilaf has chunks of butternut squash, making it a delicious meatless main course.

⅛ tsp saffron threads

3 Tbsp olive oil

1 yellow onion, finely chopped

2 cloves garlic, minced

2 cups (14 oz/440 g) long-grain white rice

2 cinnamon sticks

½ tsp ground cumin

½ tsp paprika

¼ tsp ground turmeric

Salt

3 cups (24 fl oz/750 ml) chicken or vegetable broth

4 cups (22 oz/690 g) peeled, seeded, and chopped butternut squash

2 Tbsp minced preserved lemon

⅓ cup (1½ oz/45 g) chopped pistachios

¼ cup (⅓ oz/10 g) chopped fresh mint

3 Tbsp dried currants

In a large, deep frying pan over medium heat, toast the saffron threads, stirring constantly, until fragrant and a shade darker, about 1 minute. Pour the threads into a bowl and, when cool, crumble.

Add the olive oil to the pan and warm over medium-high heat. Add the onion and garlic and sauté until the onion is soft and translucent, 3–5 minutes. Stir in the rice, cinnamon, cumin, paprika, turmeric, and saffron. Season with ½ tsp salt and cook, stirring occasionally, until the spices are fragrant, about 1 minute.

Stir in the broth, squash, and preserved lemon and bring to a simmer. Reduce the heat to low, cover, and cook until the liquid is absorbed and the rice and squash are tender, 20–25 minutes.

Transfer the pilaf to a serving bowl and fluff with a fork. Stir in the pistachios, mint, and currants and serve.

14

BRAISED CHICKEN WITH TANGERINE & STAR ANISE

serves 4

Here, vibrant tangerines, which are at their best in the winter, add a tart-sweet and exotic element to a star anise–infused braising liquid. Their fragrant juice and zest perk up the deep flavors in the dish and cut through the richness of the tender braised chicken thighs.

2 tangerines

8 skin-on, bone-in chicken thighs, about 3¼ lb (1.6 kg) total

Salt and freshly ground pepper

2 Tbsp peanut oil

1 small yellow onion, finely chopped

2 cloves garlic, minced

1 tsp peeled and grated fresh ginger

1 cup (8 fl oz/250 ml) chicken broth

2 Tbsp soy sauce

1 tsp chile-garlic sauce, such as Sriracha

2–3 star anise

2 tsp cornstarch dissolved in 1 Tbsp water

Finely grate the zest from the tangerines, then squeeze ½ cup (4 fl oz/125 ml) juice. Season the chicken with 1 tsp salt and ½ tsp pepper.

In a large, heavy pot, heat the oil over medium-high heat. Working in batches, sear the chicken, turning once or twice, until browned on both sides, about 9 minutes. Transfer to a plate.

Pour off all but 1 Tbsp fat in the pot and return the pot to medium heat. Add the onion and cook, stirring occasionally, until softened, 3–4 minutes. Add the garlic, the ginger, and half of the tangerine zest and stir until fragrant, about 1 minute. Add the broth, tangerine juice, soy sauce, chile-garlic sauce, and star anise and bring to a boil, stirring to scrape up any browned bits from the bottom of the pot. Return the chicken to the pot, reduce the heat to low, cover, and simmer until the chicken is opaque throughout, about 25 minutes.

Transfer the chicken to a platter. Bring the liquid in the pot to a boil over medium-high heat. Stir in the cornstarch mixture and cook just until the sauce thickens slightly, about 30 seconds.

Pour the sauce over the chicken. Sprinkle with the remaining tangerine zest and serve.

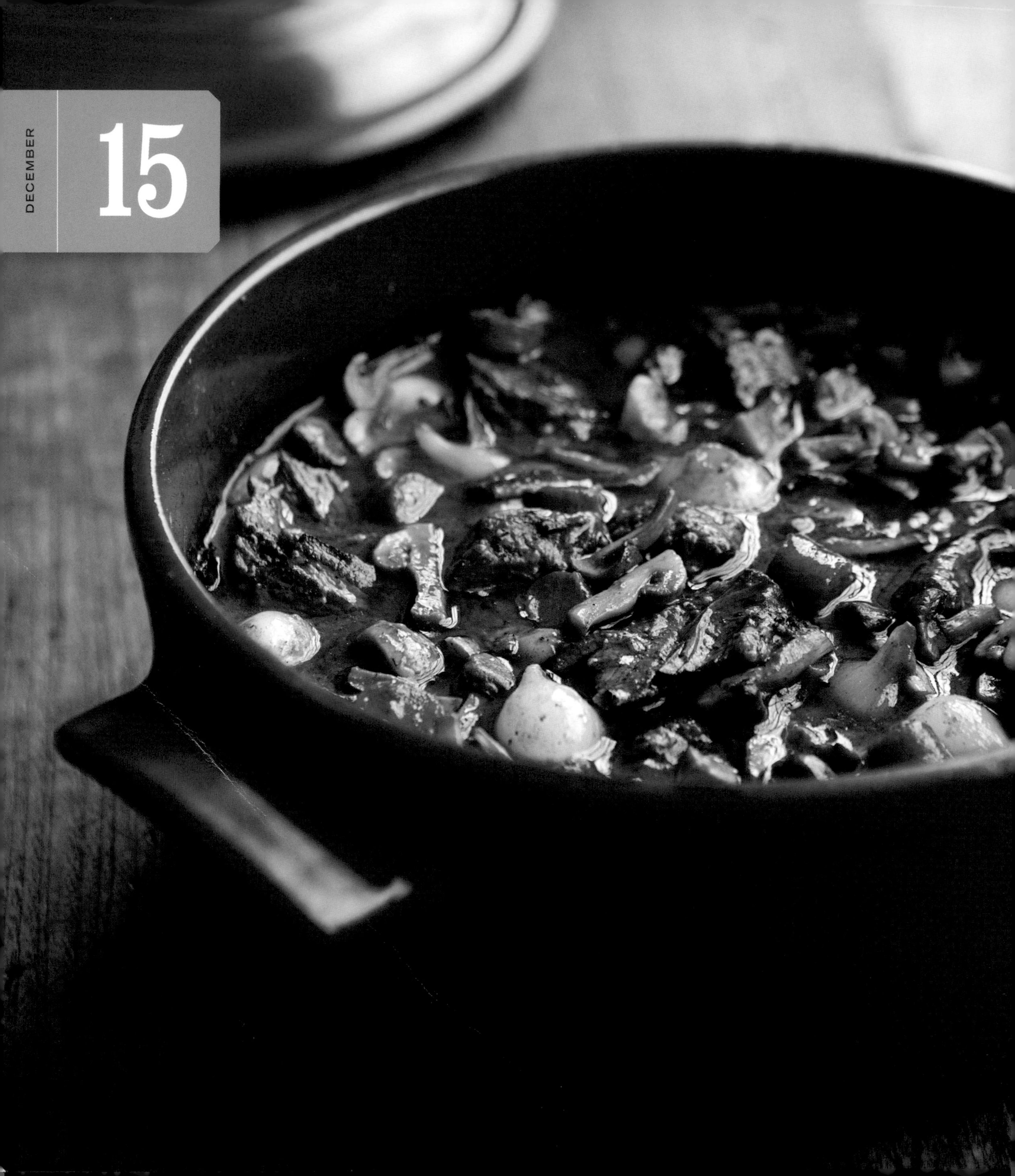
DECEMBER
15

BEEF BOURGUIGNON

serves 6–8

3½ lb (1.75 kg) boneless beef chuck roast, or a combination of boneless chuck and beef shank, cut into 2–2½ inch (5–6 cm) chunks

Salt and freshly ground pepper

All-purpose flour

1 Tbsp olive oil

6 oz (185 g) pancetta, cut into 1-inch (2.5-cm) pieces

1 carrot, sliced

1 yellow onion, chopped

3 cups (24 fl oz/750 ml) hearty red wine

2 cloves garlic, minced

1 Tbsp fresh thyme leaves, or ½ Tbsp dried thyme

1 bay leaf

1 Tbsp tomato paste

3 Tbsp unsalted butter, plus more if needed

1 lb (500 g) mushrooms, thickly sliced

20–24 jarred or thawed frozen pearl onions

Beef bourguignon represents French country cooking at its best. A tough cut of beef is transformed into a silken tour de force that can be cut with a fork. The great wine of Burgundy transforms into an unctuous sauce to which mushrooms and pearl onions are added. Serve with steamed or roasted potatoes to soak up the sauce.

Sprinkle the beef chunks with ½ tsp salt and ¼ tsp pepper. Spread some flour on a large plate. Lightly coat the cubes with the flour, shaking off the excess.

In a large, heavy pot, warm the oil over low heat. Add the pancetta and cook until crisp and golden, 4–5 minutes. Using a slotted spoon, transfer to a large bowl. Raise the heat to medium-high and, working in batches, sear the beef, turning as needed, until browned on all sides, about 5 minutes. Transfer to the bowl with the pancetta. Add the carrot and onion to the pot and cook until browned, about 5 minutes. Transfer to the bowl with the pancetta and beef.

Pour off the fat from the pot. Reduce the heat to medium, add the wine, and stir to scrape up any browned bits on the pot bottom. Stir in the pancetta, beef, carrot, onion, garlic, thyme, bay leaf, and tomato paste. Season with ½ tsp salt and ¼ tsp pepper and bring to a simmer. Reduce the heat to low, cover, and cook until the beef is somewhat tender, about 2½ hours. »→

In a frying pan, melt the 3 Tbsp butter over medium heat. Add the mushrooms and sauté until lightly browned, 4–5 minutes. Transfer to a bowl. Add the pearl onions to the pan and sauté, adding more butter if needed, until golden, about 10 minutes. After the beef has cooked for 2½ hours, add the mushrooms and pearl onions to the pot and continue to cook until the beef is fork-tender, about 1 hour more.

Transfer the beef, pancetta, and vegetables to a large serving bowl. Skim the fat from the surface of the sauce. Raise the heat to medium-high, bring to a boil, and cook until the sauce thickens slightly, 1–2 minutes. Pour the sauce over the beef mixture and serve.

BAKED EGGPLANT WITH YOGURT & POMEGRANATE

serves 4

1 cup (8 oz/250 g) plain Greek-style yogurt

1 clove garlic, crushed

5 Tbsp (3 fl oz/80 ml) olive oil, plus more for greasing

3 Asian eggplants, about 1½ lb (750 g) total, peeled and cut lengthwise into slices about ¾ inch (2 cm) thick

Salt and freshly ground pepper

1 Tbsp pomegranate molasses

Slender Asian eggplants, unlike the larger globe variety, are rarely bitter, which eliminates the need to salt and drain the flesh. This quick-to-assemble dish is given a boost of richness from a topping of creamy, thick Greek-style yogurt, and a pleasantly pungent edge from a drizzle of pomegranate molasses. It is an light, satisfying main course or an excellent side dish to grilled meats or fish.

In a small bowl, stir together the yogurt and garlic. Cover and set aside for 1 hour to blend the flavors, or refrigerate for up to 8 hours and bring to room temperature before using.

Preheat the oven to 475°F (245°C). Oil a baking sheet. Arrange the eggplant slices in a single layer on the prepared sheet. Brush the slices evenly with 4 Tbsp (2 fl oz/60 ml) of the oil. Sprinkle generously with salt and pepper.

Bake the eggplant until tender, about 15 minutes. Transfer to a platter. Remove the garlic from the yogurt. Spread the yogurt over the eggplant slices. In a small bowl, whisk together the pomegranate molasses, ½ tsp salt, and the remaining 1 Tbsp oil until combined. Drizzle over the yogurt and serve.

17

Quiche is hard to beat as a one-pan meal. A buttery, flaky pastry crust is nearly irresistible, and the possibilities for fillings are endless. Broccoli and cheddar are a universally appealing combination, making this one of the most popular versions. Serve with a frisée salad and a glass of crisp white wine.

BROCCOLI-CHEDDAR QUICHE

serves 6

1¼ cups (6½ oz/200 g) all-purpose flour

Salt and freshly ground pepper

7 Tbsp (3½ oz/105 g) cold unsalted butter, cut into small pieces

¼ cup (2 fl oz/60 ml) ice water, or as needed

2 cups (4 oz/125 g) broccoli florets

1 cup (8 fl oz/250 ml) half-and-half

2 eggs

1 Tbsp minced fresh dill

1 cup (4 oz/125 g) shredded sharp Cheddar cheese

In a large bowl, whisk together the flour and ¼ tsp salt. Scatter the butter over the flour mixture. Using a pastry blender or 2 knives, cut in the butter just until the mixture forms coarse crumbs about the size of peas. Drizzle with the ice water and toss with a fork until the mixture forms moist clumps. If the dough seems too crumbly, add a little more ice water. Form the dough into a disk, wrap in plastic wrap, and refrigerate for at least 30 minutes or up to 2 hours.

On a lightly floured work surface, roll out the dough into a round about 12 inches (30 cm) in diameter. Transfer to a 9-inch (23-cm) tart pan with a removable bottom, gently fitting the dough into the bottom and up the sides of the pan. Trim the dough, leaving a ½-inch (12-mm) overhang. Fold the overhanging dough back over itself and press it firmly into the pan sides; the dough should be doubly thick at the sides and rise about ⅛ inch (3 mm) above the rim. Pierce the dough all over with a fork. Line the dough with foil and freeze for 15–30 minutes.

Position a rack in the bottom third of the oven and preheat to 375°F (190°C). Place the dough-lined pan on a baking sheet and fill the foil with pie weights or dried beans. Bake until the dough is set and beginning to brown, about 20 minutes.

Meanwhile, bring a saucepan of lightly salted water to a boil. Add the broccoli and cook until barely tender, about 5 minutes. Drain well. In a bowl, whisk together the half-and-half, the eggs, the dill, ½ tsp salt, and ¼ tsp pepper. »→

Remove the baking sheet from the oven, and remove the foil and weights from the pan. Scatter the broccoli and the Cheddar evenly in the pastry shell. Pour the egg mixture into the shell. Return the sheet to the oven and reduce the oven temperature to 350°F (180°C). Bake on the bottom oven rack until the filling is puffed and golden brown, about 35 minutes. Let cool slightly, then serve.

18

DECEMBER

Canadian bacon is in fact closer to ham than American bacon. Cut into fine dice, it offers a boost of sweet pork flavor to the chops in this recipe, and both the bacon and chops alike become plump and juicy in the beer braise. Serve with a side of creamy mashed potatoes.

ALE-BRAISED PORK CHOPS WITH CANADIAN BACON

serves 6

6 bone-in pork loin chops, each about 1½ inches (4 cm) thick

Salt and freshly ground pepper

2 Tbsp olive oil

2 slices Canadian bacon, finely chopped

1 large yellow onion, halved and thinly sliced

6 cloves garlic, sliced lengthwise

½ cup (4 fl oz/125 ml) pale ale or lager

½ cup (4 fl oz/125 ml) chicken broth

2 Tbsp cider vinegar or white wine vinegar

Season the pork chops generously with salt and pepper. In a large, heavy frying pan, warm the oil over medium-high heat. Working in batches, sear the chops, turning once, until golden brown on both sides, 8–10 minutes. Transfer to a plate.

Pour off the fat from the pan and return it to medium-high heat. Add the bacon and onion and sauté until they begin to brown, 7–8 minutes. Add the garlic, then pour in the ale and stir to scrape up any browned bits on the pan bottom. Stir in the broth, the vinegar, ¼ tsp salt, and several grindings of pepper. Transfer the contents of the pan to a slow cooker. Stack the pork chops on top. Cover and cook on the low setting for about 7 hours. The chops should be tender.

Transfer the chops to a platter, top with some of the braising liquid, and serve.

19

This pilaf covers all of the bases—rice, veggies, chicken—making it a great one-pot meal, and perfect for feeding your family during the week. Don't worry about the small amount of water for the rice; the chicken exudes plenty of juice, and together they make enough liquid to cook the rice.

BAKED CHICKEN RICE PILAF

serves 4–6

3½–4 lb (1.75–2 kg) assorted chicken pieces, skin on and bone in

Salt and freshly ground pepper

1 Tbsp unsalted butter

1 small yellow onion, finely chopped

2 carrots, finely chopped

2 celery ribs, finely chopped

2 cloves garlic, minced

1½ cups (10½ oz/330 g) basmati rice

1 tsp chopped fresh thyme

1 Tbsp chopped fresh flat-leaf parsley

1 bay leaf

Season the chicken pieces on both sides with salt and pepper. Preheat the oven to 425°F (220°C).

In a large, heavy pot, melt the butter over medium-high heat. When the butter begins to brown, add the onion, carrots, celery, and garlic, and season with salt and pepper. Cook, stirring occasionally, until the vegetables are tender, 3–4 minutes. Add the rice and cook, stirring constantly, until lightly toasted, about 1 minute.

Remove from the heat, stir in the thyme, parsley, and bay leaf, and arrange the chicken on top of the rice in a single layer. Place in the oven and cook, uncovered, for 15 minutes. Reduce the heat to 350°F (180°C), add 1 cup (8 fl oz/250 ml) water, cover the pot, and bake until the chicken is opaque and the rice is tender, about 45 minutes.

Remove from the oven and let stand, covered, for 10 minutes. Uncover, fluff the rice under the chicken with a fork, discard the bay leaf, and serve.

20

Serve spoonbread for a quick weeknight supper, or set it out next to a spiral-cut ham for a big holiday gathering. This version combines a handful of favorites into one dish: the eggy cornmeal pudding is enhanced with crumbles of bacon, a sprinkling of sharp Cheddar, and kernels of sweet corn. You'll get some of each in every delicious spoonful.

CORN SPOON BREAD WITH CHEDDAR & BACON

serves 4–6

4 Tbsp (2 oz/60 g) unsalted butter, cut into small pieces, plus more for greasing

3 slices thick-cut applewood-smoked bacon, coarsely chopped

3 cups (24 fl oz/750 ml) milk

Salt and freshly ground pepper

1 cup (7 oz/220 g) yellow cornmeal, preferably stone-ground

3 eggs, separated

1 cup (4 oz/125 g) shredded sharp Cheddar cheese

1 cup (6 oz/185 g) thawed frozen corn kernels

2 green onions, white and tender green parts, finely chopped

Chopped fresh chives for garnish (optional)

Preheat the oven to 375°F (190°C). Butter a 2-quart (2-l) baking dish.

In a frying pan, fry the bacon over medium heat, stirring, until crisp and golden, about 6 minutes. Drain on paper towels.

In a large saucepan, bring 2 cups (16 fl oz/ 500 ml) of the milk, 1½ tsp salt, and ¼ tsp pepper to a boil over medium-high heat, being careful that the milk does not boil over. Gradually whisk in the cornmeal and return to a boil. Reduce the heat to medium-low and cook, whisking frequently, until the cornmeal is quite thick, about 2 minutes. Remove from the heat. Add the butter and whisk until melted. In a bowl, whisk together the remaining 1 cup milk and the egg yolks, then whisk into the cornmeal mixture. Stir in the Cheddar, corn, bacon, and green onions.

In a clean bowl, using an electric mixer on high speed, beat the egg whites until soft peaks form. Fold about one-fourth of the whites into the cornmeal mixture to lighten it, then fold in the remaining whites. Spread the cornmeal mixture in the prepared dish.

Bake until puffed and golden brown, about 25 minutes. Garnish with chives, if using, and serve.

21

One of the most popular Anglo-Indian dishes—a uniquely British invention—is chicken tikka masala, succulent cubes of chicken breast bathed in a sweet, spicy sauce. Plenty of ginger and spice makes it a warming dish for a cold night. Packaged naan bread is now easy to find at many supermarkets. Stack buttered and toasted slices alongside the curry.

CHICKEN TIKKA MASALA

serves 4

¼ cup (2 oz/60 g) Greek yogurt or other plain yogurt

Juice of 1½ limes

3 tsp peeled and grated fresh ginger

1 tsp ground cumin

1¼ tsp garam masala

2 tsp sweet paprika

4 skinless, boneless chicken breast halves, about 1 lb (500 g), cut into 1-inch (2.5-cm) chunks

Salt

5 Tbsp (3 fl oz/80 ml) sunflower oil

1 small yellow onion, finely chopped

1 clove garlic, minced

5 green cardamom pods

1 tsp ground cumin

1 tsp ground coriander

½ tsp ground turmeric

½ tsp ground chile

1 can (14½ oz/455 g) diced tomatoes

1 jalapeño chile, thinly sliced

½ cup (4 fl oz/125 ml) heavy cream

Juice of ½ lemon

Warmed naan or pita breads

In a nonreactive bowl, stir together the yogurt, the lime juice, 2 tsp of the ginger, the cumin, 1 tsp of the garam masala, and the paprika. Add the chicken to the marinade, stir, cover, and refrigerate for at least 1 hour or up to 7 hours.

Preheat the broiler. Remove the chicken from the marinade, shaking off the excess, and place on a plate. Season with salt, drizzle with 2 Tbsp of the sunflower oil, and toss to coat. Arrange the chicken in a single layer on a foil-lined pan and broil, turning once, until browned, 3 minutes on each side.

In a saucepan, warm the remaining 3 Tbsp sunflower oil over medium heat. Add the onion, remaining 1 tsp ginger, and garlic and cook, stirring frequently, until the onion is soft, 4–5 minutes. Add the cardamom, cumin, coriander, turmeric, and ground chile and cook, stirring constantly, for about 2 minutes. Add the tomatoes and cook, stirring frequently, until the oil separates from the tomato ⟫

mixture, 5–8 minutes. Add the jalapeño, cream, and ½ cup (4 fl oz/125 ml) water, bring to a boil, reduce the heat to low, and simmer until the mixture forms a creamy sauce, 8–10 minutes.

Stir in the cooked chicken and the remaining ¼ tsp garam masala, season with salt, and simmer until the chicken is heated through, 8–10 minutes. Stir in the lemon juice. Serve with the naan bread.

22

Winter produces the crispest, crunchiest cabbages of the year, and bok choy is no exception. Pair it with thinly sliced flank steak, and season with a few simple but bold seasonings. Serve this quick and hearty stir-fry with wide rice noodles or steamed brown rice, if you like.

STIR-FRIED BEEF & BOK CHOY WITH GINGER

serves 4

2 Tbsp dry sherry

1 Tbsp soy sauce

½ tsp Asian chile paste

1 lb (500 g) baby bok choy

2 tsp peanut oil

2 cloves garlic, minced

1 Tbsp peeled and grated fresh ginger

1 lb (500 g) flank steak, thinly sliced across the grain

In a small bowl, stir together the sherry, soy sauce, and chile paste. Cut the bok choy lengthwise into halves or quarters, depending on size.

In a wok or a large frying pan, heat 1½ tsp of the oil over high heat. Add the bok choy and stir-fry just until tender-crisp, 3–4 minutes. Transfer to a bowl.

Add the remaining ½ tsp oil to the pan. Add the garlic and ginger and stir-fry until fragrant but not browned, 15–30 seconds. Add the beef and cook, stirring, just until no longer pink, about 2 minutes.

Return the bok choy to the pan, add the sherry mixture, and cook for 1 minute until heated through. Serve.

23

An economical cut of pork becomes a special-occasion, family-style main course in this traditional French country recipe. Feel free to vary the stuffing, adding other herbs or some grated Parmesan or chopped ham. You can also add some crushed tomatoes and dried oregano to the cooking liquid for a thicker, Italian-style sauce.

BRAISED STUFFED PORK SHOULDER

serves 6–8

1 boneless pork shoulder, about 4 lb (2 kg)

1 thick slice good-quality white bread, coarsely crumbled

1 egg, lightly beaten

2 cloves garlic, minced

2 Tbsp chopped fresh flat-leaf parsley

1 Tbsp finely shredded fresh basil

½ tsp dried oregano

½ tsp dried thyme

Salt and freshly ground pepper

¼ cup (2 fl oz/60 ml) olive oil

1 cup (8 fl oz/250 ml) dry white wine

1 cup (8 fl oz/250 ml) chicken broth

2 sprigs fresh thyme

Preheat the oven to 350°F (180°C).

Lay the pork shoulder on a cutting board with the boned side facing up. Starting at the center and using a sharp knife, cut through the thickest part of the meat, working from the center to the sides and cutting parallel to the board, to create 2 flaps of meat. When opened, the butterflied pork should measure about 12 by 16 inches (30 by 40 cm).

In a bowl, combine the bread, egg, garlic, parsley, basil, oregano, and thyme. Season with ¼ tsp salt and a pinch of pepper and stir to mix well. Spread this stuffing over the pork, leaving a border of about ¼ inch (6 mm) on the long edges and about 1 inch (2.5 cm) on the short edges. Starting at a short edge, roll up the meat. Securely tie the roll at regular intervals with kitchen string.

In a large, heavy pot, warm the oil over medium-high heat. Season the pork generously with salt and pepper. Sear the pork, turning occasionally, until browned on all sides, about 10 minutes. Transfer to a plate. Add the wine to the pot and stir to scrape up any browned bits on the pot bottom. Stir in the broth and bring to a boil over medium-high heat. Return the pork to the pot and add the thyme sprigs. Cover and cook in the oven until the pork is very tender, about 2 hours. ⟫

Transfer the pork to a cutting board and cover loosely with foil. Discard the thyme sprigs. Bring the cooking liquid to a boil over high heat, and cook until it thickens slightly, about 10 minutes. Adjust the seasoning.

Cut the pork crosswise into slices about ½ inch (12 mm) thick, removing the strings. Arrange the slices on a platter, top with the sauce, and serve.

24

A quartet of cheeses enlivens this decadent risotto: triple cream mascarpone, piquant and potent Gorgonzola, sharply aged Parmesan, and meltingly smooth Asiago. Serve with a fresh salad, to balance out the richness.

FOUR-CHEESE RISOTTO

serves 6

6 cups (48 fl oz/1.5 l) chicken or vegetable broth

¼ cup (2 fl oz/60 ml) olive oil

½ yellow onion, finely chopped

2 cups (14 oz/440 g) Arborio or Carnaroli rice

1 cup (8 fl oz/250 ml) dry white wine

½ cup (3 oz/90 g) mascarpone cheese

¼ cup (1½ oz/45 g) crumbled Gorgonzola cheese

¼ cup (1 oz/30 g) grated Parmesan cheese

¼ cup (1 oz/30 g) grated Asiago cheese

Salt and freshly ground pepper

In a saucepan, bring the broth to a gentle simmer over medium heat and maintain over low heat.

In a large, heavy saucepan, warm the oil over medium heat. Add the onion and sauté until softened, about 4 minutes. Add the rice and stir until coated with oil and translucent, about 3 minutes. Add the wine and cook, stirring, until completely absorbed. Add the simmering broth a ladleful at a time, stirring frequently after each addition. Wait until the broth is almost completely absorbed (but the rice is never dry on top) before adding the next ladleful. Reserve about ¼ cup (2 fl oz/ 60 ml) of the broth to add at the end.

Cook until the rice is almost tender to the bite and looks creamy, about 20 minutes. Remove the risotto from the heat. Stir in the reserved broth and the cheeses, season with salt and pepper, and serve.

BRAISED SHORT RIBS WITH ORANGE-TARRAGON CREAM

serves 4–6

2 Tbsp olive oil

3½ lb (1.75 kg) bone-in short ribs

Salt and freshly ground pepper

½ tsp fennel seeds, lightly crushed

4 Tbsp (1½ oz/45 g) all-purpose flour

2 oz (60 g) thick-sliced pancetta, chopped

1 large yellow onion, finely chopped

1 carrot, finely chopped

6 cloves garlic, smashed

1 Tbsp red wine vinegar

2½ cups (20 fl oz/625 ml) fruity red wine

2 sprigs fresh thyme

2 bay leaves

⅔ cup (5 oz/155 g) canned crushed tomatoes

1¾ cups (14 fl oz/430 ml) beef or chicken broth

1 tsp minced fresh tarragon

Grated zest of 1 orange

¼ cup (2 oz/60 g) crème fraîche or sour cream

Short ribs respond beautifully to slow, moist braising and become melt-in-your-mouth tender. A generous amount of wine complements the meat and adds complexity to the reduced sauce. The ribs are especially good served over noodles or rice with plenty of their juices. Whisking together crème fraîche and orange zest provides a tangy, refreshing garnish to pass at the table.

In a large, heavy pot, warm the oil over medium-high heat. Season the ribs with salt, pepper, and the crushed fennel seeds, then dredge with 2 Tbsp of the flour, shaking off the excess. Working in batches, sear the ribs until browned on all sides, about 10 minutes.

Preheat the oven to 300°F (150°C). Pour off most of the fat from the pot, leaving a thin film. Reduce the heat to medium and add the pancetta, onion, carrot, and garlic. Cook, stirring occasionally, until the vegetables begin to brown, about 6 minutes.

Sprinkle in the remaining 2 Tbsp flour and cook, stirring constantly, until the flour is golden brown, about 2 minutes. If necessary, adjust the heat so the flour doesn't scorch.

Stir in the vinegar and ½ cup (4 fl oz/125 ml) of the wine and stir to scrape up any browned bits on the pot bottom. Add the remaining wine, bring to a brisk simmer, and cook until reduced by about half, 8–10 minutes. Add the thyme, bay leaves, tomatoes, and broth. Season with ½ tsp salt and plenty of pepper. ⋙

Return the ribs to the pot, cover, and cook in the oven until the meat is falling off the bones, turning the ribs about once an hour, about 3½ hours. Transfer the ribs to a platter.

Strain the braising liquid through a fine-mesh sieve placed over a large heatproof bowl, pressing on the vegetables to extract as much liquid as possible. Discard the solids. Let the liquid stand for 3–4 minutes, then skim the fat from the surface. Wipe out the pot, pour in the braising liquid, bring to a simmer over medium-high heat, and cook until slightly reduced, about 5 minutes.

Remove the bones and any chunks of fat or gristle from the short ribs. Cut the meat into bite-sized pieces. Return the meat to the pot and heat until warmed through, about 5 minutes. In a small bowl, stir together the tarragon, orange zest, and crème fraîche. Serve the meat accompanied by the orange-tarragon cream.

DECEMBER

26

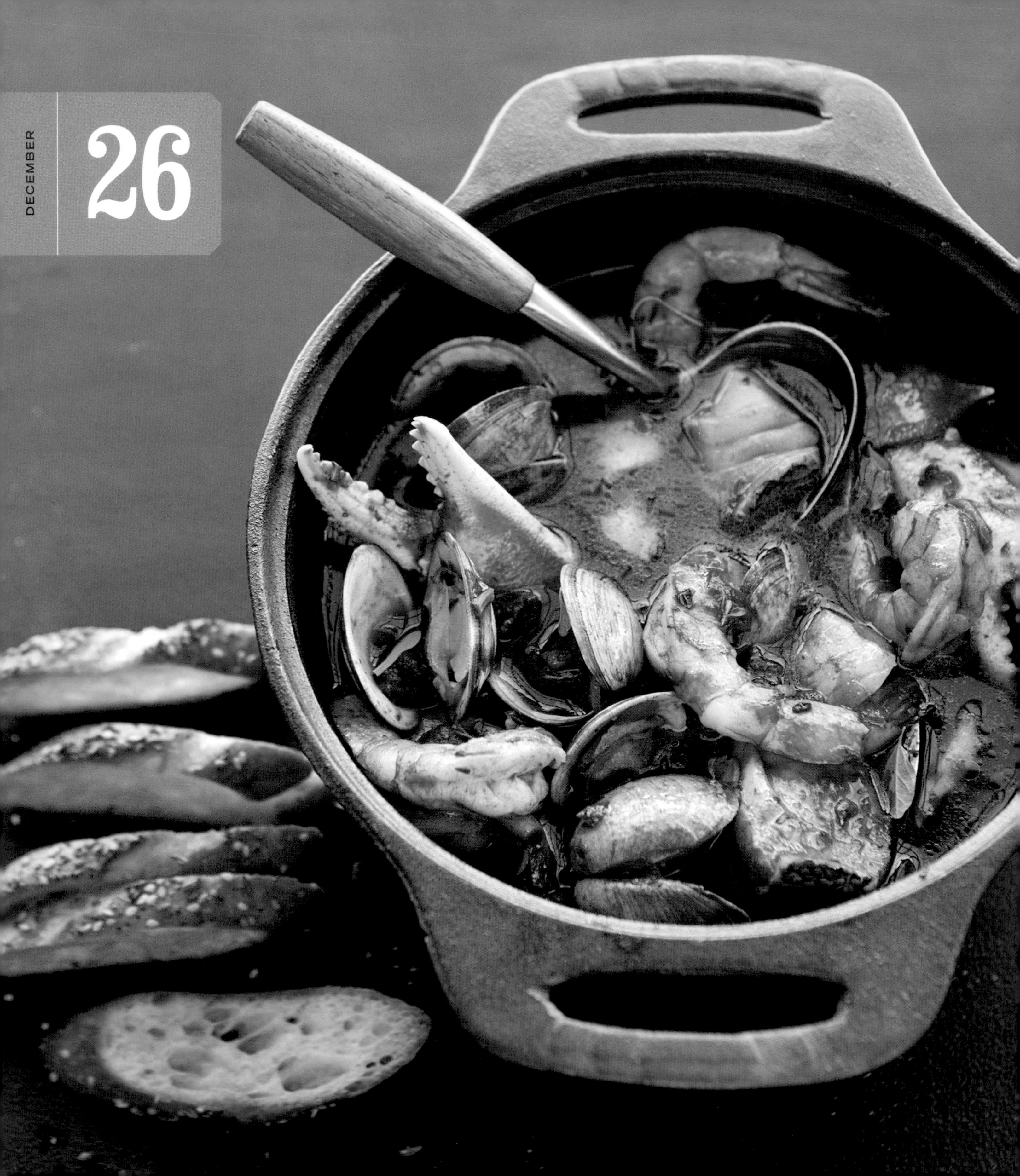

26

CIOPPINO
serves 6

¼ cup (2 fl oz/60 ml) olive oil

2 yellow onions, chopped

2 red bell peppers, seeded and chopped

4 cloves garlic, minced

2 bay leaves, broken in half

1 can (28 oz/825 g) diced tomatoes

¾ cup (6 fl oz/180 ml) dry red wine

½ cup (4 fl oz/125 ml) dry white wine

2 Tbsp chopped fresh oregano

2 Tbsp chopped fresh thyme

¾ lb (375 g) firm white fish fillets such as halibut or monkfish, cut into 1-inch (2.5-cm) chunks

1 lb (500 g) littleneck or other small clams, scrubbed and soaked

1 lb (500 g) Dungeness crab claws, or ½ lb (250 g) Dungeness or other lump crabmeat, picked over for shell fragments

20 large shrimp, heads and legs removed, or peeled and deveined if desired

¼–½ tsp hot-pepper sauce such as Tabasco

Salt and freshly ground pepper

Between holiday parties and roasts, lighten up with a seafood supper. This famous San Francisco fisherman's stew has many variations. Most include local Dungeness crab, but beyond that the seafood additions depend on the catch of the day and the whim of the cook. Following this philosophy, use whatever seafood is best in your area. If you can't find Dungeness crab, substitute good fresh lump crabmeat.

In a large, heavy pot, warm the oil over medium heat. Add the onions and bell peppers and sauté until just tender, 4–5 minutes. Add the garlic and sauté for 30 seconds. Add the bay leaves, tomatoes and their juices, and red and white wines and bring to a simmer. Partially cover, reduce the heat to medium-low, and cook until thickened slightly, about 15 minutes.

Remove and discard the bay leaves. Add the oregano, thyme, fish, and clams, discarding any that do not close to the touch. Cover and cook over medium-low heat for 5 minutes. Add the crab and shrimp, cover, and cook until the shrimp and fish are opaque throughout and the clams have opened, 3–4 minutes. Discard any unopened clams. Stir in the hot-pepper sauce and season with salt and pepper. Serve.

27

SAUSAGE & MUSHROOM STRATA
serves 6

Butter for greasing

6 eggs

2 cups (16 fl oz/500 ml) milk

1 cup (8 fl oz/250 ml) heavy cream

2 Tbsp grated Parmesan cheese

2 Tbsp chopped fresh flat-leaf parsley

Salt and freshly ground pepper

1 tsp canola oil

1 lb (500 g) Italian-style chicken sausages, casings removed

½ lb (250 g) cremini or button mushrooms, or a combination, sliced

1 loaf country-style bread, cut into slices about ½ inch (12 mm) thick

2 cups (8 oz/250 g) shredded smoked Gouda cheese

Imagine a savory baked French toast: tender slices of bread soaked in a rich custard, spicy Italian sausages, and smoky Gouda. Perfect for a cozy holiday brunch, this hearty strata is also substantial enough for dinner. Serve with a simple mixed green salad.

Butter a 9-by-13-inch (23-by-33-cm) baking dish. In a bowl, whisk together the eggs, milk, cream, Parmesan, and parsley. Season with salt and pepper.

In a frying pan, warm the oil over medium heat. Add the sausage, breaking it into bite-size pieces. Cook, stirring, until the sausage begins to lose its pink color, about 2 minutes. Add the mushrooms and a pinch each of salt and pepper, cover the pan, and cook until the mushrooms begin to wilt, about 2 minutes. Uncover and continue cooking, stirring, until the sausage is cooked through and the mushrooms are tender, about 4 minutes. Drain on paper towels.

Arrange one-third of the bread on the bottom of the prepared dish. Top with half of the egg mixture, half of the Gouda, and half of the sausage and mushroom mixture. Repeat the layers, ending with the remaining bread. Using a spatula, press on the top layer of bread to be sure it is covered in the egg mixture. Let stand for 30 minutes, occasionally pressing the bread so that it is well coated.

Preheat the oven to 350°F (180°C). Bake the strata until golden brown and puffed, about 1 hour. Halfway through the cooking time, remove the strata from the oven and press on the top layer of bread to submerge it before returning it to the oven. Let the strata rest for 10 minutes before serving.

28

Fresh winter broccoli and tender seared sirloin vastly improve this Chinese-American restaurant favorite. Tossing in some egg noodles makes it a complete meal, no accompaniments necessary. Serve with a steaming pot of green tea.

BEEF & BROCCOLI STIR-FRY WITH NOODLES

serves 4

¼ cup (2 fl oz/60 ml) oyster sauce

3 Tbsp soy sauce

2 Tbsp rice wine or dry sherry

2 tsp toasted sesame oil

1 tsp cornstarch

½ tsp sugar

Freshly ground pepper

1 bunch broccoli, about ½ lb (250 g), cut into florets

½ lb (250 g) fresh Chinese egg noodles

3 Tbsp corn or peanut oil

3 thin slices peeled fresh ginger

1 lb (500 g) sirloin or flank steak, thinly sliced across the grain into strips

In a bowl, combine ⅓ cup (3 fl oz/80 ml) water and the oyster sauce, soy sauce, rice wine, sesame oil, cornstarch, and sugar. Season with a pinch of pepper and stir to dissolve the cornstarch and sugar.

Bring a large pot of water to a boil. Add the broccoli and cook until tender-crisp, 3–4 minutes. Using a slotted spoon, transfer to a colander and rinse with cold water. Return the water to a boil, add the noodles, and cook, stirring occasionally, until just tender, about 1 minute. Drain the noodles, transfer to a large shallow serving bowl, and toss with 1 Tbsp of the corn oil. Cover loosely with foil to keep warm.

Heat a wok or large frying pan over high heat until very hot and add the remaining 2 Tbsp corn oil. Add the ginger and stir-fry until golden brown, about 1 minute. Using the slotted spoon, scoop out and discard the ginger. Add the beef and stir-fry just until browned, about 2 minutes. Transfer the beef to a bowl. Return the pan to high heat, add the oyster sauce mixture, and cook, stirring, until slightly thickened, about 30 seconds. Return the beef to the pan, add the broccoli, and stir-fry until heated through, about 1 minute. Spoon over the noodles and serve.

29

In Florence, this type of gnocchi is called nudi, because it is similar to ravioli filling minus the pasta. Start by boiling a test dumpling, and if it breaks apart, add a little more flour to the remaining mixture. You can boil the gnocchi up to 3 hours in advance, and then cover and refrigerate them until it is time to bake. If they have been chilled, add 5 minutes or so to the baking time.

GRATINÉED RICOTTA & SPINACH GNOCCHI

serves 6

2 cups (1 lb/500 g) whole-milk ricotta cheese

1¾ cups (7 oz/220 g) grated Parmesan cheese

2 eggs

¼ tsp grated nutmeg

Salt and freshly ground pepper

2 lb (1 kg) spinach, tough stems removed

4 Tbsp (2 oz/60 g) unsalted butter, plus more for greasing

1 small yellow onion, finely chopped

1½ cups (7½ oz/235 g) all-purpose flour

½ cup (2 oz/60 g) fine dried bread crumbs

In a bowl, beat together the ricotta, 1 cup (4 oz/125 g) of the Parmesan, the eggs, and the nutmeg. Season with salt and pepper.

In a pot, combine the spinach, ¼ cup (2 fl oz/60 ml) water, and a pinch of salt. Cover and cook over medium heat, stirring, until tender, 3–4 minutes. Drain the spinach, let cool, squeeze out the liquid, finely chop, and add to the ricotta mixture.

In a frying pan, melt 2 Tbsp of the butter over medium heat. Add the onion and sauté until golden, about 10 minutes. Add the onion to the ricotta mixture and stir well. Stir in the flour until the mixture is well blended and a soft dough forms.

Line 2 baking sheets with parchment paper. Scoop up a tablespoonful of the dough and, with dampened hands, shape it into a ball ¾ inch (2 cm) in diameter. Place on the prepared sheet. Repeat with the remaining dough, making sure the balls don't touch.

Fill the pot halfway with salted water and bring to a boil. Preheat the oven to 400°F (200°C). Butter a shallow 3-qt (3-l) baking dish. Reduce the heat to maintain the water at a simmer. Add half of the gnocchi and cook, stirring gently once or twice, until they rise to the surface, about 3 minutes. With a slotted spoon, transfer to the dish. Repeat with the remaining gnocchi.

Cut the remaining 2 Tbsp butter into bits and dot the surface of the gnocchi. Sprinkle with the remaining Parmesan and the bread crumbs. Bake until the butter is sizzling and the cheese is melted, about 15 minutes. Serve.

30

Broccoli rabe is well suited for braising, which mellows its sharp flavor and tenderizes its tough stems. Serving the sausages, vegetables, and abundant broth over soft, creamy polenta makes a simple, quick, yet quite elegant supper.

WINE-BRAISED SAUSAGES

serves 4

1¼ lb (625 g) sweet Italian sausages

1 cup (8 fl oz/250 ml) dry red wine

3 Tbsp olive oil

1 small yellow onion, chopped

1 small fennel bulb, thinly sliced

3 large cloves garlic, minced

1 large bunch broccoli rabe, about 1 lb (500 g), stems trimmed

1 cup (8 fl oz/250 ml) chicken broth

Creamy Polenta (page 276)

⅓ cup (1½ oz/45 g) grated Parmesan cheese

Prick each sausage in several places with a fork. Place the sausages in a large, heavy pot. Add ½ cup (4 fl oz/125 ml) of the wine and bring to a boil over medium-high heat. Cover, reduce the heat to medium-low, and cook the sausages for 5 minutes. Uncover, raise the heat to medium-high, and cook, turning the sausages occasionally, until they are browned and the liquid is evaporated, 8–10 minutes. Transfer to a plate.

Pour off all but 2 Tbsp fat in the pot, add the oil, and reduce the heat to medium. Add the onion and fennel and sauté just until tinged with gold and softened, 4–5 minutes. Stir in the garlic and sauté for 30 seconds. Return the sausages to the pot and add the broccoli rabe, broth, and remaining wine. Cover, reduce the heat to medium-low, and cook until the broccoli rabe is tender and the sausages are cooked through, 8–10 minutes.

Spoon the polenta onto a platter. Ladle the sausages and vegetables over the polenta, sprinkle with the Parmesan, and serve.

31

December marks the opening of what is probably a San Franciscans' favorite seafood: Dungeness crab. Fish markets and supermarkets sell it cooked and cleaned, but connoisseurs buy the crab live and cook their own. Cooking your own crab yields tastier meat and it leaves you with crab shells with which to flavor a risotto broth.

DUNGENESS CRAB RISOTTO

serves 4

2 cups (16 fl oz/500 ml) bottled clam juice

½ cup (4 fl oz/125 ml) dry white wine

1 large celery rib, cut into 4 pieces

¼ yellow onion

5 Tbsp (3 fl oz/80 ml) olive oil

1 cup (3 oz/90 g) thinly sliced leeks, white and pale green parts only

1½ cups (10½ oz/330 g) Arborio or Carnaroli rice

About 2 lb (1 kg) cooked lump crabmeat, picked over for shell fragments

2 Tbsp minced fresh flat-leaf parsley

1 tsp grated lemon zest

Salt and freshly ground pepper

In a saucepan, combine the clam juice, wine, celery, onion and 4 cups (32 fl oz/1 l) water. Bring to a simmer over medium heat, adjust the heat to maintain a gentle simmer, and cook for 15 minutes. Strain the broth through a fine-mesh sieve, then return to the pan. Bring the broth to a gentle simmer over medium heat and maintain over low heat.

In another saucepan, warm 3 Tbsp of the oil over medium-low heat. Add the leeks and stir to coat with the oil. Cook, stirring occasionally, until soft and sweet, about 10 minutes. Add the rice and cook, stirring, until well coated and translucent, about 3 minutes. Add the simmering broth a ladleful at a time, stirring frequently after each addition. Wait until the broth is almost completely absorbed (but the rice is never dry on top) before adding the next ladleful. It should take about 20 minutes for the rice to become al dente and absorb most of the broth. (You may not need all of the broth.) The rice should be creamy and tender yet firm in the center. Remove from the heat.

Set aside 4 large nuggets of crabmeat for garnish. Stir the remaining crabmeat into the rice along with the remaining 2 Tbsp oil, the parsley, and the lemon zest. Season with salt and pepper.

Spoon the risotto into bowls, garnish with the reserved crabmeat, and serve.

ONE POT RECIPES BY TYPE

ASIAN-STYLE DISHES

Allspice Duck with Braised Bok Choy, 18
Asian Braised Short Ribs, 56
Braised Black Cod with Shiitake Mushrooms, 280
Braised Chicken with Tangerine & Star Anise, 282
Braised Soy-Ginger Chicken, 137
Claypot Chicken with Shiitakes & Broccoli, 219
Five-Spice Chicken Soup, 12
Ginger Chicken with Green Onions, 157
Japanese Braised Salmon, 218
Sesame Chicken with Sugar Snap Peas, 113
Spicy Braised Tofu with Pork, 65
Spicy Tofu with Peas, 88
Sri Lankan Fish Stew, 52
Steamed Tofu with Greens & Peanut Sauce, 140
Teriyaki Chicken Thighs, 168
Thai-Style Brisket, 42
Vietnamese Clay Pot Fish, 255

BAKED PASTAS

Baked Pasta Primavera, 104
Baked Pasta with Lamb & Béchamel, 88
Baked Pasta with Pork Ragù, 75
Baked Pasta with Prosciutto & Peas, 19
Baked Pasta with Sausage & Dandelion Greens, 64
Baked Penne with Eggplant, Zucchini
    & Tomatoes, 142
Baked Penne with Mushrooms & Comté Cheese, 252
Baked Rigatoni with Cauliflower, Pancetta
    & Caramelized Onions, 197
Baked Rigatoni with Fennel, Sausage
    & Peperonata, 92
Baked Ziti with Cauliflower & Gruyère, 10
Baked Ziti with Ricotta & Sausage, 218
Baked Ziti with Three Cheeses, 233
Beef, Basil & Goat Cheese Lasagna Roll-Ups, 261
Chicken Lasagna with Three Cheeses, 188
Classic Macaroni & Cheese, 209
Macaroni with Farmstead Cheddar & Bacon, 45
Pumpkin-Sage Cannelloni, 204
Ricotta & Spinach Stuffed Pasta Shells, 23
Spinach Lasagna with Three Cheeses, 160
Spinach & Roasted Red Pepper Lasagna, 59
Stuffed Cannelloni with Bolognese Sauce, 270
Truffled Mac & Cheese, 279
White Vegetarian Lasagna, 229

CURRIES

Chicken & Coconut Curry, 16
Chickpea & Sweet Potato Curry, 226
Indian Chickpea Curry, 38
Indian Fish Curry, 92
Indian Lamb & Spinach Curry, 108
Lamb Curry with Squash, Chickpeas & Apricots, 146

Lentil, Potato & Spinach Curry, 21
Thai Green Chicken Curry with Asparagus, 61
Thai Green Curry Mussels, 164
Thai Pumpkin & Chicken Curry, 271
Thai Red Curry Beef, 116
Vietnamese Eggplant Curry, 188
Winter Vegetable Coconut Curry, 40

FRIED RICE & NOODLES

Chile Fried Rice with Chicken & Shrimp, 95
Crab Fried Rice, 178
Fried Rice with Pork & Shrimp, 116
Ginger Rice with Chicken, Chard & Shiitakes, 39
Pad Thai, 185
Peanut-Braised Tofu with Noodles, 48
Tofu-Vegetable Fried Rice, 136
Vegetable Chow Mein, 133
Vegetable Fried Rice, 69

GRATINS

Beef, Onion & Tomato Gratin, 178
Cod, Leek & Potato Gratin, 15
Gratinéed Ricotta & Spinach Gnocchi, 294
Potato & Cauliflower Gratin, 100

MEATLESS DISHES

Artichoke & Leek Frittata, 80
Artichoke Risotto, 241
Asparagus Risotto, 94
Baked Eggplant Parmesan, 211
Baked Eggplant with Yogurt & Pomegranate, 285
Baked Pasta Primavera, 104
Baked Penne with Eggplant, Zucchini
    & Tomatoes, 142
Baked Penne with Mushrooms & Comté
    Cheese, 252
Baked Semolina Gnocchi, 147
Baked Ziti with Cauliflower & Gruyère, 10
Baked Ziti with Three Cheeses, 233
Baked Zucchini & Tomato Tian, 163
Broccoli Rabe, Pesto & Smoked Mozzarella
    Strata, 255
Butternut Squash Risotto with Sage, 259
Cheese Soufflé, 40
Chickpea, Squash & Eggplant Tagine, 219
Chickpea & Sweet Potato Curry, 226
Classic Macaroni & Cheese, 209
Four-Cheese Risotto, 290
Fresh Corn Pudding, 155
Frittata with Herbs, Leeks & Parmesan, 108
Golden Beet & Blue Cheese Risotto, 212
Gratinéed Ricotta & Spinach Gnocchi, 294
Herbed Tomato Strata, 192
Indian Chickpea Curry, 38

Italian Tomato & Bread Soup, 197
Lentil, Potato & Spinach Curry, 21
Mushroom Ragù with Polenta, 276
Pasta with Pesto, Green Beans & Potatoes, 172
Pepper Jack & Jalapeño Spoon Bread, 224
Polenta Lasagna with Butternut Squash
    & Spinach, 266
Polenta with Cheese, Garlic & Chard, 208
Polenta with Fontina & Roasted Vegetables, 187
Potato, Goat Cheese & Dill Frittata, 143
Potato & Cauliflower Gratin, 100
Potato-Leek Soup, 62
Pumpkin & Cannellini Bean Cassoulet with
    Roasted Garlic, 238
Pumpkin-Sage Cannelloni, 204
Ratatouille, 181
Red Bean & Vegetable Gumbo, 49
Red Pepper & Goat Cheese Frittata, 137
Red Quinoa with Asparagus, Portobellos & Feta, 70
Ricotta & Spinach Stuffed Pasta Shells, 23
Ricotta & Tomato Sformato, 165
Risotto with Fresh Corn & Basil Oil, 139
Risotto with Leeks & Sun-Dried Tomatoes, 145
Risotto with Taleggio, Radicchio & Red Wine, 46
Roasted Pumpkin with Garlic, Sweet Potatoes
    & Cherry Tomatoes, 200
Root Vegetable Pot Pie, 42
Savory Bread Pudding with Asparagus & Fontina, 110
Spanakopita, 195
Spiced Cauliflower & Potatoes, 31
Spiced Rice Pilaf with Butternut Squash
    & Pistachios, 282
Spiced Squash Tagine, 230
Spicy Simmered Eggs with Kale, 16
Spicy Three-Bean Chili, 206
Spicy Tofu with Peas, 88
Spinach-Feta Quiche, 121
Spinach Lasagna with Three Cheeses, 160
Spinach & Roasted Red Pepper Lasagna, 59
Spring Vegetable Ragout, 91
Steamed Tofu with Greens & Peanut Sauce, 140
Stir-Fried Sesame Eggplant, 172
Stir-Fried Tofu with Ginger & Lemongrass, 166
Stuffed Artichokes, 117
Stuffed Poblano Chiles with Black Beans
    & Squash, 152
Tofu Stir-Fry with Black Bean Sauce, 214
Tofu-Vegetable Fried Rice, 136
Tortilla Española with Romesco Sauce, 169
Truffled Mac & Cheese, 279
Vegetable Chow Mein, 133
Vegetable Enchiladas, 128
Vegetable Fried Rice, 69
Vegetable Stir-Fry with Tofu, 182
Venetian Rice & Peas, 84
Vietnamese Eggplant Curry, 188

weldon**owen**

415 Jackson Street, Suite 200, San Francisco, CA 94111
www.weldonowen.com

ONE POT OF THE DAY

Conceived and produced by Weldon Owen, Inc.
In collaboration with Williams-Sonoma, Inc.
3250 Van Ness Avenue, San Francisco, CA 94109

A WELDON OWEN PRODUCTION

Copyright © 2012 Weldon Owen, Inc. and Williams-Sonoma, Inc.
All rights reserved, including the right of reproduction
in whole or in part in any form.

Printed and bound in China by Toppan-Leefung Printing Limited

First printed in 2012

10 9 8 7

Library of Congress Control Number: 2012938094

ISBN 13: 978-1-61628-433-6
ISBN 10: 1-61628-433-1

Weldon Owen is a division of
BONNIER

WILLIAMS-SONOMA, INC.

Founder and Vice-Chairman Chuck Williams

WELDON OWEN, INC.

CEO and President Terry Newell
VP, Sales and Marketing Amy Kaneko
Director of Finance Mark Perrigo

VP and Publisher Hannah Rahill
Associate Publisher Amy Marr
Executive Editor Kim Laidlaw
Editor Julia Humes
Assistant Editor Becky Duffett

Creative Director Emma Boys
Senior Designer Lauren Charles

Production Director Chris Hemesath
Production Manager Michelle Duggan

Photographer Erin Kunkel
Food Stylist Robyn Valarik
Prop Stylist Leigh Noe

ACKNOWLEDGMENTS

Weldon Owen wishes to thank the following people for their generous support in producing
this book: David Bornfriend, Sarah Putman Clegg, Jane Tunks Demel, Judith Dunham, David Evans,
Lesli J. Neilson, Jennifer Newens, Elizabeth Parson, and Jason Wheeler